Evaluating parental power

Manchester University Press

SOCIAL AND POLITICAL POWER

Series editor: Mark Haugaard

Power is one of the most fundamental concepts in social science. Yet, despite the undisputed centrality of power to social and political life, few have agreed on exactly what it is or how it manifests itself. Social and Political Power is a book series which provides a forum for this absolutely central, and much debated, social phenomenon. The series is theoretical, in both a social scientific and normative sense, yet also empirical in its orientation. Theoretically it is oriented towards the Anglo-American tradition, including Dahl and Lukes, as well as to the Continental perspectives, influenced either by Foucault and Bourdieu, or by Arendt and the Frankfurt School. Empirically, the series provides an intellectual forum for power research from the disciplines of sociology, political science and the other social sciences, and also for policy-oriented analysis.

Already published

Power, luck and freedom: Collected essays
Keith Dowding

Neoliberal power and public management reforms
Peter Triantafillou

Evaluating parental power

An exercise in pluralist political theory

Allyn Fives

Manchester University Press

The right of Allyn Fives to be identified as the author of this work has been
asserted by him in accordance with the Copyright, Designs and Patents Act 1988.

Published by Manchester University Press
Altrincham Street, Manchester M1 7JA

www.manchesteruniversitypress.co.uk

British Library Cataloguing-in-Publication Data
A catalogue record for this book is available from the British Library

Library of Congress Cataloging-in-Publication Data applied for

ISBN   978 1 7849 9432 7   hardback

First published 2017

The publisher has no responsibility for the persistence or accuracy of URLs for
any external or third-party internet websites referred to in this book, and does
not guarantee that any content on such websites is, or will remain, accurate or
appropriate.

Typeset by
Servis Filmsetting Ltd, Stockport, Cheshire
Printed in Great Britain by
CPI Group (UK) Ltd, Croydon CR0 4YY

For Anne Marie and Joanna

Contents

List of tables   viii
Series editor's foreword   ix
Acknowledgements   xiii

Introduction: philosophy, power, and parents   1

Part I: Paternalism and its limits   9

1   Paternalism   11
2   Caretaker or liberator?   33

Part II: Conceptual and methodological issues   53

3   Moral dilemmas   55
4   Children's agency   81
5   Parental power   98
6   Normative legitimacy   124

Part III: The moral legitimacy of parental power   145

7   Legitimacy in the political domain and in the family   147
8   Licensing, monitoring, and training parents   176
9   Children and the provision of informed consent   197
10 Sharing lives, shaping values, and voluntary civic education   222

Conclusion   243

References   249
Index   263

Tables

1.1	Two definitions of paternalism	16
1.2	The necessary and possible qualities of an agent	25
2.1	Whether receipt of care can conflict with a right to liberty	43
4.1	Four parenting styles	83
5.1	Glossary of power concepts	112
5.2	The forms of power	113
8.1	Hypothetical predictive instrument with high sensitivity/ specificity and 1 per cent prevalence of child abuse in 1,000 families	179
9.1	Legally relevant criteria for decision making capacity and approaches to assessment of the patient	204

Series editor's foreword

Bertrand Russell once argued that power is to social science what energy is to physics (Russell 1938: 10). While power is one of the most important concepts in the social sciences, it is also one of the most complex and elusive to research.

Weber's analysis of power and authority (1947 and 1978) is one of the first social scientific discussions of power and it influenced the US power debates, which developed post-Second World War. In these debates Dahl's careful analysis stands out for its clarity in providing us with a conceptual vocabulary of power (Dahl 1957 and 1968). This includes an agency-based, exercise and decision-making definition of power; conceptualized in terms of powerful actors (A) making subordinates (B) do something that they would not otherwise do. This exercise of power is distinct from resources (that may or may not be exercised) and it provides power-holders with power of specific scope. However, while providing a new set of conceptual tools to analyse about power relations, Dahl's work was subject to sustained critique from Bachrach and Baratz and others, who argued that power is also exercised through structural biases that are not necessarily reducible to overt decision-making (Bachrach and Baratz 1962). Lukes followed this critique with his theorization of the third-dimension of power (Lukes 1974), which concerns the mobilization of belief and ideology to legitimize power relations of domination. The three-dimensional model was applied in a richly textured empirical study of Appalachian mining communities (Gaventa 1982). Overall, as the three-dimensional power debates develop, the focus shifts from actions of the dominating actor A to the counter-intuitive and fascinating phenomenon that subordinate actors B often appear to actively acquiesce or participate in their own domination.

In a qualified critique of Lukes, Scott argued that appearances are often deceptive (Scott 1990). The relationship between public and private discourse renders the working of three-dimensional power more complex than any simplistic images of the oppressed willingly participating in their own domination, or internalizing false-consciousness. In turn, Scott's work has inspired an on-going power-literature on the complexities of resistance versus acquiescence.

In the 1980s, under the influence of the translation of Foucault's work (for instance, Foucault 1979 and 1982), the Anglophone power debates shifted towards more epistemic and ontological analysis, which resonated with the shift of emphasis from the powerful to the conditions of the oppressed. This gave rise to fascinating work on the relation between power and discourse; power and truth; the way power influences the ontological formation of social subjects through discipline; and how governmentality has changed systemic power relations (including Clegg 1989; Dean 2010; Laclau 2005; Flyvbjerg 1998; Hayward 2000). However, in critique, many have argued that neo-Foucauldians tend to lose sight of the significance of individual agency (Lukes 2005).

Bridging the intellectual divide between those following the Dahl–Lukes trajectory and the neo-Foucauldians, another important thread to the power debates comes from Giddens (1984) and Bourdieu's (1989) conceptualizations of structure as a verb. This way of thinking provides us with conceptual tools for making sense of how agents both structure and are structured by relations of power.

In international relations, the shift from agency towards systemic, epistemic and ontological perceptions of power took the form of a gradual move from realist focus on resources to a more idealist emphasis upon soft power (Nye 1990 and 2011). Similarly, in rational choice theory, there emerged an emphasis upon the systemic situatedness of strategic choices.

The effect of interrogating the social contexts and social ontology of agents has caused many theorists to re-evaluate the nature of power normatively, moving away from the automatic equation between power and domination to a perception of power as a condition of possibility for agency, thus freedom (Morriss 2002 and 2009). Thus, freedom and power move from being opposing categories to being mutually constitutive. Associated with this normative re-evaluation, power theorists distinguish between power-to, power-with and power-over (Allen 1998 and 1999; Pansardi 2012). To begin with power-over was considered a normative negative, suggesting oppression, while power-to and power-with were the positives. However, some theorists argue power-over can also have emancipatory, as well as the more obvious dominating, aspects (Haugaard 2012).

Allyn Fives' book *Evaluating parental power: an exercise in pluralist political theory* is a highly innovative work that seeks to theorize the normative implications of the social power that parents routinely exercise over children. All parents have power over their children; what makes some of these exercises of power relations legitimate and others illegitimate? How do we justify these conclusions? Fives answers these crucial questions through the sophisticated use of pluralist liberal political theory. His response is both significant to the practice of childcare policy, and constitutes an invaluable contribution of our understanding of the normative aspects of social power.

Overall, the book series, *Social and Political Power*, seeks to build upon these rich traditions of power analysis, which currently make the study of social and political power one of the most vibrant fields in the social and political sciences. It also builds upon the success of the *Journal of Political Power*, which provides an important forum for article analysis, while this book series facilitates longer works on social and political power.

The book series is open to any of the multiplicity of traditions of power analysis, and it welcomes research that is theoretically oriented, as well as empirical research on power or practitioner oriented applications.

Mark Haugaard
National University of Ireland, Galway, Ireland.

References

Allen, Amy (1998) 'Rethinking power', *Hypatia*, 13(1), 21–40.

Allen, Amy (1999) *The Power of Feminist Theory: Domination, Resistance, Solidarity* (Boulder CO: Westview Press).

Bachrach, Peter and Baratz, Morton S. (1962) 'The two faces of power', *American Political Science Review*, 56(4): 947–52.

Bourdieu, Pierre (1989) 'Social space and symbolic power', *Sociological Theory* (7)1: 14–25.

Clegg, Stewart (1989) *Frameworks of Power* (London: Sage).

Dahl, Robert A. (1957) 'The concept of power', *Behavioural Science*, 2(3): 201–15.

Dahl, Robert A. (1968) 'Power', in David L. Shills (ed.), *International Encyclopedia of the Social Sciences*, Vol. 12 (New York, Macmillan), pp. 405–15.

Dean, Mitchell (2010) *Govermentality: Power and Rule in Modern Society*, second edition (London: Sage).

Flyvbjerg, Bent (1998) *Rationality and Power: Democracy in Practice* (Chicago: The University of Chicago Press).

Foucault, Michel (1982) 'The subject and power', in Hubert L. Dreyfus and Paul Rabinow (eds), *Michel Foucault: Beyond Structuralism and Hermeneutics* (London: Harvester Wheatsheaf), pp. 208–26.

Foucault, Michel (1979) *Discipline and Punish: The Birth of the Prison* (Harmondsworth: Penguin).

Giddens, Anthony (1984) *The Constitution of Society* (Cambridge: Polity Press).

Gaventa, John (1982) *Power and Powerlessness: Quiescence and Rebellion in an Appalachian Valley* (Oxford: Clarendon Press).

Hayward, C. (2000) *De-facing Power* (Cambridge: Cambridge University Press).

Haugaard, Mark (2012) 'Rethinking the four dimensions of power', *Journal of Political Power*, 5(1): 35–54

Laclau, Ernesto (2005) *On Populist Reason* (London: Verso).

Lukes, Steven (1974) *Power: A Radical View* (London: Macmillan).

Lukes, Steven (2005) *Power: A Radical View*, second edition (Basingstoke: Palgrave Macmillan).

Morriss, Peter (2002) *Power: A Philosophical Analysis*, second edition (Manchester: Manchester University Press).

Morriss, Peter (2009) 'Power and liberalism' in Stewart Clegg and Mark Haugaard (eds), *The Sage Handbook of Power* (London: Sage).

Nye, Joseph S. (1990) Soft power. *Foreign Policy* (80): 153-172.

Nye, Joseph S. (2011) 'Power and foreign policy', *Journal of Political Power*, 4(1): 9–24.

Pensardi, Pamela (2012) 'Power to and power over: two distinct concepts?', *Journal of Political Power*, 5(1): 73–89.

Russell, Bertrand (1938) *Power: A New Social Analysis* (London: George Allen & Unwin).

Scott. J. C. (1990) *Domination and the Arts of Resistance: Hidden Transcripts* (New Haven: Yale University Press).

Weber, Max (1947) *The Theory of Social and Economic Organization*, ed. Talcott Parsons (New York: Free Press).

Weber, Max (1978) *Economy and Society* (2 Vols), *An Outline of Interpretive Sociology*, ed. G Roth and C. Wittich (Berkley: University of California Press).

Acknowledgements

I first began to think about and write about children and parents as philo-sophical topics in order to better understand some important questions about civic education. Some of that work was first published in an earlier book, *Political Reason*, and over subsequent years I was fortunate enough to be invited to contribute articles about these questions to volumes edited by Johannes Drerup et al. and Jacqueline Boaks and Michael P. Levine. During this time, I was also working on many empirical studies relating to children and parents, as well as being a member, and in more recent years chair, of the Research Ethics Committee at NUI Galway, where many studies involving children are considered for ethical approval. This *practical* work has helped me better understand some of the ethical considerations concerning parent–child relations, including research with children, and my work in this area has appeared in the book I edited with Keith Breen, *Philosophy and Political Engagement*.

So the current book has had a long gestation and I have been very fortu-nate during that time in the work that I have been involved in and the col-leagues I have worked with. At the outset, I want to mention Chris Curtin, who first encouraged me to write something on the topic of power and parenting. Up to that point, I had developed an interest in the normative issues concerning children's rights, but had not as yet linked this with the broader academic dialogue about power and its legitimacy. And I think it is fair to say that, despite the stellar work of David Archard, Harry Brighouse, Adam Swift, Colin Macleod and others, there has been surprisingly little interest in the *legitimacy* of parental power over their children. After I began to make some first steps in this field, Mark Haugaard then invited me to contribute something on this topic to the *Social and Political Power* book series. I also benefitted greatly from discussing with Mark many of the issues raised here, in particular that power, including coercive power, can be normatively legitimate, and the centrality of the ethical dimension to any conceptualisation of power. In this book, I also try to take seriously the challenge posed by moral pluralism, and to examine the implications of pluralism for theorists of power as well as for citizens engaged in power relations. In that regard, I must mention Peter Morriss's *Power: A Philosophical Analysis* (2012). The approach he takes to the analysis of power, and many of his conclusions about the plurality of power concepts, gave me considerable encouragement that I was on the right track in what I was trying to do here, although, I want to stress, one that he himself does not necessarily take.

Below I examine a number of case studies concerning parental power. Much of what I say here is influenced to a greater or lesser degree by empirical studies carried out in the UNESCO Child and Family Research Centre. These chapters are also informed by my experiences on our Research Ethics Committee. I examine what supports should be provided to parents and what limitations and conditions should be placed on the rights of parents, whether and how children's participation in research or receipt of medical care is justified, and what the role of civic education should be and whether participation should be voluntary. The challenge for me was to find a way to bring together such practical matters on the one hand and political philosophy on the other. What can political philosophy say about such issues? What place if any do empirical evidence and practical judgements have in political philosophy? Most importantly, often we have to answer these questions while also grappling with independent and conflicting moral claims. In trying to answer these questions I have concluded that the role of theory is, in one important respect, limited: I do not think that theory itself can provide general rules with which to resolve the tensions that arise when moral values come into conflict. Instead, we resolve moral dilemmas through the exercise of practical reason and practical judgement, and we can do so only when faced with the need to make decisions in specific contexts.

As I say at many points below, much the same conclusions about pluralism and the limits of theory were reached before me by Isaiah Berlin, Bernard Williams, Thomas Nagel, and others. In arriving at such a conclusion, I have travelled some distance from what I had to say in *Political Reason*, in that I am now wary of an approach that does not limit the role of theory in this way. But more importantly, I want to draw attention to the importance of my own practical work, mentioned above, in bringing me to see that in everyday life we do make the kinds of practical judgements I have in mind, that is, judgements where there are independent and conflicting moral claims and where we do not have a general rule to resolve the conflict. Political philosophy needs to be brought into line with this reality, I think, if political theorists are to make meaningful engagements in public matters, but without claiming for political philosophy a degree of certainty in matters of moral conflict that it does not possess.

Earlier drafts of many of these chapters were shared with friends and colleagues, who very generously gave up their time, shared their expertise, and provided a much-needed critical point of view on what I had been doing. In this regard, I am extremely grateful to Keith Breen, Louise Campbell, Mark Haugaard, and Richard Hull. At various presentations I was also lucky enough to have colleagues offer their views on this work and in particular I would like to thank Brendan Flynn, Niall Ó Dochartaigh, and Kevin Ryan. Finally, I want to thank the anonymous reviewers who commented on earlier drafts of this work.

Introduction
Philosophy, power, and parents

This is a book about parents, power, and children and, in particular, the legitimacy of parents' power over their children. It is also a book about political philosophy itself, as it examines the role of this discipline when we evaluate the legitimacy of parents' power. If parents have power, and if they exercise power over their children, what makes some power relations legitimate and others illegitimate, and how do we justify these conclusions? To begin to answer these questions let us start with the prevailing view of parental power. It is widely accepted that we should not interfere with an adult's liberty so as to promote that adult's well-being. We should not treat others in this way as, in the main, we think this type of paternalism is inappropriate as a way to structure the way we live together as fellow adults and fellow citizens. However, at the same time, it is widely accepted that parents may, indeed should, exercise power over their children in precisely this way. It is argued that, as a general rule, parents should prioritise children's own well-being whenever it comes into conflict with children's liberty. A further assumption is that these considerations are sufficient to account for the normative evaluation of parental power, as parents' power over their children can be equated with, or reduced to, this type of paternalism.

Many political philosophers who write about this topic share these assumptions. Therefore, it is in response to these assumptions that we find our starting point for thinking about parental power. In the chapters to come I want to pose a number of questions in response to the prevailing view of parental power. Why have philosophers reached these conclusions and are they justified? Why has the debate about parental power been framed in this way, namely as a debate about the legitimacy or otherwise of one form of paternalistic power? Finally, what does this tell us about the nature and role of political philosophy, in particular its role in resolving moral conflicts, such as that between the requirement to protect liberty and the requirement to promote well-being?

This last question is important, as the way in which we have come to think of the power exercised over children tells us a great deal about the way we deliberate about political issues more generally. Indeed, the debate on parental power highlights a paradox in contemporary political thought. For it is widely assumed that the job of political philosophers is, first and foremost, to identify a general rule to resolve moral conflicts, and if they do not do so their arguments are of little use in politics and have little validity in and of themselves. Moral conflict is regarded 'as a pathology of social and moral thought, and as something to be overcome, whether by theorising [...] or by an historical process' (Williams, 1981 [1979], p. 72).

This is paradoxical, first, as there is little or no evidence to suggest that political philosophers will ever reach a consensus about what that general rule is. In the history of political thought it is possible to identify areas where, over time, agreement has been reached. But there is no indication that we will soon have convergence on the general rule for resolving moral conflicts, as disagreement continues between the various schools of thought in political philosophy, including, but not limited to, utilitarian, Kantian, social contract, Aristotelian, Thomist, and republican positions. It is paradoxical for the further reason that any attempt to resolve conflicts in this way would, it seems, run counter to a number of ethical ideals in modern society, including the ideals of democratic equality, individual freedom of reflection, and respect for diversity. In a society where each citizen has equal status, where each is free to make up their own mind about matters of conscience, and where we respect reasonable, diverse moral doctrines, is it right that the political community should require citizens to resolve moral conflicts by giving priority to one value, when citizens do not already do so and when philosophical debate on the matter is unresolved?

Yet political philosophers, not least those who investigate parental power, assume they can and they should identify the general rule that will resolve moral conflicts. I want to show that, to succeed, this endeavour requires a process of moral simplification for which we have no philosophical licence, that is, a process whereby we circumscribe both the appropriate moral considerations and 'the morally relevant features of situations encountered' (Hampshire, 1978, p. 39). I also want to explore ways in which we can try to resolve moral conflicts without moral simplification and without claiming to have identified a general rule to resolve conflicts. Very much in line with the work of Thomas Nagel, Bernard Williams, and Stuart Hampshire, in this book I argue that it is through practical reasoning and practical judgement, and not alone through theoretical reasoning, that we can endeavour to resolve moral conflicts, and do so in the context of specific cases where practical decisions are required.

Nonetheless, practical reason and practical judgement are of little use by themselves. Indeed, and as this book will, I hope, illustrate, theory has a crucial role to play in thinking about these political matters. Theoretical reflection on conceptual and methodological issues is central to the moral debate on parental power, including the meaning of such concepts as paternalism, power, agency, and legitimacy, and also the methodological issue of the limits of theoretical reason and the point at which practical reason and practical judgement are called for. As I have said, the debate about parental paternalism is one instance where philosophers have tried to resolve moral conflicts through appeal to a general rule. In addition, the concept of paternalism is itself of particular interest. What I believe to be the correct definition of that concept shows that paternalism will always involve moral conflict and also that paternalism itself is not sufficient as an account of parental power. Therefore, what is called for is the very opposite of moral simplification. Not only is moral conflict unavoidable when parents act paternalistically, the plurality of moral considerations appropriate to parental power, and the plurality of morally relevant features of these power relations, is such that we must address various non-paternalistic forms of parental power as well.

I want to say some more about the prevailing or dominant approach to the analysis of parental power. An important source for much that is said about parental power now is J. S. Mill's rejection of one type of paternalism in the 1850s. When Mill devised his 'principle of liberty' or 'harm principle' he also rejected paternalistic interference with another's liberty:

> The object of this essay is to assert one very simple principle, as entitled to govern absolutely the dealings of society with the individual in the way of compulsion and control, whether the means used be physical force in the form of legal penalties or the moral coercion of public opinion. That principle is that the sole end for which mankind are warranted, individually or collectively, in interfering with the liberty of action of any of their number is self-protection. That the only purpose for which power can be rightly exercised over any member of a civilised community, against his will, is to prevent harm to others. His own good, either physical or moral, is not a sufficient warrant. (Mill, 1985 [1859], p. 68)

According to Mill, then, for power to have legitimacy, it must *not* be exercised paternalistically in the sense referred to above. We may not interfere with others' liberty, without their consent, for their own good.

At the same time, Mill believes, parents *are* entitled to exercise power over their children in precisely this way. The principle of liberty does not apply to those 'incapable of self-government', and where that capacity

is absent, as is the case concerning children, according to Mill, we may
interfere with their liberty for their own good: 'protection against themselves is professedly due to children and persons under age' (ibid., p. 147).
Mill is not alone in concluding that, while paternalistic interference with
an adult's liberty is clearly and unambiguously illegitimate, nonetheless
parents may legitimately interfere with their children's liberty for paternalistic reasons. Geoffrey Scarre accepts there is an 'asymmetry' in the
'calculation of the relative importance of liberty and well-being' among
adults and among children. Liberty is more cherished for adults, well-being
for children. Unlike children, it is 'better for adults to suffer from the consequences of their own unwise decisions rather than be subjected to the
decisions of others' (1980, p. 120).
    What do these comments of Mill (and Scarre) suggest? As we shall see
below, although the debate on parental power is marked by controversy
and disagreement, nonetheless there is a considerable, even surprising,
degree of consensus. The following are two widely-held assumptions in
political philosophy regarding parental power:

(1) If children lack the qualities of an agent, parents' exercise of power
    over their children is for that reason justified;
(2) Parents' power is paternalistic, and this means that parents interfere
    with their children's liberty, without their consent, and for their chil-
    dren's own good.

These assumptions are evident in two diametrically opposed positions on
parental power. First, they are evident in the caretaker thesis, which can
be represented as follows: children lack the qualities of an agent (except
for many of those who have reached late adolescence); therefore, parents'
exercise of power over children is justified; and parents' power is paternalistic (as defined above). The same assumptions are evident in the opposing
liberation thesis, which can be represented as follows: children often do not
lack the qualities of an agent; once children are capable of agency, parents'
exercise of power over children is then unjustified; and parents' power is
paternalistic (as defined above).
    So those who hold diametrically opposed views on whether parental
power is legitimate, nonetheless share the same assumptions about how
to arrive at those conclusions. They merely differ concerning whether children possess the qualities of an agent, and this in turn leads them to give
priority to different moral claims, the promotion of children's well-being
in one instance and the protection of children's liberty in the other. This
brings us to a third underlying assumption evident in this debate:

(3) When two or more moral claims appear to be in conflict, the conflict can be resolved at the level of philosophical (abstract and general) reflection by identifying the general rule for deciding which moral claim is fundamental.

Therefore, the role of the philosopher is to engage in abstract philosophical reflection so as to identify the general rule for the resolution of moral conflicts, and philosophers can hope to attain some degree of success in this role.

Let us look at an example of how political philosophers tend to approach moral conflicts. Amy Gutmann attempts to resolve a conflict between the requirement to protect parents' (and children's) rights to freedom of religion, on the one hand, and the requirement to protect children's rights to an adequate education (and by extension, the duty to promote the autonomy of the adults children will one day be), on the other hand. This is what she says:

> We *rank* children's rights to education above their rights to religious freedom since we believe that this restriction of their present liberty is necessary to create the conditions for future enjoyment of religious and other freedoms. Without education, liberal freedoms lose a great deal, even if not all, of their value. We are left with the problem of *ordering* the religious freedom of parents and the right of children to an adequate education. The *appropriate rule* is that a child's right to education be given *priority* over his or her parents' right to religious exercise. (Gutmann, 1980, pp. 349–50; emphasis added)

I have placed some of Gutmann's argument above in italics. In Gutmann's work, which as we shall see is far from idiosyncratic in the approach adopted to moral conflicts, we are faced with the problem of ordering (ranking) competing moral claims, and we do so by identifying a general rule that can be applied to such cases of apparent moral conflict so as to establish which claim is fundamental, and has priority, and in this way dissolve the conflict.

As I said, we can discern the same assumptions in the debate between those who propose the caretaker thesis and those who defend the liberation thesis. Utilising similar methods to those suggested by Gutmann, what is considered to be an apparent conflict between the requirement to promote children's well-being and the requirement to protect children's liberty is resolved by the caretaker thesis (where priority is given to the promotion of well-being) and by the liberation thesis (where priority is given to the protection of liberty). In each case, it is claimed that there is a general rule for resolving moral conflicts of this sort. Note, although they each claim to have identified a general rule for resolving this conflict, their claims are contradictory and their recommended policies incompatible. And yet we are encouraged to believe that the role of philosophy is to identify *the* general rule for ordering competing claims and therefore for resolving moral conflicts, and that it is through this means that any subsequent decisions and actions can claim to be principled or morally justified. As I said above, I think this goal is symptomatic of a deeply paradoxical view of political philosophy. So what is the alternative?

If we examine cases where conflicts arise, we will see that, very often, there can be no general rule for their resolution. That is, often, we are faced with a genuine, real moral dilemma, rather than merely the appearance of a conflict that quickly dissolves thanks to the efforts of the theoretician. Why are we faced with situations where moral claims conflict and there is no general rule for their resolution? I will tackle this question in greater detail below. Specifically I will try to show that talk of moral dilemmas is not contradictory and also that there are occasions when, even if we have done what is right, it is rational to feel regret at the moral items not acted upon (see Chapter 3). However, for now it is sufficient to say that we are faced with real moral dilemmas for the reason that the justification for our actions is not unitary, as 'value has fundamentally different kinds of sources' (Nagel, 1979 [1977], p. 132). And so the 'enterprise of trying to reduce our conflicts [...] by constructing a philosophical *ethical theory* (in the sense of systematising moral belief) is a misguided one' (Williams, 1981 [1979], p. 80; emphasis in original). There is a variety of moral values that resists all efforts at reduction, through some process of systematising, including the one whereby one value is held up as fundamental, whether we think the latter is utility, autonomy, liberty, virtue, or whatever. It is because of the irreducible plurality of both the morally relevant features of a case and the moral considerations appropriate to a case that we cannot satisfactorily make moral judgements on the basis of a theoretical account maintaining to have identified the general rule for resolving moral conflicts. And when we are faced with moral dilemmas, this indicates the limit point of theory, and the point at which practical reason and practical judgement are required.

There are two things to note at this point about practical reason. My argument is that, given its limitations, we must turn away from theory, and that these limitations are a reflection of something unavoidable about moral values, their irreducible plurality. However, and this is the second point, not all approaches to practical reasoning are of equal merit. In this book, I will argue for an approach influenced in part by Rawls's account of reasonableness (1999 [1997]) and Nagel's account of 'public justification in a context of actual disagreement' (1990 [1987], p. 315). What I propose will have little in common with communitarian, and even less so with

Nietzschean, approaches to practical reason and practical judgement (see Fives, 2008b; 2009; 2010).

Although my thesis is that theory has its limits, theory does play an important role. It can contribute to our understanding of moral phenomena through conceptual analysis and it can guide us, methodologically, in our efforts to resolve moral dilemmas through practical reasoning. And it is through such theoretical argumentation that, in this book, I hope to defend the approach taken here, including the scope given to practical reason and practical judgement, as well as the form the latter should take. This is very much in line with what Jonathan Wolff has called 'problem-driven philosophy', to distinguish it from 'ideal theory' (Wolff, 2011). To put the same point another way, what political philosophy cannot do, I contend, is resolve moral dilemmas as a theoretical exercise. This is the case as moral dilemmas resist resolution in accordance with general rules.

If we are not aware of the limits of political philosophy there is a danger that we will measure our success against unattainable standards. In doing so, one of two things can happen. We can give way to despair and nihilism, concluding that, as philosophers seem unable to identify general rules for resolving moral conflicts, this shows that conflicts can only be resolved through a-rational and a-moral means, through conflict rather than through argumentation. This is the position of the Nietzschean. Alternatively, we may find ourselves in a state of denial, refusing to admit that we have failed in our efforts to identify the general rule needed to resolve all conflicts. Those working in this way strive to convince that they have identified the desired general rule, but cannot agree on what that rule is. At best, all we can say is that they cannot all be right; at worst, that they are all wrong to see the aims and objectives of their work in this way.

One final thing before beginning in earnest. The following chapters are organised around three tasks. The first is to examine the prevailing view about parental power: namely that it is a certain form of paternalism, that it is justified treatment of those who lack the qualities of an agent, and that it does not generate moral conflicts. I will propose an alternative, pluralist view of paternalism in Chapter 1, while in Chapter 2 I will try to show that even paternalism properly understood is of limited application when we evaluate parental power. Parents exercise power over their children in ways that are not paternalistic, and in many cases they do so legitimately.

The second task is to propose an alternative approach for the evaluation of parental power. What I argue for here is that we can be faced with moral dilemmas (Chapter 3), and this is the case when we consider children's agency (Chapter 4) and the forms of parental power (Chapter 5), as with each there is an irreducible plurality of morally relevant considerations and of morally significant features. Thus, when we consider the legitimacy of parental power (Chapter 6) we shall have to address moral conflicts.

The final task is to illustrate what has been argued for regarding conceptual and methodological issues and this is done through a series of case studies. However, I first address the counter-argument that issues of legitimacy arise in the political domain and not in respect of parent–child relations (Chapter 7). I then proceed to examine the 'right to parent' and whether parents should be licensed, monitored, or trained (Chapter 8); children's voluntariness and competence, and the right to provide informed consent for medical treatment and research participation (Chapter 9); and finally, parents' efforts to share a way of life with their children and the State's efforts to shape the values of future citizens through civic education (Chapter 10). As already indicated, in these case studies the approach taken is very much in line with problem-driven political philosophy as opposed to ideal theory. In each case study, I start by examining the practical reality in which such decisions are to be made, and on that basis, I address a number of ethical questions through practical reason and practical judgement.

Part I

Paternalism and its limits

When parents exercise power over their children, are they acting paternalistically? Indeed, must parents behave towards their children in a paternalistic fashion for their power to have legitimacy? These are the questions addressed in the next two chapters. I first ask, what is paternalism (Chapter 1)? We shall see that there are two very different definitions of paternalism that political philosophers employ. My argument is that the most widely used of these definitions, the one most closely associated with Mill's liberalism, is the least satisfactory. I will make the case for an alternative, pluralist, definition of paternalism, according to which paternalism does involve moral conflicts, it does not always involve interference with another's liberty, and it is only exercised over those possessing the qualities of an agent.

I will then ask, is parental power always paternalistic (Chapter 2)? Based on an extended analysis of the caretaker thesis and the liberation thesis, I argue that parental power often is not paternalistic, as understood by my preferred definition. Therefore, the concept of paternalism is not sufficient for our normative evaluation of parental power. Parents exercise their power in ways that are not paternalistic but may, nonetheless, be justified. However, the concept of paternalism, correctly defined, does shed light on both the nature of power and also the role of the philosopher in considering its legitimacy. Namely, it puts to the forefront the fact that power takes many forms and that in the evaluation of power we can be faced with moral dilemmas. In subsequent chapters, in Part II of this book, I explore the various ways in which power is exercised and also the various considerations appropriate to its justification.

1

Paternalism

In this chapter, I introduce the central themes of the book. These themes can best be presented as questions, as follows: When parents exercise power over their children, what are the various forms power takes and what forms of power can be morally justified? When we evaluate the legitimacy of parental power, can we be faced with moral dilemmas, and if so how can we resolve such conflicts? Finally, in what ways may parents exercise power over children who lack the qualities of an agent, those who are capable of agency but are incompetent, and those who are fully competent? I do not claim to answer all of these questions in full in this chapter. However, by examining two competing definitions of paternalism I think we can highlight what are the pertinent issues that we must explore further, while I will also endeavour to make clear the arguments to be made in the coming chapters.

Although it is widely accepted that parents may exercise paternalistic power over their children, there is considerable controversy over the meaning of paternalism itself. All accept that when parents act paternalistically they do so for their child's own good and without the child's past, present, or immediately forthcoming consent. However, that is where the consensus ends. According to the prevailing, 'liberal' view, paternalism involves interference with another's liberty (Dworkin, 2005), it does not lead to moral conflicts (Hershey, 1985), it is justified through retrospective consent (Dworkin, 1972), and it is justified treatment for those who lack the qualities of an agent (Brighouse and Swift, 2014). According to a diametrically opposed position, the one defended here, the 'pluralist' view, paternalism need not entail interference with another's liberty, it does entail moral conflict, it is not justified through retrospective consent, and finally, paternalism is only exercised over those who have the qualities of an agent (Gert and Culver, 1976; Palmeri, 1980).

This debate over the meaning of paternalism is important for a number of reasons. We may judge that parents should act paternalistically. However, it does not follow that the children in question lack the qualities of an agent or are incompetent. Nor does it follow that there are no moral dilemmas in doing so. And nor does it follow that, in all cases, parents are justified in infringing their children's liberty. The debate on paternalism is important also as it is illustrative of a wider controversy about the nature and role of political philosophy, in particular with respect to moral conflicts and how they are to be resolved.

The liberal and pluralist views on paternalism

We are interested in the legitimacy of parents' power. So let us start by asking what is *power*? A relationship of power involves a controlling unit (an agent exercising power over another) and a responsive unit (an agent subjected to the exercise of controlling power) (Dahl, 2002 [1968], pp. 10–11). And what is *paternalistic* power? In the literature on paternalism, there is agreement on two points, namely that paternalism involves benevolence and that the paternalist controlling unit acts without the past, present, or immediately forthcoming consent of the responsive unit. However, there is significant disagreement about other central aspects to the meaning of paternalism. I begin with the prevailing, liberal view.

Gerald Dworkin sums up the liberal view as follows: 'By paternalism I shall understand roughly the interference with a person's liberty of action justified by reasons referring exclusively to the welfare, good, happiness, needs, interests or values of the person being coerced' (1972, p. 65). That is, paternalism involves interfering with the liberty of some other person, 'manipulating or coercing another person' (Brighouse and Swift, 2014, p. 67). It is also argued that paternalism is justified only in situations where the responsive unit lacks the qualities of an agent. Paternalism 'is justified when people cannot make the choices they would make if they were fully rational and autonomous' (Archard,[1] 2004, p. 78). Therefore, paternalism is not justified in respect of those who do possess the qualities of an agent, and so, all things being equal, it is unjustified treatment of adults. At the same time, it is argued that paternalism is justified by the retrospective consent of the person over whom power is exercised. Children's consent cannot authorise parental paternalism in the present moment. Nonetheless, a wager is made that the adults children will one day become will provide retrospective consent for their parents' paternalistic behaviour towards them as children (Dworkin, 1972; Gutmann, 1980). Finally, it is assumed that paternalism does not entail any unresolved moral conflict (Hershey, 1985). It is right, all things considered, to paternalistically interfere with children's liberty, and thus, it is claimed, parents are not faced with conflicting moral judgements here.

I have provided a very brief outline of the prevailing, liberal view on paternalism. Let us now look in detail at one such defence of parental paternalism. The argument for paternalism I want to consider is based on utilitarian moral and political philosophy, although later (Chapter 2) we shall find the same assumptions evident in a non-utilitarian, Kantian argument.

According to the utilitarian, 'actions are right in proportion as they tend to promote happiness, wrong as they tend to produce the reverse of happiness' (Mill, 1998 [1861], p. 137). The philosopher who provides us with this formula also is a firm opponent of paternalistic interference with liberty in relations between adults, as we saw in the Introduction. According to Mill's principle of liberty, the only reason why power may be exercised over members of a civilised community, against their will, is to prevent harm to others. Their own good does not provide sufficient warrant. However, as we saw, for Mill, the principle of liberty does not apply to those 'incapable of self-government', which for Mill includes children (Mill, 1985 [1859], p. 147). Therefore, this position starts from a liberal opposition to paternalism in relations between adults capable of agency, and justifies paternalism in those cases where the responsive units are unable to govern themselves.

Geoffrey Scarre agrees with Mill that children are incapable of self-government, and for that reason parental paternalism is justified, and, like Mill, on the grounds that this is necessary for children's own happiness. Like Mill, Scarre is here concerned with paternalistic interference with liberty: 'paternalistic interventions are backed by altruistic motives [...] they involve for all that an infraction of [...] human freedom' (Scarre, 1980, p. 117). Scarre also believes that paternalistic parents are not left with an unresolved moral conflict here. This is the case as 'it is possible to justify our usual intuition that subjecting children to paternalistic coercion *does not infringe their rights*, and to remove any suspicion that we treat children and adults according to a morally invidious double standard' (ibid., p. 118; emphasis added). Paternalistic interference with an adult's liberty is wrong and we have sympathy with the normal adult wish to be free, but, Scarre claims, children 'are incapable of forming life plans'; and 'indeed the capacity to form coherent purposes and the development of the will-power to stick by them are part of what distinguishes adults from children' (ibid., pp. 119–20). How should we interpret this argument? Scarre is arguing that there is only the appearance of moral conflict when parents act paternalistically. As the children subjected to paternalistic power lack the qualities of an agent, they are incapable of self-government, in Mill's terms; they are neither free nor rational, as Scarre puts it, and so when parents interfere with children's liberty they do not thereby infringe children's rights.

Scarre accepts an 'asymmetry' in the 'calculation of the relative importance of liberty and well-being' among adults and among children (ibid.,
p. 120). Liberty is more cherished for adults, well-being for children.
Following Mill's conclusions, Scarre contends that it is 'better for adults
to suffer from the consequences of their own unwise decisions rather than
be subjected to the decisions of others' (ibid.). How can Scarre justify this
'asymmetry'? What we need to appeal to is a consideration that 'must be
applicable impartially', he contends: it 'must locate a feature of persons,
without distinction' (ibid., p. 121). For example, why is it not unjust to
intervene in the affairs of (to use his now dated terminology) 'mentally
handicapped' and 'otherwise inadequate' adults, he asks, and why is this
not the thin edge of a wedge? He believes it can be 'justifiable to trade a
person's liberty as the price of other advantages to him' (ibid.). This is so
because liberty is not a thing of absolute value (ibid., p. 122). Liberty is
important because of the advantages, the happiness, it brings; and if it
ceases to produce those advantages it loses its importance: 'If happiness is
the normal objective of liberty, it is right to curtail liberty in the case of children, for allowed complete freedom from adults' coercion it is hardly credible that they should achieve happiness (or even, in many cases, survive at
all)' (ibid.).

What qualities or characteristics of children justify the conclusion that
children's freedom from adults' coercion will not bring them happiness?
Before examining what Scare has to say, let me make the following distinction. First, agents are capable of *liberty of action*, of acting as they intend, of
forming and acting on their own intentions. Second, agents may or may
not also be *competent*, as competence is the ability to perform a task or
range of tasks, and competent decision making is the ability to make decisions adequately. I return to a detailed discussion of this distinction later
in this chapter. I introduce it now because Scarre's argument applies to
both concepts but he does not acknowledge the difference between them.
In what we have seen so far of his argument, it entails we are justified
intervening in the affairs of those who lack *liberty of action*: they are incapable of forming and acting on intentions; they are, in his terms, 'mentally
handicapped' and 'otherwise inadequate'. There is then a very important,
but unacknowledged, change of tack, as the implication of what Scarre
goes on to say is that the relevant feature is the responsive unit's *competence*
to make decisions. Thus, Scarre proposes the following rule for paternalist
intervention: 'the paternalist should intervene in an individual's affairs
only when there is reason to believe his decisions are not based on rational
considerations, and that they are likely to result in a diminution of his stock
of existing good, or under-achievement of his possible stock of good' (ibid.,
p. 123). This is a significant change in his argument, as those who are *not*

'mentally handicapped' or 'otherwise inadequate', that is, those capable of
liberty of action, nonetheless in any one case may make an incompetent
decision, that is, in Scarre's terms, a decision that is not rational and that is
not best designed to promote their own good. Indeed, most adults who fall
within normal parameters for liberty of action will, at one point or another,
make incompetent decisions in this sense.

What does he say about children's incompetence? Scarre derives his rule
for paternalistic intervention from empirical claims about human reasoning that bear the imprint of utilitarian moral philosophy. People's rational
actions generally have two characteristics, he argues: first, rational actions
are 'directed to maximizing the expected utility of the agent'; and second,
they 'typically manifest themselves as elements of a systematic approach
adopted by an agent for maximizing his good' (ibid.). On the basis of these
considerations, Scarre believes it is justified 'to impose a *general* paternalist
regime on children' (ibid.). Not only may parents act paternalistically in
respect of their children, parents must impose comprehensive 'systems of
purpose' on their children. There is one restriction placed on paternalism.
This is the prohibition against interfering at all in the affairs of people, say
older adolescents, who in general manifest the ability to consider their
actions rationally (ibid., p. 124).

Scarre's line of argument is that liberty is valuable only insofar as it
promotes the individual's own happiness; that children's liberty will not
promote their own happiness; and this is the case because they do not manifest the capacity for *liberty of action*, or, at other points, they are not *competent* to act so as to maximise their own expected utility and to act as part
of a systematic approach to maximising their utility. Therefore, there is
only the appearance of moral conflict in paternalistic interference with
children's liberty. Interfering with children's liberty may seem to violate
a moral rule in relation to children. In fact, the moral conflict no sooner
arises than it is resolved, as such interference does not violate children's
right to liberty. As it is 'justifiable to trade a person's liberty as the price of
other advantages to him', it is justifiable to violate children's liberty when
it (liberty) will not lead to children's happiness, that is, when they are incapable of liberty of action or are incompetent.

Now I turn to the alternative, pluralist conceptualisation of paternalism.
Bernard Gert and Charles M. Culver define paternalism as follows:

A is acting paternalistically towards *B* if and only if *A*'s behavior (correctly)
indicates that *A* *believes that*:
1) his action is for *B*'s good
2) he is qualified to act on *B*'s behalf
3) his action involves violating a moral rule (or doing that which will require
   him to do so) with regard to *B*

Table 1.1 Two definitions of paternalism

		The liberal view on paternalism	The pluralist view on paternalism
1	Intention	Always benevolent intention	Always benevolent intention
2	Forms of power	A interferes with B's liberty	A controls B (and may or may not interfere with B's liberty)
3	Pluralism	No moral conflict	Moral conflict
4	Consent	Justification through retrospective consent	Justification does not require consent
5	Agency	B lacks the qualities of an agent	B is capable of liberty of action

4) he is justified in acting on B's behalf independently of B's past, present, or immediately forthcoming (free, informed) consent
5) B believes (perhaps falsely) that he (B) generally knows what is for his own good. (Gert and Culver, 1976, pp. 49–50; emphasis in original)[2]

There is some overlap between the pluralist and liberal definitions of paternalism, as we have said. For both, the controlling unit (A) acts with the intention of promoting the other's (B's) good. Therefore, the paternalistic action is always benevolent in intention. And although there is disagreement over the role of consent in the justification of paternalism, it is agreed that the paternalist does not wait on the responsive unit's past, present, or immediately forthcoming consent before acting. However, deep disagreement characterises their views on the remaining features of paternalism (see Table 1.1).

Forms of power

Let us start with the various forms paternalistic power can take. In Chapter 5, we examine various ways in which one person can exercise power over another, and I will use Peter Morriss's definition of 'power over' there. To have power over others is to control others, as follows: to *affect* something or someone is to alter or impinge on that thing or person in some way, whereas to *effect* something is 'to bring about or accomplish it' (Morriss, 2002, p. 29; see Wrong, 1995 [1979]). Therefore, *to have 'power over' others is to affect others and produce effects for others.* Now let us consider the different ways in which the paternalist exercises power.

Gert and Culver explain that there are various ways in which the paternalist can control the person over whom power is exercised:

We regard coercive action, which involves the use of threats, as a subclass of attempts to interfere with liberty of action. Attempts at such interference are, in turn, a sub-class of attempts to control behavior. Thus, by showing that we can have paternalistic action which does not even involve an attempt to control behavior, we can show that paternalistic action need not be coercive nor involve an attempt to interfere with liberty of action. (1976, p. 46)

Gert and Culver here illustrate the various ways in which paternalistic power can be exercised, and in doing so draw attention to the various forms of 'power over'. First, coercion refers to instances where A affects B in such a way that B is given an irresistible incentive and is compelled to comply with A. Second, obstacles to possible choices and activities count as interference with liberty, but such obstacles may or may not bring with them coercive sanctions. Finally, power can be exercised so as to merely control someone's behaviour or someone's experiences, beliefs, or emotions (see also Komrad, 1983; Hershey, 1985; Shiffrin, 2000; Clarke, 2002).

It is essential to make these conceptual distinctions, as I can control you without controlling your behaviour, and I can control your behaviour without interfering with your liberty of action, and interfere with your liberty without coercing you. I will have much more to say about this as we proceed, but for now we can note the importance of acknowledging that my having power over you does not entail your loss of freedom. This should not be confused with the claim, which we will have more to say about as well, that I can exercise power over you, and even interfere with your liberty, and yet in doing so promote your autonomy. For example, this is the case with 'transformative' leaders who exercise power so as to empower their followers (see Fives, 2015; see also Haugaard, 2012).

What does an interference with liberty involve? I interfere with your liberty only when I place an obstacle to your possible choices and activities (Berlin, 2004 [1958]). Let us bring this back to parental power and in particular parental paternalistic power. In the following two examples (see Chapter 10 for a fuller discussion of these cases), parents act paternalistically so as to promote their children's autonomy and in so doing interfere with their children's liberty:

(a) The government has introduced a civic education programme, the aims of which include promoting children's capacities for critical reflection, along with other qualities, including relatedness and moral and political understanding. The programme for eleventh grade students (sixteen–seventeen years of age) is a form of service learning, which combines practical civic involvement in the community with classroom-based instruction. In our example, one group of students wish to be excused from the classroom-based component of the course, which they feel to be a waste of their time. They offer to make up the missed time with extra community-based work, which they believe to be worthwhile as a way to directly engage with and learn about the needs of others in the community. However, their parents insist that the children attend the classroom-based components of the course. Their parents interfere with their children's liberty, and do so in order to promote the autonomy of the adults the children will one day be.

(b) A second group of students are happy to engage in the classroom-based component of the civic education course, but they are not happy with what they see as a teacher-led and adult-oriented pedagogical approach. They request greater input into the design and delivery of the course, which would require a democratic and participatory approach to civic education, on the grounds that this is appropriate for such a course in a liberal democratic society. Once again, the parents refuse to support their children's requests, and instead insist the children attend the teacher-led and adult-oriented classes, and once again interfere with their children's liberty for the sake of their children's future autonomy.

In examples (a) and (b), the parents act paternalistically to promote their children's future autonomy, and in doing so interfere with their children's liberty. Let us look at an example where parents interfere with their children's liberty for some other objective. In example (c), a parent prevents the performance of an action, and in that way interferes with the child's liberty, but does so for the sake of the child's immediate safety:

(c) While out walking in the countryside with my fifteen-year-old son, I stop him from doing something that I judge to be highly dangerous for him, namely walking on a slippery wooden plank across a deep gorge. Unlike the example of a man unaware that the bridge he is about to cross is unsafe (Mill, 1985 [1859]), in this example, my son knows that the wooden plank is slippery and dangerous. I know that I am doing something that is *prima facie* (that is, *at first sight*) wrong, as it is something that involves my violating a moral rule. I do so with the intention of promoting my child's good, in this instance, preventing him from acting in a way that could lead to his suffering a serious physical injury. However, in this case I interfere with my son's liberty by stopping him from walking across the slippery plank.

So in all three examples, parents act paternalistically, and in so doing interfere with their children's liberty (and in two of the three examples do so in order to promote their children's autonomy). In some cases, however, a parent can act paternalistically and *not* interfere with the liberty of the child, as in the following example:

(d) I find out that my son is being bullied by a fellow student in his civic education class, and as a result, is afraid to attend class. I believe that civic education is good for my son. And without looking for my son's consent, I threaten the bully and warn him not to harass my son again. I have acted paternalistically, as I have acted so as to promote my son's good and without his consent, but I have not interfered with my son's liberty in doing so.

As we saw above, for the liberal, paternalism involves interference with the liberty of the person whose good the paternalist wishes to promote. However, there is no interference with liberty in example (d), even though this is a paternalistic act. I have not interfered with my son's liberty just because I have acted in a way that will (presumably) change the way the bully acts towards him and therefore change the environment in which my son makes choices and engages in activities. I have not removed choices and options from my son. Indeed, it is more accurate to say I have removed choices and options from the bully, and even that I have coerced him in addition, but this is not at issue. Rather, the example shows that in acting paternalistically towards my son, I need not interfere with *his* liberty. So this example would suggest that there is a plurality of forms of power generally and a plurality of forms of paternalistic power more specifically, a pluralism denied by the liberal view on paternalism.

In considering whether there is a plurality of forms of power, we can also employ the terminology of the three 'dimensions' of power debate.[3] According to Robert Dahl, power terms 'refer to subsets of relations among social units such that the behaviors of one or more units (the responsive units, B) depend in some circumstances on the behaviour of other units (the controlling units, A)' (Dahl, 2002 [1968], pp. 10–11).[4] This is referred to as the first face or dimension of power, focusing as it does on A's participation in the making of decisions that affect B. For Dahl, power always at least controls behaviour, but this leaves open the possibility that the exercise of power may or may not interfere with liberty and may or may not coerce, as we have seen in our examples above.[5] While Dahl's is a pluralist approach, therefore, in contrast, in the second and third dimensions, power is equated with only one of its various forms.

For Peter Bachrach and Morton Baratz, power is not only exercised in decision making, but also in agenda setting. They refer to the latter as the second face of power: 'power may be, and often is, exercised by confining the scope of decision-making to relatively "safe" issues' (2002 [1962], p. 30). This is the case when parents take one possibility 'off the agenda', for example, the possibility of their children simply not attending civic education classes at all. In doing so, parents interfere with their children's liberty, although it is a separate matter whether they do so legitimately (Haugaard, 2012, p. 39). Finally, there is the third dimension of power, as formulated by Steven Lukes. For Lukes, power is exercised only where there is a conflict of interests between ruler and ruled, and sanctions are threatened or imposed (2005 [1974], p. 36). Here power serves an ideological function, as those over whom power is exercised are not even aware that their interests are not thus promoted. As we shall see in Chapter 5, although he leaves open the possibility that power can be exercised paternalistically, for example in the case of parents and children, the crucial point is that, for Lukes, power is, simply, coercion. In contrast, in Chapter 5 I will try to show that there is an irreducible plurality of power concepts and so we cannot reduce power to coercion or interference with liberty.

Pluralism

The second area of profound disagreement between liberals and pluralists concerns whether or not paternalism involves moral conflict. According to Gert and Culver, the paternalist, A, believes that his action violates a moral rule with regard to B. That is, to act paternalistically requires not doing what one would otherwise be required to do with regard to some other person. Others have objected to this part of Gert and Culver's definition, and have argued that A can behave paternalistically towards B without violating a moral rule towards B. The following example from Gerald Dworkin (1983), which is thought to support this point, is reiterated by David Archard: 'A husband is under no moral obligation to inform his suicidal wife of the whereabouts of *his* sleeping pills. He acts paternalistically when he fails to do so, but violates no moral rule by his failure' (Archard, 1990, p. 37; emphasis in original).

An alternative interpretation of this example is that this *is* illustrative of a moral conflict. Dworkin and Archard, in their separate arguments, contend that the husband is 'under no obligation'. Indeed, we may judge that the husband is acting correctly, all things considered, when he refuses to tell his wife where his pills are. However, the husband does act without his wife's consent, and in addition this particular act does represent what Archard elsewhere refers to as the 'usurpation of a person's present choices or will' (1993, p. 341). The fact that the pills belong to the husband does not change the fact that he removes an option from his wife. It is *prima facie* wrong for a husband to prevent his wife from acting on her own choices, and therefore in this example the husband does violate a moral rule towards his wife, namely the requirement not to interfere with another's liberty. It is merely that, all things considered, we are likely to judge the husband acts correctly in violating this moral rule because in doing so (we presume) he acts in a manner best suited to saving his wife's life. Therefore, the husband *is* faced with a moral conflict, although many will agree with the manner in which he resolves it.

Let us look at one other argument claiming to show that paternalism need not involve moral conflict. Paul Hershey argues as follows:

> Suppose, for example, that it is the duty of a father to make sure his child learns to read and some father, not thinking of this, decides to teach his child to read whether the child likes it or not. Suppose further that the child offers no resistance to the lessons and instruction given by the father. Certainly this is a case of paternalism which does not need justification, and no moral rules are, or are believed to be, violated. (1985, p. 175)

However, if we can interpret the phrase 'the child offers no resistance' as meaning that the child 'assents' or even 'consents' to the father's actions in this example, then the father is *not* acting paternalistically. What we can say is that this is an example of someone acting so as to promote good consequences for someone else, and therefore it is an act of *beneficence*. Much more is needed for it to count as paternalism in addition. For example, let us imagine that the child sincerely does *not* want to learn to read, and therefore, whether tacitly or explicitly, does not consent to being taught to read. Then, if the parent nonetheless proceeds to teach the child to read, the parent would be acting paternalistically, and not merely beneficently.

That the paternalist violates a moral rule captures something necessary about paternalism and distinguishes it from non-paternalistic beneficence and also non-paternalistic non-maleficence. If I simply do something that will be of benefit to someone else (for example, teach the other person to read) or that will prevent harm to someone else (for example, inoculate the other person against disease) it does not follow that I am acting paternalistically. However, if I teach someone to read against their wishes, or if I inoculate someone without their knowledge, then I am meeting one necessary requirement of paternalism, in that I am violating a moral rule in regard to the other person. That some moral rule, whatever it is, is violated explains why it is felt that the paternalist has something to answer for and something to explain.

Consent

For John Locke, and other liberals, power has normative legitimacy when it is exercised on the basis of the consent of the governed (see Chapters 6 and 7). The prevailing, liberal view on paternalism does rely upon arguments from consent (Gutmann, 1980). However, I am not convinced of the importance of this issue for the liberal argument itself. This is the case because these are arguments about future (retrospective) consent, rather than past, present, or immediately forthcoming consent. Therefore, there may in fact be no disagreement between the liberal and pluralist arguments here, or at least no disagreement that amounts to a significant difference of opinion.

For instance, Gerald Dworkin argues that parents who treat their children paternalistically may do so if their children will one day consent to what happened: 'Parental paternalism may be thought of as a wager by the parent on the child's subsequent recognition of the wisdom of the restrictions. There is an emphasis on what could be called future-oriented consent – on what the child will come to welcome, rather than on what he does welcome' (1972, pp. 76–7). As Gert and Culver state in their definition, paternalists believe they are justified in acting independently of the other person's 'past, present, or immediately forthcoming (free, informed) consent'. I think everyone is in agreement on that point. However, the liberal argument is that paternalists make the wager that they will receive consent from their child when that child has reached adulthood, and such retrospective consent justifies the paternalistic action.

As I said, I am not convinced that the requirement of retrospective consent is a significant feature of the liberal position. As the parent cannot know whether the child will consent as an adult, the speculation that the child one day will do so surely is just that, speculation. It may be a good idea for parents to ask themselves whether their children will one day retrospectively consent to what they are now doing. This is *one* way to evaluate the moral legitimacy of their current actions. It is a thought experiment of the following kind: I am acting paternalistically towards my daughter, and I believe I am acting correctly if I can genuinely believe that the adult she (my daughter) will one day be will consent to this treatment. However, we can adopt such an approach without requiring actual consent for justification, and indeed all agree that paternalism is *not* based on past, present, or immediately forthcoming consent. Therefore, I think we can put to one side the requirement that adults will provide retrospective consent for the paternalistic actions of their parents without making any noticeable difference to the concept of paternalism itself.

Agency and rights

As we have seen, a widely held assumption among liberals is that paternalism is justified treatment of those who lack the qualities of an agent. As we shall see now and in the next chapter, this is of great significance, as it ties in with assumptions about moral conflicts and their resolution, as well as assumptions about what rights are or are not owed to children. It is commonly assumed that, as the children subjected to paternalistic power lack the qualities of an agent, their parents are not morally bound to respect their (the children's) liberty, and therefore interfering with their liberty does not infringe children's right to liberty and as a result does not lead to a moral conflict. What is the alternative, pluralist view?

As we saw, Gert and Culver argue that paternalists must believe that the people over whom paternalistic power is exercised do generally believe they generally know what is for their own good. If that is the case, the paternalist (A) must believe the person over whom paternalistic power is exercised (B) is capable of forming and holding such a belief. But not everyone over whom power is exercised has that capacity: 'Thus we cannot act paternalistically toward infants and animals unless we believe them to have this sort of self-consciousness' (1976, p. 53). Parents cannot act paternalistically towards their very young infants, unless they believe that their very young infants believe that they (the infants) generally know what is for their own good. The situation is different with children who have passed through further stages in cognitive and emotional development, where such self-consciousness *is* a possibility. What distinguishes very young infants from older children is that the latter, all things being equal, will have passed through various stages in development and will have cultivated capacities for agency.

As we said, for the liberal view of paternalism, the subordinate party (the child) lacks the qualities of an agent. Given the significance of these assumptions, I want to devote some space here to elaborate on precisely what is meant when it is claimed that children *lack the qualities of an agent*. We have already seen that Scarre's position is ambiguous here. At some points, his argument entails that children are incapable of agency in a global sense, they are incapable of *liberty of action*; while, at other points, the implication is that children are merely *incompetent*, that is, although they are capable of liberty of action they make bad decisions. Given this lack of specificity in the use of the concept by some, let us carefully examine what is meant by agency.

Albert Bandura defines human agency as follows: 'To be an agent is to influence intentionally one's functioning and life circumstances' (2006, p. 164). He identifies the following four properties of agency:

(i) *Intentionality*: We can define agents as those who 'form intentions that include action plans and strategies for realizing them';
(ii) *Forethought*: Agents 'set themselves goals and anticipate the likely outcomes of prospective actions to guide and motivate their efforts';
(iii) *Self-reactiveness*: Agents are self-regulators, as agency involves the ability to make choices and action plans, 'but also the ability to construct appropriate courses of action and to motivate and regulate their execution'; and

(iv) *Self-reflectiveness*: Agents 'reflect on their personal efficacy, the soundness of their thoughts and actions, and the meaning of their pursuits, and they make corrective adjustments if necessary'. (ibid., pp. 164–5)

It should be noted that this definition of agency does not entail ontological assumptions of an atomistic kind. In fact, it is assumed that agents are subject to various constraints and influences. The exercise of self-influence is seen as 'part of the causal structure' that includes 'intrapersonal, behavioural, and environmental determinants' (ibid.).

So what is agency? First, all agents possess some qualities. These are what I will call the *necessary* qualities of an agent. And agents may go on to develop some or all of the further *possible* qualities of an agent. However, it is precisely this distinction that has not been made by Scarre and others. What I will try to show is that, just because children have deficits in respect of some possible qualities of an agent, it does *not* follow that they lack the necessary qualities of an agent and it does not follow that their parents are not duty bound to protect their right to liberty. Insofar as children do have the necessary qualities of an agent, on that basis they are owed a right to liberty, even if they lack some or all of the further possible qualities of an agent, and even if, as a result, we are faced with a moral conflict, and may decide in a given case that we should not respect their right to liberty. It is this possibility of moral conflict that the prevailing, liberal view on paternalism denies, and which I want to defend. However, I should note, in this chapter I can only introduce many of the concepts and arguments involved, and do so in a very schematic way. It is in subsequent chapters that I will elaborate on these points with the level of detail they require.

As Table 1.2 illustrates, agents are capable of liberty of action, of acting as they intend, of forming and acting on their own intentions. While this is the one necessary quality of an agent, there are other qualities it is possible but not necessary for an agent to possess. Thus, anyone capable of forming and acting on their own intentions has liberty of action, but it does not follow that they are competent, rational, autonomous, or virtuous, or that they can execute each and every decision, or that their actions will be voluntary. I will elaborate on these distinctions very briefly below.

First, we should distinguish between liberty of action, on the one hand, and the *execution of decisions*, on the other hand. One may have the qualities of an agent needed for liberty of action, and yet be unable to execute one's decisions in a particular area or sphere. Children capable of influencing intentionally their functioning and life circumstances, that is, children who are agents, nonetheless may be unable to perform an action because of their stage of development (e.g. they may lack the motor skills for a specific task, such as to drive a car), or injury or illness (e.g. they may have a

Table 1.2 The necessary and possible qualities of an agent

Necessary quality of an agent	Different possible qualities of an agent	What this quality entails	Necessary conditions for possession of this quality
Liberty of action		Acting as one intends	Able to form and act on intentions
		Global capacity	
	Execution of decisions	Use of resources or exercise of necessary skills or strengths to execute decisions	Able to form and act on intentions
			Possess and exercise relevant resources, skills, or strengths
	Voluntary action	Free from liberty-infringing influence of others	Able to form and act on intentions
		Free from excessive un-noticed or un-controllable urges and compulsions	Sufficiently free from internal and external impediments
	Competent decision making	Sufficient access to information, understanding of information, appreciation of how it applies to oneself, and/or rational deliberation	Able to form and act on intentions
			Meet specific criteria of competence
	Rationality	Sufficient rational deliberation in decision making	Able to form and act on intentions
			Meet specific criteria of rationality
	Autonomy	Exercise of self-government	Able to form and act on intentions
			Meet specific criteria of self-government
	Virtue	Acting from a stable disposition to do what is good	Able to form and act on intentions
			Foster ethically valuable character traits

broken leg that restricts their mobility), or a life-long disability (e.g. they may have significant lack of voluntary muscle control), or lack of resources (e.g. material poverty) or learnt skills (e.g. reading and writing). Many children who do not lack the qualities of an agent may nonetheless face significant execution deficits, deficits that, in many instances, others could remedy with various forms of assistance. In Chapter 2 there will be a fuller treatment of this distinction.

Voluntary action is different again. Here, individuals capable of forming and acting on their intentions are not prevented from doing so, either by some external impediment (i.e. a liberty-infringing exercise of power) or by some internal impediment (e.g. an uncontrollable fear). We shall explore various ways in which parents can control their children's behaviour, and also examine which forms of control are compatible with children's voluntariness, in Chapters 6 and 10.

It is also the case that I may have liberty of action and yet fall short in terms of competence, rationality, or autonomy. *Competence* refers to the ability to perform a task or range of tasks, and competent decision making is the ability to make decisions adequately. Some believe that standards of competence cannot be equated with the requirements of being either autonomous or rational. They conclude that people's decisions may be incompetent because they have not had access to the relevant information, have not fully understood the information, and do not appreciate how this information applies to them in their current situation (Culver and Gert, 1990). However, others believe the competent decision is also autonomous (Appelbaum, 2007). And *autonomy* is synonymous with an exacting standard of self-governance. I am autonomous in so far as I govern my life in accordance with rational, moral laws that I have chosen myself. I am autonomous insofar as I am the author of the commands I obey (Wolff, 1990 [1970], pp. 26, 29). Finally, decisions and actions can be judged against expectations of *rationality* as well; and some argue that a competent decision must also be a rational decision. That is, individual are competent only insofar as they have the ability to 'give a rational reason' for the decision in question (Beauchamp and Childress, 2009, pp. 114–15). We will explore children's autonomy in Chapter 3, and we will then examine children's competence in Chapter 9.

It is also the case that an agent may or may not go on to develop moral virtues. *Virtue*, therefore, is a further possible but not a necessary quality of an agent. Virtuous behaviour entails acting from a stable disposition to do what is good, a commitment to 'what is good or best unqualifiedly' (MacIntyre, 1988, p. 30). When defining virtue, some emphasise the social context, as virtue 'requires for its application some prior account of certain features of social and moral life in terms of which it has to be defined and explained' (MacIntyre, 1988, p. 186). For others, in contrast, character traits are virtues insofar as, based on certain facts about humanity, they benefit us and help us resist temptations and weaknesses (Foot, 2001). To foster and exercise such character traits, one must be capable of forming and acting on one's intentions, but not all those capable of agency can be said to be virtuous. As we shall see in Chapter 4, psychologists have focused on children's development of pro-social qualities, while political philosophers have examined among other things whether autonomy is a precondition of virtue.

I want to link what has been said here about agency to arguments about children's right to liberty. I have distinguished liberty of action from other possible qualities of an agent. Later, starting in Chapter 4, we will also distinguish *negative* freedom from *positive* freedom, and the latter distinction is closely related with the former.

As formulated by Isaiah Berlin, negative freedom refers to an 'area' in which a person 'is or should be left to do or be what he is able to do or be, without interference by other persons'; whereas positive freedom derives from the idea of being my own master (2004 [1958], pp. 169, 179). This distinction is important as, it is claimed, the 'plea for civil liberties and individual rights' can be made on the grounds that they protect one's negative freedom, and do so independent of whether one is also in a condition to exercise positive freedom. Such a plea arises from the notion that 'all coercion is, in so far as it frustrates human desires, bad as such' (ibid., p. 175). That is, one's *right* to protection against such coercion is not conditional on one's choosing competently, of having the correct 'desires', and so on: that is, it is not conditional on one's positive freedom. We must wait until Chapter 4 before I can defend the claim that the right to negative freedom has value independently of the promotion of positive freedom. For now, without any justifying argument, I merely want to register the idea that children capable of liberty of action have a legitimate claim to rights protecting the exercise of that liberty.

Soft and hard paternalism

I have given only a very brief introduction to the agency concepts that will be explored in greater depth later in this book. For now, I want to focus on one distinction that has particular significance for the debate on paternalism. We have already said there has been insufficient attention paid to the distinction between the necessary qualities of an agent, on the one hand, and an agent's competence, on the other. Indeed, often when it is claimed that children lack the necessary qualities of an agent in fact it is incompetence that is being referred to, and this lack of clarity has been damaging to the quality of the debate on children's right to liberty. In contrast, Gert and Culver's definition of paternalism allows for this distinction, and I will focus on it and its implications here, namely the appropriateness of the soft and hard forms of paternalism.

In the paternalistic power relation between A and B, B is an agent, as B is capable of influencing intentionally B's functioning and life circumstances. As we have seen, it is necessary that A believes that B believes that B generally knows what is for B's own good. In some instances, A judges B's beliefs in this regard to be 'perhaps false'. However, even when A does judge B's beliefs to be perhaps false, this does not affect B's status as an agent. If A is correct in judging B's belief to be perhaps false, it follows that B's decision making will not be 'competent' in this instance, but B is still capable of influencing intentionally B's functioning and circumstances, as the following example will illustrate:

(e) If a ten-year-old girl (B) believes that she should eat chocolate every day and that to do so is for her own good, and if B is capable of eating chocolate without help from others (that is, she has the dexterity required to open chocolate bars and to eat their contents), then, for the purposes of this case, B is capable of influencing intentionally her functioning and life circumstances. If B puts this plan into effect she may bring about certain harms for herself, including tooth decay. After reflection, B may be content to continue with her course of action, deciding, among other things, that tooth decay is a small price to pay for the pleasure of eating chocolate every day. The paternalist, A, intervenes here because A believes that B's belief that she generally know what is for her own good is perhaps false. A judges that eating chocolate every day is not for B's good and in addition acts to ensure that B does not do so.

Bandura's definition of agency does not require that agents will always act in such a way that no harms will arise for them. Agents are required to reflect on the soundness of their thoughts and actions. Therefore, we would require that B is capable of doing so. However, after reflection, B may still want to do the kinds of thing that A believes are harmful for B.

What are the implications of the above for our discussion of paternalism? To answer this question, we need to make the following threefold distinction between:

(1) Persons incapable of liberty of action,
(2) Persons capable of liberty of action who are judged competent, and
(3) Persons capable of liberty of action who are judged incompetent.

This distinction is important for the following reason. Gert and Culver's argument entails that (1) those incapable of liberty of action cannot be treated paternalistically. However, paternalism may be exercised over (2) those capable of liberty of action who are judged competent to make such a decision, which is referred to as *hard* paternalism, and (3) those capable of liberty of action but judged incompetent to make a decision in a given case, which is referred to as *soft* paternalism (Feinberg, 1986; Arneson, 2005). Of course, as we have seen, depending on the criteria employed, 'competence' can include the requirements of 'rationality' and 'autonomy', and 'virtue' may be equated with competence as well. However, I shall not make these distinctions here, but instead focus on what can be said generally about liberty of action and competence.

(1) The first category, those *incapable of liberty of action*, can include adults with profound and multiple intellectual disabilities or severe mental illness, or adults in a continuous state of unconsciousness. In such cases, the medical condition must be such as to render the individual not just incompetent to make a decision in a given case but incapable of agency generally. My argument is that, while it is possible to exercise power over such adults, it is not possible to act paternalistically towards them.[6] However, our focus here is on children. Children may be incapable of liberty of action because they have reached only the very earliest stages of development in terms of cognition, emotional development, motor skills, verbal communication, and so on. It is not possible to behave paternalistically towards children in this category, although it is possible to control their lives so as to promote their well-being (non-paternalistic beneficence) or protect them from harm (non-paternalistic non-maleficence).

(2) The paternalist may act for others' good even when the people in question are competent to make the decision by themselves. If *A* believes that *B* is competent to make a decision but nonetheless acts paternalistically towards *B* this would be an instance of *hard* paternalism. This is illustrated by a revised version of example (d):

(d) My daughter is being bullied in school. Although she accepts that it would be beneficial to her if I spoke with her teacher so that her teacher would help bring the bullying to an end, she has come to the conclusion that I should not do so. She has reasoned carefully about the likely consequences of each course of action, she accepts that my speaking to her teacher would most likely produce good consequences for her, but she also believes that her parents should no longer 'fight her battles for her'. Although I accept she is competent to make this decision, nonetheless, because I have significant concerns about letting the bullying continue unchecked, I go ahead and speak to my daughter's teacher.

In contrast (3), *soft* paternalism refers to interventions in 'the life of another person on grounds of beneficence or nonmaleficence' when that person is *not* competent. With respect to the treatment of adults, this refers to cases such as 'poorly informed consent or refusal, severe depression that precludes rational deliberation, and addiction that prevents free choice and action' (Beauchamp and Childress, 2009, pp. 209–10).

Let us pause for a moment to consider the ways in which both hard and soft paternalism are conceptualised in the literature. Hard paternalism, it is contended, refers to efforts to 'prevent or mitigate harm to or to benefit a person, despite the fact that the person's risky choices and actions are *informed, voluntary, and autonomous*' (ibid., p. 210; emphasis added). Sometimes it is necessary to protect even competent individuals 'from the harmful consequences even of their fully *voluntary* choices and undertakings', it is argued (Feinberg, 1986, p. 12; emphasis added). Let us turn now to the way in which 'soft' paternalism has been discussed in the literature. If people are incompetent, it is thought that their actions display 'substantially *nonvoluntary* conduct' (Beauchamp and Childress, 2009, p. 210; emphasis in original). Soft paternalism, as a result, is seen as a form of 'protection to a person from his own *non-voluntary* choices' that is compatible with a general commitment to liberty, as such choices 'are just as alien to him as the choices of someone else' (Feinberg, 1971, p. 112; emphasis added). If we do intervene in someone else's choices in this way, it is argued, this does '*not* involve a real conflict between the principles of respect for autonomy and beneficence' (Beauchamp and Childress, 2009, p. 210; emphasis added).

I want to take exception to these discussions of hard and soft paternalism. To accept them would require equating competence (the ability to perform a task or range of tasks) with autonomy (self-governance), and both of these with liberty of action (the ability to form and act on intentions) as well as voluntary action (being sufficiently free from internal and liberty-infringing external impediments). Rather, as I have said, I can be an agent, I can have liberty of action, if I am able to form and act on intentions. It does not follow that I also meet any specific criteria of competence generally, or more specifically of rationality, or autonomous self-governance, or even voluntary action. I have tried to show, very briefly, that these concepts are distinct, and I will elaborate on this argument in the coming chapters. What is the benefit of maintaining these conceptual distinctions? As we shall see in the next chapter, a central issue here is the right to liberty. In the prevailing, liberal view it is argued the paternalist does not violate a right to liberty when the paternalist interferes with a child's liberty, and as we have just seen, it is argued that soft paternalism is compatible with a general commitment to liberty.

I have already indicated an alternative position, based in part on Berlin's arguments, one that I will defend in the next chapter. I will argue that, just in virtue of being an agent, I have a right to liberty, and I have such a right even when I am not deciding in a way that is competent, rational, or autonomous, never mind virtuous. A central part of the argument there is that, because children have a right to liberty, we may be faced with particular kinds of moral dilemmas. As Berlin, again, accepts, there may be good reasons to interfere with my liberty (for example, for the sake of my own well-being), but for all that, it is, in the first instance, an interference with my liberty and therefore a violation of my right to liberty (Berlin, 2004 [1958], p. 172). I return to this point in the next chapter, where I critically examine arguments intended to show that paternalistic interference with children's liberty do not violate a right to liberty. I will argue that such attempts fail.

Conclusions

The debate on paternalism is central to our understanding of parental power. I have criticised the prevailing, liberal view that paternalism involves interference with liberty, that it is justified treatment of those who lack the qualities of an agent, and that it does not entail moral conflict. This argument is important, for we may judge that parents should act paternalistically but it does not follow that parents are justified in infringing their children's liberty, or that children lack the capacity for liberty of action, or that there are no moral dilemmas in doing so. The debate on paternalism also is illustrative of a wider debate about the nature and role of political philosophy. I shall take up this theme further in later chapters, but the central lesson is that political philosophers have been engaged in a process of moral simplification, a tendency we should resist. Rather, when we evaluate parental power what we discover is an irreducible plurality of moral considerations and of morally significant features. As we have already seen, there is a plurality of forms of power, there are diverse moral considerations that can come into conflict when we evaluate such power relations, and we must consider such questions as the power that can be exercised over children who lack the capacity for liberty of action, those who are capable of liberty of action but are incompetent, and those who are competent.

Notes

1   It should be noted that David Archard does not claim that paternalism involves the infringement of liberty (Archard, 1993), the first common assumption discussed earlier.

2 In the quote taken from Gert and Culver I have replaced their use of 'A' and 'S' with 'A' and 'B' for consistency with the remaining discussion.
3 For an account of the fourth dimension of power, namely discipline, see Haugaard (2012).
4 In this quote, I have replaced Dahl's use of 'C' and 'R' for the more commonly used 'A' and 'B' to refer, respectively, to the controlling unit and the responsive unit.
5 Dahl does not reduce or equate power to 'coercion, command, or compulsion', as David Baldwin notes, despite the many commentators who have claimed the contrary concerning Dahl's conceptualisation of power, as Baldwin also details (2015, p. 220).
6 However, there is one important qualification to make. It is possible to behave paternalistically towards an adult once capable of liberty of action but who is currently incapable of liberty of action. One possible example is if B is currently incapable of liberty of action, if A knows what B's wishes and preferences are, for example, through an advanced directive, and A puts B's wishes and preferences to one side so as to promote B's well-being.

2

Caretaker or liberator?

In the last chapter, we examined the concept of paternalism in some depth, paying attention to a number of key conceptual issues. We looked at the different forms of 'power over', the nature of moral conflicts, the agency of those over whom paternalistic power is exercised, and also the rights children may enjoy. In this chapter, I continue this analysis of paternalism by exploring the way that concept has been utilised in the 'caretaker thesis' and the 'liberation thesis'. Are parents caretakers or liberators? Is the role of parents to act in a paternalistic fashion so as to take care of their children or is it instead to set their children free? According to the caretaker thesis, parental power makes up for the deficits in children's agency, and for that reason children should be subjected to standard institutional paternalism (see Purdy, 1996; Burtt, 2003; Archard, 2004; Brighouse and Swift, 2014). The liberation thesis stands at the other end of the spectrum concerning children's rights. According to the liberation thesis, we tend to underestimate children's capacity for agency, and we ignore the fact that many children have the required capacity to exercise the rights that adults enjoy (Holt, 1975; Harris, 1996; Freeman, 2007).

In this chapter, I argue that those who defend the caretaker thesis do so on the basis of the commonly held beliefs criticised in the previous chapter, the assumptions characteristic of the liberal view on paternalism. It is assumed that paternalism entails interfering with another's liberty, that it does not involve moral conflicts, and that it is justified treatment of those who lack the qualities of an agent. In addition, no clear distinction is made between children who lack the qualities of an agent and children who are merely incompetent. What is more, the same assumptions underlie the liberation thesis. Indeed, both the caretaker thesis and the liberation thesis are questionable because they operate with a definition of paternalism that is highly problematic. I also want to make one further argument here. Namely, even an adequate conceptualisation of paternalism is insufficient as a general account of parental power, as there are non-paternalistic forms of parental power as well. Therefore, independent of their shortcomings as accounts of paternalistic power, we should expect both the caretaker thesis and the liberation thesis to be unsatisfactory because paternalism itself as a concept is of limited application. It is for these reasons that we must move beyond paternalism.

The caretaker thesis

To understand the caretaker thesis, it is helpful to start with the general liberal argument concerning legitimate power. Liberals believe that, as humans have a fundamental right to personal freedom, as they have rights of self-determination, the power exercised over them is legitimate only when 'justified by their prior free grant of permission to the exercise of power' (Archard, 2010, p. 46). For power to have legitimacy, the rational, autonomous persons over whom it is exercised must first give their consent. These are the liberal considerations used to evaluate power relations between adults, the power exercised in the 'political domain' (Rawls, 2003 [1989]). However, many liberal thinkers do not apply these considerations, or at least not without significant qualification, to the evaluation of power relations between parents and their children (Brighouse and Swift, 2014, p. 15). Why is this inconsistency considered justified? It is argued that 'children are not in a position to give permission', because they 'lack the mature capacities of reason and independent volition that are needed for the giving and withholding of permission to be possible' (Archard, 2010, p. 46). Given children's deficits in agency, therefore, they do not have rights of self-determination, and parental power cannot be justified by children's prior consent.

This can be thought of as the *deficit* conception of legitimacy. According to this line of thought, parents may exercise power over children only insofar as children lack the qualities of an agent and only insofar as parental power makes up for the deficits that legitimate their subordination:

> The reason we exclude them [children] from the community of social and political equals is that they lack a range of social, emotional, and cognitive capacities that cannot be developed apart from their subordination to caring adults who take responsibility for their education and that, when developed, ground the possibility of their successful integration into a larger political and cultural community. (Burtt, 2003, p. 258)

Thus, parents exercise paternalistic power over their children; and paternalism is justified by children's agency deficits: either it is justified 'when people cannot make the choices they would make if they were rational and autonomous' (Archard, 2004, p. 78); or when they 'lack the mature capacities of reason and independent volition' (Archard, 2010, p. 46).

A central premise of the caretaker thesis is that parental power makes up for children's agency deficits. It is also assumed that, because children lack the qualities of an agent, they have no right to liberty. Paternalism, it is argued, 'denies to children' the rights of 'self-determination', as it is assumed that 'children should not be free to make autonomous decisions' (Archard, 2004, p. 77). This is the case even with Archard's proposed 'compromise position' between the liberation and caretaker theses. The 'compromise' in question is the 'presumption that younger children cannot whereas older children, that is teenagers, can exercise rights of self-determination' (ibid., p. 93). His is not a compromise between the competing values of children's liberty and children's well-being, as he will give priority to children's well-being whenever it is in conflict with children's liberty, as we shall see. Rather, it is a compromise between those who, on the one hand, contend that *all* children should have *all* of the rights of self-determination enjoyed by adults, and on the other hand, those who contend *no* child should have *any*. For Archard, it is still the case that those without the 'capacity' for 'rational autonomy' simply have no rights of self-determination.

The caretaker thesis rests on the claim that parental power makes up for children's agency deficits. So what is meant, for example, when Archard refers to a child not being rational and autonomous? He highlights three aspects of rational autonomy: rationality, maturity, and independence. I want to look at each in turn. First, he notes that children can be 'incapacitated compared to adults' regarding the 'acquisition of knowledge and experience', which is required for *rationality*, understood as 'the forming of generally reliable beliefs about one's surroundings, having a relatively coherent set of desires and consequently being able [...] to order one's preferences consistently between alternative courses of action'; second, children who lack *maturity* are 'more likely than adults to make decisions whilst in the grip of strong emotions, which can change from one moment to the next'; and finally, third, children are less likely to have *independence*, in the sense of being able to 'actually act out their choices' because certain 'physical abilities [...] are straightforwardly beyond a child', and also the possibility 'of having a mind of one's own' is less likely (ibid., pp. 93–5).

What more can we say about these deficits? It seems that, to use the terminology from Chapter 1 (see Table 1.2), what we have here are, simultaneously, (1) deficits in liberty of action, (2) deficits in competence, and (3) deficits in execution:

(1) At one point, it is quite clear that Archard is referring to deficits in *liberty of action* and not incompetence: it is, he argues, 'the incapacity

to choose and not the folly of any particular decision which justifies the paternalist in usurping that choice' (ibid., p. 67). In this vein, Archard refers to children having not yet developed the 'cognitive capacity' required for making intelligent decisions, and also their 'emotional inconstancy' (ibid., p. 78). Such children are incapable of forming and acting on intentions, and it is this that justifies parental power, and not the incompetence (the folly) of the decisions they make.

(2) However, at other points, Archard can be interpreted as arguing that paternalism is justified because of the folly of a child's decision; that is, because of the child's *incompetence*: 'So the paternalist caretaker must choose what the child would choose if competent to make choices, and choose with regard to the interests of the adult the child will become' (ibid.). Indeed, when Archard refers to children's lack of 'rationality', this can be interpreted as a lack of competence, as it is the absence of the information and experience necessary for competent decision making. Such children have the capacity for liberty of action, but the decisions they will make will not be competent. Similarly, when children are said to lack 'maturity', what they lack is the self-control and self-mastery needed to order one's desires and choose rationally; that is, what is required to choose competently.

(3) Yet again, at other points it seems that Archard has in mind children's *deficits in execution*. For example, he refers to the physical abilities 'straightforwardly beyond a child'. This can be the case of children capable of agency, and even competent to choose, but, given their stage of physiological development say, cannot act as they choose.

Why does it matter that no clear distinction has been made between liberty of action, competence, and execution of decisions? First, it matters as some of the situations included here in a discussion of paternalistic power are not paternalistic, namely, when power is exercised over children incapable of liberty of action. As we saw in the Introduction, we cannot act paternalistically towards animals and young infants. It matters for the further reason that paternalistic power exercised over those capable of liberty of action but incompetent to make a decision is *soft* paternalism. And soft paternalism leads to moral conflict, as is the case if the paternalist usurps the choice of an individual who is capable of choice but incompetent to make the decision in question. One reason why it leads to moral conflict is because people capable of agency have rights of self-determination: they have a right to liberty insofar as they can form and act on intentions, even if they do so incompetently, a right that, in this instance, has been violated by the paternalist. Third, the distinction is important as children can be capable of liberty of action, and also competent, yet lack some skill or resource needed to execute their decision. Again, in such cases they do have rights of self-determination, although they may need assistance from others to enjoy those rights. Also, there need be no moral conflict at all here between the right to liberty and the need for assistance. For example, this may be the case in a situation where children have the capacity to learn from formal schooling, have decided competently they wish to attend school, but, because of a physical disability that impairs their mobility, they can do so only with the assistance of their parents and other caring adults. I will return to this point later in this chapter.

At this point let us recap before moving on. For the caretaker thesis, parents' power is paternalistic, and paternalism involves interference with children's liberty. However, although there is agreement that parents' power is to make up for some deficit in their children's agency, there is disagreement here over what it is that does justify the power of the caretaker parent.

One line of argument is that we must give priority to the duty to promote the autonomy of the adults children will one day be. As Joel Feinberg has argued, the rights of parents to act as caretakers are justified by their ensuring children's 'right to an open future', and parents do this by maximising chances for self-fulfilment (1980, p. 135). Brighouse and Swift accept that tensions may emerge between our duty to tolerate diverse ways of life and our duty to promote autonomy, but when parental practices pose a threat to the development of autonomy, we decide straightforwardly in favour of autonomy: 'The principle of toleration does not extend to tolerating practices that are harmful to non-consenting others. So we can regulate child rearing to promote autonomy without being intolerant' (2006, p. 83). Brighouse and Swift are cognisant that very often it is parents who create for their child the 'emotional cost of breaking from the views in which she was raised' (2014, p. 173). This is all the more reason for parents to promote the autonomy of the adults their children will become. Their conclusion is that 'children have a right to be treated paternalistically' given the interests they have in becoming autonomous as well as their interests in their own well-being (ibid., p. 70).

However, according to a second line of thought, from David Archard, the rights of parents are conditional on their discharging the duty to ensure their children have a 'minimally decent existence' (Archard, 2010, pp. 43, 52). Parental rights are not unconditional, and parental duties have priority over parental rights. However, parents are *not* required to 'bring up their children in the light of liberal principles' in either of the following two ways (ibid., p. 45). As we have already seen, Archard does not apply the general liberal approach concerning legitimacy to the evaluation of parents' power, and so he rejects the liberal idea that parents' power must be and can only be based on the prior consent of their children. However, he also rejects Feinberg's argument that parents should ensure for their children an 'open future'. Archard concludes that any such attempt to ensure parents exercise power in line with liberal principles would have three negative consequences: it 'would severely limit permissible kinds of upbringing'; it would involve 'the concession of enormous powers to official agencies' to enforce this requirement; and also, as it would be harmful to the 'privacy and exclusivity' parents require in discharging their duties, it would prevent the family from serving its functions (ibid., pp. 45, 48).

Therefore, for the caretaker thesis, parental paternalism is justified treatment for children who lack the qualities of an agent, it involves interference with children's liberty, and it is justified by the children's interests *either* in a minimally decent existence *or* in becoming autonomous adults. A further feature of the caretaker thesis is the assumption that we will not be faced with irresolvable moral conflicts when we act paternalistically. For Brighouse and Swift, moral conflicts can be resolved because, as a general rule, when the two come into conflict autonomy has priority over toleration. For Archard, our duty to ensure children have a minimally decent existence has priority over our duty to promote the autonomy of the adults children will one day be. They disagree over which value has priority but agree that one value does, as a general rule, have priority and as such removes moral conflict when evaluating parental power.

Is the caretaker thesis justified? It is insofar as it is possible to justify its distinction between those to whom rights of self-determination are owed and those to whom they are not. However, what we have already argued in Chapter 1 suggests the following. Children who are capable of liberty of action have, for that reason, a right to liberty, and it is *prima facie* wrong to interfere with a right to liberty. The same is true of those who are merely incompetent. Those who defend the caretaker thesis believe that the paternalistic parent is not faced with moral dilemmas. However, if children capable of liberty of action also do have a right to liberty, as I have argued, and if caretaker parents, in some cases, are required to interfere with their children's liberty so as to promote their children's well-being, then we will be faced with a moral conflict, and considerations relevant to resolving such conflicts include whether and in what way the children's decisions are incompetent and the children themselves are unable to execute their decisions. As I have said, we return to this point later this chapter.

I am questioning the claim made in the caretaker thesis that children do not have rights of liberty. Given the nature of these criticisms, let us return again to the philosophical and ethical foundations of paternalism. In the previous chapter, we outlined Scarre's *utilitarian* argument for the caretaker thesis, according to which the fundamental moral principle is the requirement to promote utility. In the next section of this chapter, I examine Onora O'Neill's *Kantian* defence of the caretaker thesis, according to which the fundamental moral principle is the requirement to respect autonomy. Each believes they have identified a general rule for resolving what appear to be moral conflicts when we act paternalistically. Which of them is correct? Or are they each mistaken for assuming that they can identify such a general rule?

The Kantian argument from a duty of care

According to O'Neill, the 'fundamental' moral consideration in relations between parents and children is *not* children's right to liberty but *rather* parents' duties of care towards their children (O'Neill, 1989, p. 188). She thus concludes by saying there 'are good reasons to think that paternalism may be much of what is ethically required in dealing with children, even if it is inadequate in dealings with mature and maturing minors' (ibid., p. 204). Her conclusion is based in part on the premise that children do not have the required capacities that rights of liberty would protect. As with Scarre, O'Neill assumes that paternalism involves interference with another's liberty, and is justified when children have agency deficits, and also, as with Scarre, she concludes that we are not faced with any irresolvable moral conflict when we act paternalistically in this way. So how does she arrive at these conclusions?

A 'fundamental' moral consideration in their relations with children is parents' duty of care. This is the duty to be 'kind and considerate in dealing with children – to care for them – and to put ourselves out in ways that differ from those in which we must put ourselves out for adults' (ibid., p. 190). This obligation is not universal, as we do not owe it to all children, and when abstracted from any one social context it is incomplete or imperfect. That is, this obligation is owed neither to all others nor to specified others, and so there are no right holders, no one who can demand care as a right. It is true that we can institutionalise the duty of care, for instance in the roles of social worker, parent, teacher, and so on, and in that way establish certain positive special obligations to which certain positive (institutional) rights correspond. For O'Neill, such rights are derivative; they exist only because of the more fundamental duty of care. In addition, the obligation to care for children requires more than ensuring that children enjoy their institutional rights. The mother who did nothing more than guarantee her children's institutional rights would be failing in her duty of care, in her duty to be kind and considerate, O'Neill contends.

O'Neill does accept that children have some rights that are fundamental. The obligation to refrain from abuse and molestation of children, whether or not they are specifically in our charge, is owed by all adults to all children. It follows that all children have a right to be free from abuse and molestation. However, what O'Neill is objecting to is a 'rights-based' ethics, which would entail that what is fundamental is an 'open-ended "right to liberty"' (ibid., p. 191). What is objectionable about this? She believes that if our morality were 'based' on the right to liberty, if the right to liberty were 'fundamental', we would have no reason to hold parents duty-bound to show care and consideration for their children. Children's lives are particularly vulnerable to unkindness, to lack of involvement, cheerfulness or good feeling from a parent. Parents 'can wither children's lives' even if they violate no rights (ibid., p. 192). The argument here would seem to be that, if children's right to liberty were fundamental, then it could trump parents' duty of care towards their children. Then, we would have no reason to hold parents duty bound to care for their children in any situation where the two moral claims came into conflict.

I want to look at this argument in more detail. O'Neill concludes that imperfect obligations of care are morally binding because they are universalisable. This follows from one of Immanuel Kant's formulations of the Categorical Imperative: 'Act only on that maxim through which you can at the same time will that it should become a universal law' (Kant, 1956 [1785], § 51). Kant believed it was not possible for humans consistently to reject the duty of care, because we cannot universalise the rejection of this duty:

> I have no wish to contribute anything to his [someone struggling with great hardships] well-being or to his support in distress [...] For a will which decided in this way would be in conflict with itself, since many a situation might arise in which the man needed love and sympathy from others, and in which, by such a law of nature sprung from his own will, he would rob himself of all hope of the help he wants for himself (ibid., § 56–7).

The duty of care is universalisable. This is the case because, although humans are rational and capable of autonomy, they are also vulnerable and needy beings; their rationality and independence 'is incomplete, mutually vulnerable and socially produced' (O'Neill, 1989, p. 198).

However, O'Neill's argument here raises some serious questions. For if it is the case that, as she claims, the duty of care can be willed by all, it follows that all humans are dependent and in need of care. Therefore, children are not unique in needing care and consideration and in being dependent on others for the provision of such care. If that is the case, what is it about children's lives that is different from adults' lives and that justifies the distinction O'Neill makes between adults' and children's right to liberty?

For O'Neill, children are dependent on adults, and unavoidably and rightly so. That is, children's dependence on adults is not analogous to the dependence of oppressed groups. For example, women and minorities have sought 'recognition and respect for capacities for rational and independent life and action that are demonstrably there and thwarted by the denial of rights' (ibid., p. 202). Children are different, because such capacities are *not* demonstrably there and are *not* thwarted by the denial of rights: 'Younger children are completely and unavoidably dependent on those who have power over their lives. Theirs is not a dependence that has been artificially produced (although it can be artificially prolonged); nor can it be ended merely by social and political changes; nor are others reciprocally dependent on children' (ibid., p. 203). While 'younger children' lack capacities for rational and independent life, such capacities begin to develop in adolescence. For that reason, '"mature minors" may find themselves in a position partly analogous to that of oppressed social groups. Their minority may sometimes be prolonged unnecessarily by civil disabilities and modes of life that damage their social development and postpone competence' (ibid.).

Children's dependence on adults (and adults' paternalistic power over children) is not an artificially produced social constraint that thwarts children's capacities for rational and independent life, she contends. It is not in children's interests to enjoy the right to liberty, given they do not have the required capacities that such rights would protect. Children are *completely and unavoidably dependent* on adults. However, this is a questionable conclusion.

Let us start with the requirement that all moral principles be universalisable. The requirement of universalisability was appealed to in justifying the duty of care: because all humans are to some extent dependent it is not possible for any human to will a moral law that rejected the duty of care. As O'Neill herself makes clear, not even the most fortunate adult is without dependence. Nonetheless, O'Neill concludes that such imperfectly and incompletely rational and independent adults, including women and minorities, should be guaranteed the right to liberty. It follows, adults may be guaranteed the right to liberty even though others have duties of care towards them. Therefore, being the rightful recipient of someone else's care does not make one ineligible to claim a right to liberty.

This tells us a lot about universalisability. It tells us that human beings can will separate moral principles that may at times pull in opposing directions and require differing and even incompatible treatment: adults can will that their right to liberty be respected and yet at the same time that they be cared for. It is only when O'Neill turns her attention to children that her approach changes. She denies that children's rights of liberty are fundamental, she denies that they '"trump" appeals to other considerations'. We can agree with her on that point, but this is not the issue. For she argues not just that children's right to liberty should not trump the duty of care towards children, but that children do not have such a right to liberty. There seems no good reason for reaching the second conclusion. Indeed, without assuming that such rights are trumps, it is possible to make a Kantian argument for children's right to liberty along the following lines: because all humans are to some extent rational and independent it is not possible for any human to will a law that rejected the right to liberty.

Like Scarre before her, O'Neill denies that there is a moral conflict when parents interfere with their children's liberty in acting paternalistically. And as with Scarre, we are left unsatisfied with the argument in support of the caretaker thesis. What can be said before moving on? The inconsistency in O'Neill's treatment of children's and adults' right to liberty may be explained by her failure to distinguish liberty of action from competence. What is unsatisfactory in O'Neill's argument could be remedied with such a distinction, and also by accepting that merely incompetent children do have a right to liberty.

Children's right to liberty and moral conflict

I have spoken already about competence and liberty of action. Now I want to focus on a further distinction, namely between execution of decisions and liberty of action. This is necessary so as to examine the general claim that children do not have a right to liberty. I have argued that children with the capacity for liberty of action are owed a right to liberty even when they are incompetent and/or cannot execute decisions. Therefore, we will be faced with moral conflicts when acting paternalistically towards such children and interfering with their liberty of action.

We have already seen that, for Bandura, to be an agent 'is to influence intentionally one's functioning and life circumstances'. Very young children are incapable of agency, they lack liberty of action. They cannot form and act on intentions. For that reason, we have argued, such children are not owed a right to liberty. In contrast, all things being equal, older children develop the capacity for agency, although when they do form and act on intentions they may make either incompetent or competent decisions. Further, among this second category, some will experience execution deficits, whether due to developmental stage, injury or illness, a life-long disability, or the lack of some learnt skill or external resource. Children in this third category do have a right to liberty, we have argued, although there may be situations where we are faced with a moral dilemma, and must decide whether or not to violate that right. Let us examine now cases in which the receipt of care does and does not come into conflict with the right to liberty of children in each of these categories.

First, children incapable of liberty of action do not have a right to liberty

Table 2.1 Whether receipt of care can conflict with a right to liberty

		Incompetent decision	Competent decision
Children's capacity	Incapable of liberty of action	1. No conflict as no right to liberty	2. n/a
	Capable of liberty of action	3. Conflict possible	4. No conflict as no need for care
	Execution deficit	5. Conflict possible	6. Can exercise right to liberty with assistance

as they do not in a meaningful sense have options that they choose from. While parents may treat such an infant in ways that are *prima facie* wrong, including by restricting the child's movements in ways that are wrong (such as by the excessive use of force), it does not make sense to say that, in doing so, they have interfered with the infant's liberty. Therefore, the infant's receipt of care cannot come into conflict with any right to liberty (see cell 1, Table 2.1), while such children also cannot be competent given they are incapable of liberty of action (cell 2).

All things being equal, children go on to develop agency and therefore the capacity to form intentions. If children are able to recognise options and also have the ability to choose between them, they do have a right to liberty as well. For example, my four-year-old daughter may have the capacity to choose to start playing football and specifically to choose to attend football training sessions on the weekend. In the first instance at least, she has a right to do so, as has anyone else capable of making such choices. It is a separate issue whether she has reasoned well in making this choice. This is a question of her competence to make the choice. And if the reasoning was incompetent (see cell 3, Table 2.1) this may give us a very strong rationale, in this instance, to not respect her choice and so to violate her right to liberty by not permitting her attend football training. For example, let us imagine she has decided she wants to play football with children twice her age, and has done so without adequately understanding the risk of injury this poses for her. In such a situation, there is a very real conflict between two moral claims; it is not the case that my daughter simply does not have a right to liberty here.

In some cases, children can make competent decisions even though they require others to assist them put such decisions into effect because of some execution deficit of their own. For example, let us imagine my daughter has made a competent decision to attend football training with children her own age. However, because she is unable to drive, because at four years of age she does not have this one skill (leaving to one side the legal objection to someone her age driving a car), she needs her parents' help to put that decision into effect. Therefore, the fact that an individual lacks skills in one area does not entail that the individual is incompetent to make decisions, never mind that the individual does not have a right to liberty with respect to such decisions (see cell 6, Table 2.1). Alternatively, my daughter may experience an execution deficit and also make an incompetent decision (see cell 5, Table 2.1). For example, my daughter has made an incompetent decision to attend football training with children twice her size (as before), and my daughter is unable to drive herself to the training (as above). Once again, a moral conflict is possible, as there may be a clash between children's right to liberty and parents' duty to protect them from the consequences of their own incompetent decisions.

Children do have a right to liberty when they are capable of liberty of action, I have argued. However, there are also scenarios where children have a right to liberty and where such a right may come into conflict with the duty to care for those children. In resolving such conflicts we may give priority to children's liberty or instead to the duty of care, but it is not the case that, as a general rule, children do not have a right to liberty. This all counts against the caretaker thesis.

The liberation thesis

If we have found reason to question, and even reject, the caretaker thesis, does this leave a door open for its polar opposite, the liberation thesis? First let us consider what exactly is demanded by the liberation thesis on behalf of children. It is argued that the rights, privileges, and duties of adults should be made available to any young person who wants to make use of them. According to John Holt, these would include the following:

1. The right to equal treatment at the hands of the law [...]
2. The right to vote [...]
3. The right to be legally responsible for one's life and acts.
4. The right to work, for money.
5. The right to privacy.
6. The right to financial independence and responsibility [...]
7. The right to direct and manage one's own education.
8. The right to travel, to live away from home, to choose or make one's own home.
9. The right to receive from the state whatever minimum income it may guarantee to adult citizens.
10. The right to make and enter into, on a basis of mutual consent, quasi-familial relationships outside one's immediate family – i.e. the right to seek and choose guardians other than one's own parents and to be legally dependent upon them.

11. The right to do, in general, what any adult may legally do. (1975, pp. 143–4)

Holt believes that any young person should be left to choose which, if any, of the above rights they wish to claim. He also believes that granting such rights would take time, and would be part of a process. Just as in Western democracies (putting to one side discrimination based on class, gender, religion, and race) the age thresholds for such rights were reduced over time, the rights he highlights could be granted to ever-younger cohorts of children on a step-by-step basis over time.

How is the liberation thesis justified? When we look at the arguments for children's liberation, we see repeated many of the assumptions found in arguments for the caretaker thesis, assumptions that we have strongly criticised here. In particular, it is assumed that paternalism involves interference with another's liberty, that paternalism is justified only as a treatment of those incapable of liberty of action, and that in arguing the case one way or another we will not be left with unresolved moral conflicts. And in addition, no clear distinction is made between liberty of action and competence, leading to a lack of clarity and precision in the arguments made. Let us look in detail at one such argument.

For John Harris, children have 'in most cases the same moral and political status as most adults' and also 'children are entitled not only to the same concern, respect and protection as is accorded to any other member of the community [...] but also are entitled to the same freedoms and self-determination' (1996, p. 137). He rejects the caretaker thesis, where it is assumed that 'rights are possessed by beings with certain capacities', and children lack those capacities (ibid.). However, Harris also uses 'capacity', 'competence', and 'autonomy' interchangeably to refer to the qualities he believes children do possess and which as a result undermine arguments for the paternalistic subordination of children (ibid., pp. 139–40). This lack of specificity where it is required most is something we found when discussing the caretaker thesis as well.

His central argument is that *both* adults and children have deficits in autonomy, which he categorises as follows: (1) when one is not in complete *control* of one's desires or actions or both; (2) when one's *reasoning* is impaired; (3) when the *information* needed to make a decision is defective; and (4) when *preferences change* over time, thus affecting the reality of one's choices (ibid., p. 140). What are the implications of such deficits for an individual's right to liberty? Although adult decision making often is defective in these ways, 'yet it is seldom suggested that this fact constitutes grounds for paternalistic control [of those adults]' (ibid., p. 145). For instance, if adults choose a high cholesterol diet, or smoke cigarettes habitually, or

drink alcohol to excess, it may be the case that they do not fully comprehend these dangers because of defects in their autonomy. However, Harris
concludes, it does not follow that we are entitled to impose upon them,
against their will, a healthy diet or abstinence from alcohol, and so on.
Rather, we may only appeal to their reason, and point out the dangers that
they are creating for themselves.

Based on what we have said in this and the preceding chapter, we know
that what Harris is referring to here is incompetent decision making rather
than a lack of liberty of action. If I choose to smoke cigarettes because I
have reasoned poorly about the likely consequences of doing so, I have
the capacity to make a decision but I have made a bad one. Therefore, the
implication of Harris's argument is that we do not condone *soft* paternalism
with respect to adults, and we should not condone it in respect of children
either. One counter argument is that, actually, we do condone soft paternalism with respect to adults when, to use Harris's terms, 'clearly their
decision making is defective' (ibid., p. 144). For example, family members
and physicians may decide to take a decision out of my hands about an
upcoming operation because I am clearly not thinking competently about
it. Thus the shortcomings of the liberation thesis are the mirror image of
those we noted for the caretaker thesis. Just as the caretaker thesis does
not acknowledge that we guarantee rights of liberty to incompetent adults,
so the liberation thesis does not acknowledge that we justify paternalism
in the case of incompetent adults. To put this point another way, Archard
(the caretaker thesis) would agree with Harris (the liberation thesis) about
what counts as deficits in autonomous decision making. However, while
Harris rejects soft paternalism in such cases, Archard does not. Archard
dealt with moral conflict by giving priority to children's well-being. Harris
faces the same conflict and, in sharp contrast, deals with it by privileging
children's liberty.

Harris's argument for children's liberation is based upon the principle
of respect for persons' autonomous decisions: 'those who respect persons
will respect their autonomous decisions at whatever age such decisions
are made and will not assume, or be permitted to act on the assumption,
that a decision is not autonomous because of the chronological age of the
decider' (ibid., p. 145). The argument for children's liberation is that, when
children's decisions are autonomous, they should be respected. That is,
children should have a right to liberty that protects them when they make
autonomous decisions, and therefore requires parents to respect those decisions and prevents parents from taking those decisions out of their hands.
However, as we have seen, Harris also objects to soft paternalism, that is,
paternalistic intervention where the responsive unit is not fully competent
(or 'autonomous', in his terms). Surely it follows for Harris that parents'

paternalism would be unjustified only when children are acting autonomously, and therefore soft paternalism *would* be justified on this argument.

However, Harris copper-fastens his rejection of soft paternalism by arguing that individuals may autonomously decide to live with some defects in the autonomy of their decision making: 'And it is clearly better, from the point of view of autonomy, for the individual to do this than live subject to the paternalist control of others. Where the individual has so chosen the paternalist cannot claim to be acting in the interests of the individual's autonomy when she claims the moral right to control that individual's behaviour for her own good' (ibid.). This should be a right of children as well as adults, Harris argues. That is, if children are capable of making an autonomous choice to live with the defects of their own decision making, their parents are not entitled to interfere with those choices for the good of the children.

The implication of this final contention is that, for Harris, parents' soft paternalism in respect of one of their children's decisions (e.g. the decision not to attend school because they prefer to stay at home and watch television) is not justified if the children have made a competent decision to live with the defects in their decision making about whether or not to go to school. This is very important, as it places one moral value above all others as the fundamental claim when there is moral conflict. Namely, because we should respect autonomy, we should consider the duty to protect the child's liberty as fundamental whenever it comes into conflict with the duty to promote the child's well-being and the duty to prevent harm to the child.

We should also note the very considerable overlap between this argument in defence of children's liberation and the arguments made in defence of the caretaker thesis. The first area of overlap is that this is an argument about parents' interference with children's liberty. The other ways in which parents exercise power over their children are given little consideration here. The second thing to note is that this is an argument about competence (which is equated with autonomy here) rather than liberty of action as such. That is, according to the liberation thesis, when children are competent (or autonomous) to make decisions, parents should respect those decisions. Finally, it is assumed that the philosopher's argument has resolved any apparent moral dilemma. As a general rule, one identified by Harris, when children are competent, then the duty to respect their autonomy and protect their right to liberty trumps other moral considerations.

Beyond the liberation and caretaker theses

So far we have examined the caretaker thesis and the liberation thesis. I have not been happy with the way in which parental power is conceptualised in either approach. Indeed, there is considerable overlap between the two approaches, notwithstanding their arriving at diametrically opposed normative and political positions. In this section, I want to draw together the reasons why we should look beyond both theses.

The shortcomings of both the liberation thesis and the caretaker thesis can be highlighted by considering Ann Palmeri's work. She starts with Gert and Culver's definition of paternalism, as we have done. Again as we have done, she focuses on the requirement that the controlling unit believes the responsive unit 'is capable of thinking about what is for his or her own good' (Palmeri, 1980, p. 107). She then makes the necessary distinction between children's *liberty of action* and whether they make (or are perceived to make) irrational, *incompetent* decisions. As we have seen, this distinction is lacking from the liberation thesis and the caretaker thesis, and is crucial for a clearer and more comprehensive account of parental power. On the basis of this distinction, Palmeri characterises the viewpoint of soft paternalist parents: 'One thing, though, is clear – children *do not fail* to make decisions and plans on matters that they know about. What we really think of them is not that they cannot make decisions but rather that they are *incapable* of making *good* ones' (ibid., p. 114; emphasis in original).

In some cases, parents wrongly assume their children to be incompetent. However, in other cases children make decisions that are not fully rational or competent. This is the case when an eight-year-old girl wants to eat only chocolate, as Palmeri notes. In such situations, it is the parent's responsibility to take the decision out of the child's hands but also, crucially, to educate the child about why her choice was not a good one. There is a moral conflict here. It does not follow that the parent should not act paternalistically, as the liberation thesis claims in situations where the child autonomously chooses to live with the defects of her decision making. Nor does it follow that the parent does not need to justify such a violation of the child's liberty, and do so in each case, as it is assumed in the caretaker thesis. Rather, in such cases the parent should offer an 'acceptable moral justification presumably demonstrable to others' (ibid., p. 114).

What Palmeri's work provides is a much better insight into the plurality of moral considerations, as well as the plurality of morally relevant features, when we evaluate any particular instance of parental power. As she says, in some situations parents may be justified not respecting their children's autonomy, and doing so in order to promote and nurture their children's development. However, in any such situation, moral justifications are required given the fact that we have been faced with moral conflicts.

Beyond paternalism

The liberation thesis is based on the assumptions that we have already questioned when analysing paternalism generally and the caretaker thesis more specifically. Although in Chapter 1, I argued strongly for an alternative, pluralist, definition of paternalism, even paternalism correctly understood has its limitations. In this, our last section, I want to draw attention to the various ways in which parents can exercise power that are *not* paternalistic. That is, there is good reason to believe paternalism, even when correctly defined, is not sufficient to account for parental power. We should move beyond paternalism, for the following five reasons at the very least.

First, as we have already seen, we cannot act paternalistically towards those who cannot even think about what is their own good (Palmeri, 1980, p. 107). Paternalism applies only to situations where A believes that B believes (perhaps falsely) that B generally knows what is for B's own good. And as we have seen, *parental power is exercised over children who do not have and are not capable of such self-consciousness, in particular very young infants*, as the following example illustrates:

(f) The parent of a girl born profoundly deaf decides to obtain a cochlear implant for her. Planning for the operation begins when the child is a number of months old and the operation takes place when the child is twelve months old.

As the example suggests, parents may act on behalf of their very young infant, and so as to promote their very young infant's well-being, they may believe they are qualified to do so, and they may do so without seeking their child's consent. However, such actions are *not* paternalistic given that the parents are not acting despite believing that their children are agents who believe that they (the children) generally know what is for their own good. In addition, in such situations the parents may not be violating a moral rule in relation to their children. (It is a separate issue whether, as some have argued, cochlear implants are harmful to 'Deaf culture' (Sparrow, 2010).) For example, there simply may be no need to deceive and/or coerce very young infants in this case, and precisely for the reason that very young infants do not believe that they (the infants) generally know what is for their own good.

Second, parents exercise power over children in instances where parents are *not* doing so from a benevolent intention to promote their children's own good. *Parents often make decisions so as to promote their own (the parents')* *interests*, as in the following example:

(g)   A mother decides to take a job offer in a distant location and decides to move her entire family to the new area. She is making decisions for her children and enforcing those decisions on her children and doing so in order to promote her own self-interest.

Such a decision may be made without seeking the consent of the children affected, the mother may believe that the children believe that they (the children) know what is best for them, and it may involve the violation of a moral rule, for instance the rule prohibiting interference with another's liberty. Nonetheless, if a mother makes the decision so as to promote her own self-interest then it does not count as paternalism (see Brighouse and Swift, 2006). The consequences of the decision may well improve the well-being of the children, but it may not, and in any case that was not the intended outcome. The limits of parents' rights to make such decisions will be discussed in Chapter 8 when we address the licensing, monitoring, and training of parents.

Third, paternalistic parents act so as to promote their children's current good, or the good of the adult the child will one day be. However, parents may act for the sake of their children in a quite different sense. That is, *parents may act so as to protect their children's liberty qua children.* For example, I may guarantee my child has a wide range of options to choose from with respect to subjects studied at school, social and sporting activities engaged in, religious practices, and so on. What the paternalist thesis does not take account of is the power exercised by parents so as to protect the child's liberty as a child. I return to this theme again in Chapter 10 when we examine civic education.

Fourth, paternalism involves the exercise of power without the prior consent of the child, an assumption shared even by those who believe paternalism is justified by retrospective consent. However, *parents may exercise power with the prior consent of their children*, as can be seen in the revised example below:

(e)   My daughter wants to eat chocolate every day. There are paternalistic ways in which I may respond so as to promote her good, but other options may be available. For example, I may discuss with her the risks of a high-sugar diet, and give her access to information and the opinions of experts, answer any questions she may have, and discuss possible alternative options. I may also decide to adhere to whatever agreement we reach. For instance, we may reach a compromise position whereby she agrees to eat chocolate no more than once a week, and my role is to monitor her behaviour to ensure that she complies with this agreement.

In such a situation, I exercise power over my daughter by establishing a procedure for making a decision together and also by then monitoring her behaviour for compliance with that agreement. I am not acting paternalistically, however, as I exercise power on the basis of my child's prior consent. Such situations are discussed further in Chapter 9 when we examine informed consent.

Finally, fifth, our concern in this book is with the phenomenon of parental power. However, as with any power relation, the controlling unit may cease to exercise power over the responsive unit, and the latter may gain power over the former. *Children may exercise power over their parents*, as can be seen by the example of a young carer providing care to her mother (see Fives et al., 2013):

(h) Mary is sixteen years old and provides intimate care for her mother who has a physical disability. Mary's caring roles include domestic chores around the home, directly helping her mother with mobility, providing medical care, and providing intimate care, including toileting and dressing. Mary does not merely carry out her mother's instructions, as she also exercises power over her mother in numerous ways. For example, she removes options from her mother by refusing to provide the help necessary for their attainment; in particular when her mother wishes to take unnecessary risks and attempts to do things she is unable to do safely.

Therefore, children may exercise power over their parents, with respect to some if not all the decisions made and actions taken in their relationship.

Conclusions

This chapter has continued our examination of paternalism, in particular as that concept has been utilised in the caretaker thesis and the liberation thesis. This chapter has shown that both theses are problematic, but also I think it has made clearer where we should focus our efforts to better understand parental power. Although offering diametrically opposed prescriptions, the same problems are evident in arguments for the caretaker thesis and the liberation thesis. Both equate parental power with paternalism, and both define paternalism as paternalistic interference with another's liberty, and as justified treatment for those lacking the qualities of an agent.

I have argued against each of these assumptions over the last two chapters, and I will continue those lines of argument now. However, before moving on, we should recall the many instances where parental power is not paternalistic. Therefore, even when it is properly understood, paternalism is not sufficient as a normative concept when we account for parental power.

Finally, both those who defend the caretaker thesis and those who defend the liberation thesis believe that their role, as theorists, is to find a general rule(s) to resolve moral conflicts when evaluating parental power. Instead, I have argued it is possible to question the claim being made that one moral consideration is fundamental and therefore has priority over others, not least because we have so many examples of philosophers disagreeing over which consideration has priority. This is one reason why the caretaker thesis is unacceptable. As children capable of liberty of action are owed a right to liberty, then even when we have good reason to interfere with children's liberty, in particular so as to promote children's well-being, this does not change the fact that the right is owed to children in the first place. We are faced with a real moral dilemma here. It is to this issue of moral conflicts and how they can be resolved that I turn in the next chapter.

Part II

Conceptual and methodological issues

How are we to evaluate parental power? In the next four chapters, I will look at the conceptual and methodological issues raised by that question. I make the case for a pluralist approach to methodology generally and the conceptualisation of power more specifically. This is necessary, I will try to show, as efforts to reduce plurality fail. When we evaluate parental power, there is an irreducible plurality of morally significant features and of relevant moral considerations. In addition, because of this irreducible plurality, we can be faced with moral dilemmas.

As we shall see in Chapter 4, findings from psychology strongly support the view that parents can use their power so as to promote their children's agency. Nonetheless, empirical findings such as these do not by themselves resolve the moral conflicts that can arise when parents exercise power for this purpose. Even when parents successfully promote their children's social, cognitive, and emotional development, they can be faced with moral dilemmas, conflicts which call into question the legitimacy of their power.

And although it is commonly assumed that power means coercion, in fact this is only one possible form power can take. As Chapter 5 shows, there is an irreducible plurality of power concepts. I can have power (for example, 'power to' and 'power with') without at the same time exercising power over others, and I can exercise power over others without at the same time either coercing them or interfering with their liberty. Therefore, when it comes to normative evaluation, we should judge what parents do with their power, that is, the type of power they exercise and what impacts it has.

Nonetheless, as we shall see, the fact that parents and children are in an asymmetrical relation also has normative significance, independent of the exercise of power by parents. I address this issue in Chapter 6, where the legitimacy of parental power is examined. In that chapter, I will try to show that it is not possible to reduce the issue of legitimacy to an evaluation of just one form of power, and that even when we do evaluate any one form of power we can be faced with conflicting moral claims.

The possibility of moral dilemmas presents us with our central methodological and conceptual challenge, and it is to this that I now turn (Chapter 3). If moral claims can pull in different directions, demanding different and incompatible things from us, how are we to make moral judgements? In the next chapter, I will try to show that we cannot do so by identifying the general rule for the resolution of moral conflicts. Instead, we will be required to work through moral dilemmas where they arise, that is, by engaging in practical reasoning and practical judgement in the contexts where individuals are tasked with making decisions and taking action.

3

Moral dilemmas

In Part I of this book, I argued that paternalism is inadequate as a general account of parental power. And as both the caretaker thesis and the liberation thesis equate parental power with paternalism, their adequacy as theories of parental power is questionable for that reason. However, of greater significance for our present purposes is the fact that, according to each thesis, when we evaluate parental power, we will not be faced with irresolvable moral conflicts. There are two aspects to this argument, and they are the focus of this chapter. First, it is believed that, when moral claims come into conflict, we can identify a general rule for their resolution. Second, when we decide between competing claims in this way, we should feel no regret at the claim that is not acted upon as it is no longer morally binding for us. For example, among those who defend the caretaker thesis, both Scarre and O'Neill believe that parental paternalism does not involve violating a moral rule in relation to those over whom power is exercised, as the duty to promote children's well-being, as a general rule, trumps other competing moral considerations and, it follows, we are no longer required to protect children's right to liberty.

As I shall argue in this chapter, both aspects of this approach to moral conflicts are unsatisfactory. First, at a high level of generality, there is no justification for the claim that, as a general rule, when moral claims come into conflict, one is fundamental and has priority over all others. That is, philosophers are unable to resolve the debate among themselves about which consideration is fundamental in this sense. Second, we can ensure that we do not feel regret in situations of moral conflict only by engaging in a process of moral simplification and moral disengagement, and, as Bernard Williams in particular has argued, we have no justification to diminish the significance of competing moral considerations in this way (1965; 1978; 1985). The argument of this chapter is that we can be faced with genuine, real moral dilemmas, that is, moral conflicts for which there is no general rule for their resolution and conflicts that leave us with moral regret at the item not acted upon. For example, as Gert and Culver have shown, there is a moral conflict involved in every act of parental paternalism. When I, as a parent, act paternalistically, in attempting to do what is best for my child I violate a moral rule in regard to my child.

If we cannot identify a general rule for their resolution, how can we resolve moral conflicts? In this chapter I try to show that we can do so through practical reasoning and practical judgement. In doing so, I will borrow from John Rawls and his account of reasonableness (1999 [1997]) and Thomas Nagel's account of 'public justification in a context of actual disagreement' (1990 [1987], p. 315). However, we must be cognisant of a number of possible dangers here. In particular, we must ensure that we do not impose a 'liberal' political solution on moral conflicts and in that way ourselves become guilty of the moral simplification we have been critical of in others. In any case, before proceeding, we must address the counter argument that moral dilemmas do not arise.

The thesis that moral dilemmas do not arise

As I said, some argue that moral dilemmas do not arise. According to this line of thought, when moral claims come into conflict, we *can* identify a general rule for their resolution. And when we decide between competing claims in this way, the claim that is not acted upon is no longer morally binding for us and so we should *not* feel regret. Let us look at this counter argument in more detail now.

According to this line of thought, when we ought to do X and we ought to do Y, and we can do either X or Y but cannot do both X and Y, nonetheless we can resolve such a conflict on the basis of a general rule of the form that if X and Y come into conflict then we should consider X more fundamental than Y. And as we know, many moral and political philosophers believe that we *can* identify such a general rule for the resolution of conflicts. One example is Rawls's argument for the lexical priority of his first principle of justice, concerning individual rights to liberty, over his second principle of justice, concerning social and economic inequalities (1971, p. 302). Only with such an ordering of principles will we avoid intuitionism and also ensure there is a final court of appeal in ordering conflicting claims and principles (ibid., p. 135). The implication is that we are *never* justified in surrendering individual liberty so as to successfully promote social and economic justice. We may only sacrifice liberty for the sake of liberty, not for the sake of any other, and in Rawls's view lesser, moral claim (cf. Hart, 1973). And as we shall see below, Philippa Foot speaks of moral absolutes in much the same way, such as the absolute prohibition on torture. While

Rawls concludes that we are *never* permitted to violate someone's liberty for the sake of some other good, even for the sake of bringing about a significant reduction in unjustified social and economic inequalities, for Foot, as a general rule we are *never* permitted to torture someone, regardless of what may be gained in doing so. I return to this side of the matter below.

However, I begin by considering Foot's argument that, when we resolve a moral conflict by making a decision, it is irrational to feel moral regret at the item not acted upon. Foot's argument is that, insofar as the moral decision has a rational justification, any feeling of regret is contrary to reason. And so, by extension, if one does feel regret in such situations, this feeling does not provide evidence for the existence of a real, genuine moral dilemma. This argument is made in response to Williams's observation that, even when there is a moral justification for an act, it can still leave what he calls a 'moral remainder, the uncancelled moral disagreeableness' (1978, p. 63), and this is the case because 'to end it [moral conflict] in decision is not necessarily to eliminate one of the conflicting items: the item that is not acted upon may, for instance, persist as regret' (1965, p. 117).

For Foot, in contrast, any talk of moral dilemmas involves a logical contradiction. If it is possible for two judgements about what we ought to do to be in conflict, it follows that one or both of these is merely a *prima facie* requirement, and that only one of these can be considered what one ought to do all things considered:[1] Some 'ought statements [...] tell us the right thing to do, and [...] this means the thing that is best morally speaking [...] It is implied that for one for whom moral considerations are reasons to act there are better moral reasons for doing this action than for doing any other' (Foot, 2002 [1983], p. 44). Therefore, when we speak of a moral dilemma we must be mistaken, for it cannot be that, all things considered, we ought to do X and also, and at the same time, all things considered, we ought to do $Y\neg X$ (that is, Y not X). Therefore, as one is not bound by the *prima facie* ought that is not acted upon, it is irrational to feel moral regret in acting as one ought all things considered.

Others agree with Foot in distinguishing what, at first sight, one ought to do from what, all things considered, one ought to do. According to this line of thought, moral dilemmas are 'impossible' because they represent 'logical contradictions' (de Haan, 2001, p. 283). It is a logical contradiction, and therefore an impossibility, to say that a person morally has a duty to do X and morally has a duty to do Y, if he cannot do X as well as Y. In contrast, it is quite a different thing to say that a person has a *prima facie* duty to do X and a *prima facie* duty to do Y, but cannot do both X and Y. In the latter case, when it is decided that, all things considered, one has a duty to do X, say, then 'not only do you have no conflict of duties, you do not even have the ghost of a conflict' (Donagan, 1993, p. 19). That is, the conflict will disappear, and so there will not be even the ghost of a conflict, and therefore no reason to feel regret.

How do we make this distinction between a *prima facie* ought and an all things considered ought? According to Foot, there are different types of ought statement. The 'practical ought' speaks of what should be done all things considered. But ought may also apply to a second class of propositions stating among other things 'the existence of rules, promises, engagements, and considerations about good and harm to oneself and others' (2002 [1995], p. 177). For instance, the practical ought may be that, all things considered, I should drive an accident victim to the hospital; and this may come into conflict with an ought from this second class of propositions, for instance, an engagement I have made to meet my friend for a social occasion (see Ross, 2013 [1930], p. 756). What Foot is arguing is that, while there is a conflict between two oughts, there is no reason for moral regret if I have done what is right all things considered, namely taken the accident victim to hospital.

However, let us look at this example once more. If we do I think we will see that it is not the absence of moral regret that characterises this situation, as Foot claims. It is the case that, as Foot notes, even if I do not keep my promise to meet my friend for a social occasion, nonetheless I am confident that, all things considered, I have done the right thing in bringing the accident victim to hospital. But note the type of comparative judgement required to reach this conclusion. I judge that it is right to bring an accident victim to hospital when the only other competing commitment I have is to keep a promise to meet my friend for a social occasion. That is, the judgement is made by examining the relative significance of the varied moral considerations that apply to me at this point in time. Therefore, this example does not show it is irrational to feel regret when we have done what is right all things considered. Rather, it shows that, in situations where a moral conflict arises and where the relevant moral considerations are of *vastly unequal significance*, it is irrational to feel anything more than minimal regret. In not keeping my engagement with my friend I have done something wrong. The wrong done will be lessened somewhat if my friend is not put out or upset at having been stood up. However, even here, I am breaking an engagement, and this is a wrong, although, again, one that is vastly outweighed by the alternative course of action, namely bringing the accident victim to hospital.

The outcome should be different when faced with the following conflict: one ought to bring an accident victim to hospital and one ought to stay at home to care for one's bed-ridden and seriously ill child. In this scenario, it is no longer clear that to bring the accident victim to hospital is the right thing to do, all things considered. But this is the case because the all things considered judgement now must take into consideration conflicting moral requirements that are of near equal significance. Once again, in this situation, no matter what I do, although I will be doing what I ought to do all things considered, it is rational to feel regret at 'the item that is not acted upon', in Williams's terms. The difference between the two examples is a matter of the seriousness of the claim left unfulfilled, and therefore, the severity of the regret one should feel. But, in each case, regret is a rational, justifiable response.

Indeed, it follows that, in some situations, bringing the accident victim to hospital may be wrong, all things considered. And surely Foot would agree it would be rational to feel regret in a situation where one was unable to bring the accident victim to hospital. However, it seems, Foot will not allow for the possibility that it could be right all things considered to *not* bring the accident victim to hospital. In addressing this aspect of Foot's argument we will also engage with her more general point that, when moral claims come into conflict, we can identify a general rule for their resolution. Foot's argument emerges when she considers 'tragic' choices that leave us morally speaking with 'dirty hands'. Although such examples from situations of extreme crises often may be unhelpful for a discussion of everyday moral judgement, nonetheless what she says here is highly informative of her more general position on moral conflict. Here she insists on the existence of 'moral absolutes'. She criticises what she calls (in an unfortunate, inappropriate choice of terms) a 'schizophrenic tendency among moral philosophers who cannot bring themselves to say there is any kind of action that is wrong in any circumstances whatsoever, and who yet feel that certain actions – say torture – cannot ever be justified' (2002 [1995], p. 187). Foot then states that her position is one of 'absolute moral prohibitions', such that 'each and every torturer acts wrongly' (ibid., p. 188). And, we presume, based on what she has said about our previous example, each and every individual who does not bring an accident victim to hospital 'acts wrongly'.

She also states that moral absolutes relating to intentional actions cannot come into conflict. We may be faced with the choice between, on the one hand, torturing B and, on the other hand, *not preventing* some other horrible outcome from coming about (that is, an event that we could only prevent if we had access to information that, we have good reason to presume, could be uncovered through the torture of B). But the absolute moral prohibition on torture remains, and therefore there should be no moral regret at not having tortured B, no matter how terrible the outcome one has therefore not prevented. Similarly, if there is an absolute prohibition on not aiding the accident victim, once again we cannot be faced with a dilemmatic choice between this and any other, conflicting moral requirement.

In this context, Foot refers to the 'dirty tricks' that the French Resistance used when fighting the Nazis. She asks, 'has he really been wronged if harmed, even if it was a *justified* action that harmed him? I should have thought not' (ibid., p. 186; emphasis in original). In this example it is difficult to work out initially the identity of the harmed person, and yet this is crucial to deciding whether *he* has been harmed. If it is an innocent bystander whose life has been sacrificed in an explosion that furthered the cause of the Resistance, this is one thing; if he is a morally guilty Nazi soldier whose life has been lost in the explosion, it is another. However, based on what Foot says about moral absolutes, it is reasonable to infer that she is not referring to an innocent bystander. For Foot, the Resistance fighter would *not* have been justified in taking the life of an innocent bystander, even if this was necessary so as to further the cause of defeating Nazism. For Foot, we can *never* have a duty to kill innocent civilians. Therefore, we can never be faced with a real or genuine conflict between the duty to help defeat Nazism and the duty not to kill innocent civilians.

There are two different arguments at work in Foot's overall rejection of moral dilemmas, as we have seen. The first is that moral dilemmas are a logical contradiction and therefore not possible. Foot's second line of argument is that there are moral absolutes, and they provide the general rules for resolving moral conflicts. Foot acknowledges that her argument is based on the work of Aristotle, Aquinas, and others. And it is the case that, for Aquinas, any moral theory that generates moral dilemmas 'must be inconsistent and so false' (Donagan, 1993, p. 10; see also MacIntyre, 1988). Foot is defining moral regret as irrational on the basis of a claim that, if some action is prohibited by a moral absolute, then we can never be required to perform that action, and therefore, it is irrational to feel moral regret at not having performed the action.

However, this line of argument is unsatisfactory. Foot makes it a matter of definition that we can never be required to perform certain actions. Her argument collapses whenever we find examples of actions that, all things considered, we ought to do, even though Aristotle or Aquinas (or Foot) conclude that the actions are prohibited by moral absolutes. For example, people are put in situations of tragic choices, where performing torture is one of their options. Those who recognise the possibility of moral dilemmas are not guilty of a (in Foot's terms) 'schizophrenic' attitude here. They *do* accept that torture is always wrong. However, they are aware also that the prohibition on torture is not the only moral consideration we have to take account of. They acknowledge the irreducible plurality of moral considerations. Therefore, at the same time, those who refuse to torture the prisoner cannot insist that they have 'clean' hands if, as a result of their omission, terrible consequences for innocent humans are made more likely.

Against moral simplification and moral reduction

Foot has argued that moral conflicts are only apparent and not real. One aspect of that argument is the claim that there are moral absolutes we are never justified in violating. The alternative view, defended here, is that moral dilemmas are real rather than apparent. And my justification for such a position is a pluralist stance on moral considerations: It 'regards some conflicts as real conflicts between independent moral considerations, rather than as merely conflicting partial judgements which simply give way without trace to an all-things considered judgement' (Raz, 1986, p. 404).

Foot tries to make it a matter of definition that, once a decision has been made concerning what all things considered one ought to do, it is irrational to feel regret. Similar claims are made in the debate on paternalism. As we have seen, it is argued that whenever there is an apparent moral conflict, we can resolve it by giving priority to what is said to be the fundamental moral claim. The following are some of the moral claims that, it has been argued, are to be given priority:

(1) the promotion of children's happiness (Scarre);
(2) to be kind and considerate, and care for children (O'Neill);
(3) the promotion of the autonomy of the adults children will one day become (Brighouse and Swift); and
(4) the protection of children's right to liberty (Harris).

In each instance, it is argued that one moral claim is, as a general rule, more fundamental than other conflicting claims. However, in each instance, this assumption is questionable. That is, it is not irrational or illogical to ask, 'Is this claim as a general rule more fundamental than another, conflicting moral claim?' My argument is that it makes sense to ask this question when the moral considerations are independent and when the moral conflict is real.

I want to analyse the philosophical approach to moral conflict evident in the arguments we analysed in Chapter 2. Each proceeds as if moral conflicts can be resolved through abstract and general philosophical reflection. More precisely, whenever the presence of moral conflicts is acknowledged, it is assumed that we can identify a generally applicable rule for their resolution. Therefore, such conflicts are only apparent rather than real to begin with. For instance, Scarre's argument is that, while it may appear that we have a duty to protect children's right to liberty, in fact we do not have such a duty when to guarantee children's liberty would increase children's misery. Therefore, while it may appear that the requirement to promote children's happiness and the requirement to protect children's right to liberty are in conflict, Scarre's own abstract and general philosophical reflection can illustrate that this is the mere appearance of moral conflict. Thus, when we infringe children's liberty we have violated no moral rule and therefore should feel no moral regret.

In each of the arguments presented above, it is contended that we must resolve conflicts between moral claims in a certain manner for the reason that one is, as a general rule, more fundamental. However, in philosophical debate there is no consensus on which is the more fundamental claim and so there is no consensus on the general rule said to resolve such conflicts. One way to address this situation is to go back to the drawing board, as it were, and attempt to establish, once and for all, which of these claims is more fundamental, and somehow, through general and abstract philosophical analysis, show this to be the case in such a way as to silence all rational and fair-minded dissent. Yet, philosophers have spent many centuries in attempting to do just this, with different philosophers doggedly defending opposing positions, as is the case, for example, with the ongoing debate between Kantians and utilitarians. The persistence of these (and other) opposing philosophical positions now concerning which moral claim has priority strongly suggests that philosophers have failed in this task. And this history of failure argues for a change of tack.

What else does this history of failure suggest? Let us return again to Foot's work. Her argument is that a moral dilemma is impossible, as to believe oneself to be faced with such a situation is to be in contradiction with oneself. However, it is informative to note that Foot's Aristotelian and Thomist position is representative of just one possible moral doctrine among many. It may be that those who are committed to the same doctrine will quickly find agreement about what is right, all things considered, and it may be that, for this select, like-minded group, in situations of apparent moral conflict all opposing moral considerations will fall away leaving not even the 'ghost of a conflict'. However, it does not follow that those who do not share this doctrine will resolve conflicts in the same way. In addition, unless we assume there is only one true moral doctrine, it is not possible for Foot to establish that those who do not share her moral doctrine and do not resolve moral conflicts as she does are, as a matter of definition, in error.

From the conflicts that arise between individuals (i.e. two-party conflicts) let us turn to the conflicts individuals may experience within themselves (i.e. one-party conflicts) (Williams, 1981 [1979], pp. 72–3). Any one person can look at a decision from different and sometimes incompatible moral points of view: for example, when making a decision about my daughter, I can look at it from the point of view of her well-being and also from the point of view of her liberty (and so on). Some may believe that we should eliminate this source of uncertainty, and in our deliberations give priority to one of those points of view. That is, in situations of conflict, we should simplify our moral outlook and reduce our moral commitment, thereby removing one (or more) of the conflicting claims. However, so far they have failed to convince us of this through philosophical analysis, as for every philosopher insisting that the right to liberty should give way whenever it conflicts with utility, there is another insisting that it is utility that should give way.

It would seem therefore that there are plural and sometimes conflicting points of view available to us when we make moral judgements. But why is it that we encounter resistance whenever our aim is moral simplification and moral reduction? Why is it, as Stuart Hampshire says, we cannot circumscribe 'the morally relevant features of situations encountered' (1978, p. 39)? One explanation is the plurality of fundamental types of value.

According to Nagel, there are five different fundamental types of value, as follows: (1) we have specific *obligations* to people or institutions, obligations which are always incurred; (2) there are general constraints on every person's actions that arise from other people's *rights*; (3) *utility* is 'the consideration that takes into account the effects of what one does on everyone's welfare'; (4) there is the *perfectionist* consideration that certain achievements or creations also have intrinsic value, such as scientific discovery or artistic creation; and finally (5) *personal commitment* 'to one's own projects or undertakings' is a value because 'our projects make autonomous claims on us, once undertaken' (1979 [1977], pp. 129–30). Not only are there different types of value, they can come into conflict. The most serious forms of conflict, 'genuine dilemmas', occur when values conflict and one does not outweigh the other:

> The strongest cases of conflict are genuine dilemmas, where there is decisive support for two or more incompatible courses of action or inaction [...] when each seems right for reasons that appear decisive and sufficient, arbitrariness means the lack of reasons where reasons are needed, since either choice will mean acting against some reasons without being able to claim that they are *outweighed*. (ibid., pp. 128–9; emphasis in original)

Although there is a plurality of values, there would be no dilemmas if we could establish 'a system of priorities among them' (ibid., p. 131). However, any attempt to establish a system of priorities will be 'absurd' because of its 'absoluteness', for example, the absolute requirement that obligations can never outweigh rights. Indeed, it is possible to imagine scenarios where parental obligations towards their children do outweigh children's rights. For example, parents' obligations to care for and nurture their children may be such as to outweigh the children's right to make decisions for themselves when those decisions put their own welfare at risk. In contrast, there may be other situations where it is children's rights that outweigh parental obligations. For example, in some situations parents should protect their children's rights to make even those decisions that may be harmful to themselves, as may be the case when the children wish to act altruistically.

Of course, Nagel is justified in rejecting such a system of priorities only if it *is* the case that, as he claims, 'value has fundamentally different kinds of source', and therefore it is *not* the case that 'all values represent the pursuit of some single good in a variety of settings' (ibid., p. 132). If Nagel is right, we would expect to encounter genuine dilemmas. In support of Nagel's position, in the next section, I look at Williams's account of what genuine dilemmas are and how they arise.

What genuine dilemmas are and how they arise

As we saw, some contend that we can identify a general rule for the resolution of moral conflicts. If that is the case, moral conflicts would be apparent rather than real to begin with. Therefore, the question that needs to be asked is, can we be faced with moral dilemmas that are real rather than apparent, and therefore that will resist our efforts to resolve them through general and abstract philosophical analysis? Williams has tried to show that, yes, we can be faced with such genuine moral dilemmas. In discussing his argument, it is helpful to start with what he has to say about the ways in which *ethical* reasoning differs from *scientific* reasoning.

In ethical matters, 'disagreement does not necessarily have to be overcome', Williams concludes (1985, p. 133). It is not that agreement, or 'convergence', will never happen in ethics. It is rather that the explanation for convergence and its absence is different in science and in ethics:

> In a scientific inquiry there should ideally be convergence on an answer, where the best explanation of the convergence involves the idea that the answer represents how things are; in the area of the ethical, at least at a high level of generality, there is no such coherent hope. The distinction does not turn on any difference in whether convergence will actually occur [...] It might well turn out that there will be convergence in ethical outlook [...] even if this happens, it will not be correct to think it has come about because convergence has been guided by how things actually are. (ibid., p. 136)

In science, then, *how things are* explains convergence. Williams gives as an example the 'perception' of secondary qualities, such as colour.

'A part of the physical world may present itself as one color to one kind of observer, and another to another; to another it may not exactly be a color at all' (ibid., p. 149). We can explain why humans perceive the world in such a way, namely that it is a 'method of finding our way around the physical world'; the physical world presents itself to us in 'reliable and useful ways' (ibid., pp. 149, 150). Because of our development as a species, humans perceive the world in a particular way, while other species, with their own history of evolutionary development, perceive the world in different ways. And scientific theory can explain as well as justify these perceptions: 'In the case of secondary qualities, the explanation also justifies, because it can show how the perceptions are related to physical reality and how they can give knowledge of that reality, which is what they purport to do' (ibid., p. 150). In addition, scientific theory can explain 'errors' in our perception. My perceptions are in error when they no longer relate to and give me knowledge of physical reality.[2]

No ethical theory can do the same for differences in ethical belief and practice, Williams argues. This is the case because such an ethical theory would have to consider not just whether ethical beliefs and practices were a method for finding our way around the social world (as opposed to the natural world). In addition, if ethical theory is to justify beliefs, as scientific theory does, it has to answer the question of whether each promotes a *good* way of living when compared with others. That is, such an ethical theory would have to have a theory of error, and so account for 'the tendency of people to have what, according to its principles, are wrong beliefs' (ibid., p. 151). Another way to put the distinction between science and ethics is that there *can* be a systematic body of scientific truths but there can*not* be a systematic body of ethical truths (ibid., p. 148). For instance, it may be that there will be convergence on the ethical issue of the legitimacy of parental power, but if it happens it will not be explained by *how things are*. That is, those who disagree with us about how to resolve conflicts between children's well-being and children's liberty are not in error in the same way that those who are unable to distinguish the colour red from the colour green. It follows, ethical thought 'at a high level of generality', that is, abstract and general philosophical reflection, does not provide us with a systematic body of ethical truths with which to show which of two competing ethical claims are in error. To put the same point another way, ethical thought is such that it will never identify general rules for the resolution of moral conflicts.

Why is this distinction between science and ethics important for our discussion of moral dilemmas? A situation where two *beliefs* are in conflict is different from a situation in which two *moral judgements* are in conflict. Two beliefs are in conflict when, for some empirical reason, they cannot both be true. An example is my belief that a certain person is a Minister who took up political office in the last year and my belief that he is also a member of the Blue party. If it is pointed out to me that no such Minister is a member of the Blue party (because the Blues are not the party in office), and I become conscious of the conflict between my original beliefs, this also 'tends to weaken one or more of the beliefs' (Williams, 1965, p. 109).[3] Indeed, one of the beliefs will be not just weakened but invalidated. That is, I should feel no struggle in letting go of the mistaken belief. It is the case that, if I am a fervent supporter of the Blues, I may feel some regret that the Blue party is not, as I originally thought, in power. However, such a feeling of regret relates to my *desire* that this party be in power. In contrast, I should feel no regret in letting go of the mistaken belief *qua* belief.

Let us focus on conflicts between moral judgements. A *moral* dilemma is a case 'where there is a conflict between two moral judgments that a man is disposed to make relevant to deciding what to do' (ibid., p. 108). More precisely, there are two basic forms the dilemma can take. The first is where 'it seems I ought to do each of two things, but I cannot do both' (ibid.). For example, it is equally correct to say of a teenage girl's parents they ought to promote her well-being *and* they ought to protect her liberty. However, if it is not possible to do both, for instance, in a situation where the teenager wishes to make what her parents believe to be the risky decision of enrolling in a clinical trial, then they are faced with a moral dilemma, where to protect her liberty will not promote her well-being. They are faced with a dilemma when, if they promote her well-being they are doing the right thing, but for that reason they are unable to do what they ought to do, namely protect her liberty. Formally, this dilemma can be represented as follows:

(1) I ought to X
(2) I ought to $Y\neg X$
(3) I cannot both X and $Y\neg X$.

The second form a dilemma can take 'is that in which something which (it seems to me) I ought to do in respect of certain of its features also has other features in respect of which (it seems) I ought not to do it' (ibid.). For example, it is equally correct to say of the teenage girl's parents (above) they ought to respect the decision she has made about enrolling in a trial as in doing so they will protect her liberty *and* they ought not to do so because the girl's decision will actually bring harm to herself. If these are mutually exclusive options, the parents involved cannot do both and are faced with a moral dilemma. Formally, this dilemma can be represented as follows:

(1) I ought to Z
(2) I ought to $\neg Z$
(3) I cannot both Z and $\neg Z$.

A dilemma is a conflict where, even when we do what we ought to do, we are forced to do something that, morally speaking, we ought not to. That this is very different from a conflict between two beliefs is illustrated by the fact we should feel no regret on discovering that a belief is mistaken. In our example above, let us assume the parents at one point believed that their daughter was competent to provide informed consent. Let us also assume that they then came to realise they were mistaken. Although the parents may desire this were not the case, as they may wish their daughter to be competent, they have nothing to regret concerning the mistaken belief itself. In contrast, in moral dilemmas, we should feel regret, even if we are confident that, all things considered, we have acted for the best in trying to resolve the conflict. This is the case because of what Williams refers to as 'the moral remainder, the uncancelled moral disagreeableness' (1978, p. 63) of such dilemmas, for example, the disagreeableness of preventing my children from providing informed consent even when I do so in order to promote their well-being.

One further point can be made about ethics and science. Scientific find-ings may be such as to justify our beliefs about an issue, and yet insufficient to resolve genuine moral dilemmas that arise about the very same issue. Let us stay with the example of a teenage daughter who wishes to enrol in a scientific study. Scientific findings may show that, if parents engage in joint decision making with their children about such issues as research partici-pation, there is a very high degree of probability (satisfying the requirement of statistical significance) that children's decision making competence will in that way be improved. Nonetheless, if parents do act in this way they may still be faced with a moral dilemma, in particular if parents can do so only by interfering with their children's liberty, for example by removing from children the option of making the decision in question by themselves rather than jointly with their parents. The empirical evidence is certainly relevant when we face this dilemma, as it shows what, to a high degree of probability, will result from the parents' actions. However, if parents act in this way, and even if the action has the hoped for beneficial consequences for the child in question, they should also feel regret at the moral item not acted upon.

So far in this section we have addressed the issue of whether we can iden-tify a general rule for the resolution of moral conflicts. For Williams, we cannot, as, at a high level of generality, we cannot have a systematic body of ethical truths. We have also addressed the second issue, raised by Foot and outlined above, namely that moral dilemmas are not possible, as they involve logical contradictions, and for that reason we should feel no regret at the item not acted upon. I want to focus again on this latter issue and two things that Williams says which are relevant to this discussion. First,

Williams stresses that, in a moral dilemma, 'the conflict arises from a contingent impossibility' (1965, p. 119). There is no inherent inconsistency in the two moral oughts that, to return to our earlier example, we ought to fight so as to defeat Nazism and that we ought not to harm innocent civilians. Rather, the conflict comes 'in the step to action: that as things are, there is no way of doing the first without doing the second' (ibid.). There is no logical contradiction here, as Williams is *not* saying that I cannot do both X and Y, and that I ought to do both X and Y. Rather, he is saying that I ought to do *each* of the two things, but, because of the facts of the case, I cannot do both.

Williams's second point in respect of this argument is as follows. As I ought to do each of the two things, just because I cannot do one of them, $Y\neg X$, it does not follow that I cannot say that I ought to do $Y\neg X$ (ibid., p. 122). When I end a moral conflict in decision, e.g. the decision to do X, it does not necessarily eliminate the conflicting item, $Y\neg X$ (ibid., p. 117). As we have seen, moral conflicts are unlike conflicts of belief. When beliefs are in conflict I should eliminate the conflicting belief that is shown to be mistaken. This is the case because the mistaken belief does not serve the purpose of a belief, as it is does not give me knowledge of reality. In contrast, simply because the contingencies of the case are such that I cannot do $Y\neg X$ (that is, I cannot do X *and* $Y\neg X$), it does not follow that I am mistaken to think that I ought to do $Y\neg X$. Moral conflicts are not 'systematically avoidable', for the reason that to avoid moral conflicts one would have to be 'free to restructure [one's] moral outlook so as to withdraw moral involvement from the situations that produce conflict' (ibid.).

So it is possible to make moral dilemmas systematically avoidable, but to do so will be morally speaking costly. To systematically avoid moral dilemmas we need to engage in wide-ranging moral simplification and withdrawal of moral commitment. This does not refer to a withdrawal of commitment from morality as such, but rather a withdrawal of commitment from the item not acted upon in a moral conflict, and a simplification of morality in that sense. For instance, some may conclude that we should withdraw commitment to perfectionist ideals whenever they are in conflict with utilitarian considerations, or withdraw commitment to rights whenever they come into conflict with incurred obligations, and so on. Williams's argument is important for us here as it highlights that moral simplification and withdrawal of moral commitment will be involved in any such attempt to systematically avoid moral dilemmas. Williams's argument is important for the further reason that it shows ethical theory does not justify such an approach to moral dilemmas. Or as Nagel has argued, we cannot hope to arrive at a theoretical justification for the resolution of all moral dilemmas because moral claims do not have the unitary source required for such a systematic avoidance of dilemmas.

How to resolve moral dilemmas

My argument so far is that moral dilemmas are real or genuine conflicts between independent moral considerations. I have criticised the opposing view that moral dilemmas are a logical impossibility and that what appears as a moral dilemma is just that, an appearance, and nothing more, and so we should feel no regret at the item not acted upon. I have also criticised the related point that we can identify a general rule for the resolution of moral conflicts, the rule that specifies which moral claim is fundamental. The view of moral dilemmas defended here entails also that the role of theory has its limits, and in particular, theory will not identify a general rule for the resolution of moral conflicts. If so, we can only hope to resolve moral conflicts through a form of non-theoretical, that is practical, reasoning. I return below to just how we can do that. However, let us first start by examining the alternative position, namely that it is through theoretical reflection we can resolve moral conflicts.

Theory without limits

I have already spoken at length of the view that moral conflicts are only apparent rather than real. The related assumption is that the role of theory is to dissolve such apparent conflicts, as theory can identify a general rule for their resolution. This is the role given to theory by, for example, Geoffrey Scarre, when using utilitarian moral philosophy to resolve apparent moral conflicts that arise when parents exercise paternalistic power, as utilitarianism shows that the duty to promote well-being is the fundamental moral claim. What is distinctive about this approach is that no limits are placed on ethical theory, as theoretical reflection, by itself, is sufficient to resolve moral conflicts and make moral judgements.

More formally, the utilitarian approach to moral dilemmas is to give consequentialist principles lexical priority over non-consequentialist principles. According to Richard (R. M.) Hare, there are two levels of moral reasoning. The 'intuitive' level involves appeal to everyday, *prima facie*, moral intuitions, such as duties to respect autonomy, to avoid deceit, to refrain from harming others, and so on. In conflict situations, 'in which two *prima facie* principles require two incompatible actions', our task is to 'determine which of these principles should be applied to yield a prescription for this particular situation' (Hare, 1978, p. 179). This happens at the 'critical' level of moral reasoning, where 'the shortcomings of the intuitive stage for complex and difficult cases are removed by recourse to utilitarian calculation' (Donagan, 1993, p. 18). Therefore, for the utilitarian, *difficult cases* create only the appearance of dilemma, as any conflict can be resolved by utilitarian calculation. When faced with conflicting values, we should adopt an impartial standpoint, sum the benefits and burdens of all those affected by the proposed courses of action, and impartially choose the one that best promotes happiness. For instance, with respect to the competing positions on paternalism, the utilitarian will compare the caretaker thesis and the liberation thesis and evaluate which is the most likely to have the greatest contribution to happiness. As we have seen, Scarre adopted this approach, and concluded that parents are not obliged to respect children's right to liberty when to do so would not promote children's happiness.

However, while others agree that the role of theory is to resolve moral conflicts they disagree about how this is to be done. Of particular interest for us is the position that gives non-consequentialist principles lexical priority over consequentialist principles. For instance, in the sphere of medical ethics and clinical research ethics, Robert Veatch has argued that consequence maximising principles are secondary to non-consequentialist principles. Thus, the duty to do no harm (non-maleficence) and the duty to promote the good (beneficence) 'by themselves can never justify breaking a promise, telling a lie, violating autonomy, killing another, or distributing goods unjustly' (Veatch, 1995, pp. 211–12). If we apply this position to the debate on parents' power, then we are given unequivocal guidance on how we should resolve moral conflicts. If a paternalistic action is necessary for the child's own welfare, but if the action of necessity requires that we violate a non-consequentialist principle, for example by depriving the child of liberty, then the paternalistic action cannot be permitted.

Both the consequentialist and the non-consequentialist believe we should feel no regret in situations of moral conflict. The item not acted upon is no longer binding; it is no longer morally prescriptive for us. The problem, as we have seen, is that while some believe it irrational to feel regret at non-consequentialist principles not acted upon when they conflict with consequentialist principles, others believe that to act in that way *would* be cause not for regret, but rather remorse, and even guilt. Should we give priority to a utilitarian calculation in resolving moral conflicts, or instead make utilitarian calculations secondary to non-consequentialist principles? As we know, after a great deal of philosophical reflection, over the course of many centuries, no definitive answer to this question has been found. Therefore, as we have said already, we do not have philosophical licence for insisting that we should resolve all value conflicts through a utilitarian calculation, or alternatively through appeal to non-consequentialist principles.

Theory within limits

An alternative approach is to acknowledge that theory has its limits. Although theoretical reflection can take us so far in addressing moral conflicts, on many occasions it will not be sufficient. This can be seen in the impartial-rule theory of Bernard Gert and K. Danner Clouser. An adequate theory, they argue, will provide 'a clear, coherent, and comprehensive system that can actually be used to solve real moral problems that arise in medicine and other fields' (Clouser and Gert, 1990, p. 233). That is why a list of moral principles or a list of moral duties by itself is not sufficient for moral decision making. Such a list 'does not tell the agent what or how to think, or how to deal with the value in a particular instance – but it reminds him to consider it' (Clouser, 1995, p. 223). Therefore, for this line of thought, the role of theory *is* to tell the agent what and how to think so as to solve moral problems for that agent. However, even when individuals take direction from theory in this way, Gert and Clouser acknowledge that moral dilemmas may still arise. Although the authors contend that protection from harm is the fundamental moral consideration, they accept that 'equally impartial, rational persons can disagree on which harms are preferable', and for that reason we should not expect that there will always be just one solution to a moral dilemma (Clouser, 1995, p. 233).

Although I do not accept that non-maleficence is the fundamental moral consideration, on this last point I am in agreement. It is rational to feel regret at the elements not acted upon in a moral dilemma, including when equally impartial, rational persons could resolve the dilemma in different ways. That is, regret is justified when it is understandable that equally impartial, rational persons would come to different conclusions about what, all things considered, morality requires of us. But if that is the case, we must ask, how do we *justify* the way that we do in fact resolve a moral dilemma when we make a decision one way or the other? I do not think Gert and Clouser's answer to this question is satisfactory. For they believe that, when we reach this point, when theory can go no further, moral reasoning as such also can go no further:

> from that point on, the dispute is no longer a moral one, but rather a matter of accommodation that can involve many other interests and commitments – political, aesthetic, religious, or personal. Knowing where moral reasoning can go no further is a significant bit of knowledge, and giving an account of it represents a significant difference between our theory and other moral theories. Utilitarianism, for example, holds that there is one and only one correct answer to any moral problem. (Clouser, 1995, p. 233)

We can indeed be faced with moral dilemmas. However, is it the case that, once theory can no longer tell us what and how to think, moral and ethical reasoning can go no further? If this were so, we would be left with a particularly abject view of moral reasoning. For it entails either that those engaged in moral reasoning will be told what and how to think by moral theory and moral theorists, or else that there will be no moral reasoning as such, and instead issues will be resolved by an a-moral and a-rational process of *accommodation*. What this denies is the possibility of practical reasoning as a way to resolve moral conflicts. I turn now to the question of how practical judgement can complement theoretical reasoning when faced with moral dilemmas.

Practical reason and practical judgement

In this section, I outline an approach to practical reason and practical judgement that will be defended here before being applied to various case studies in the final chapters of this book. I want to first distinguish practical judgement from theoretical reasoning. I also want to look at the kinds of consideration that we employ when making practical judgements, including empirical data and the views and wishes of others. And I distinguish one approach to practical judgement, inspired by the work of Rawls as well as Nagel, from others.

Let us recap briefly. We have argued that ethical theory has its limits. Because in ethical reasoning agreement or convergence is not explained by how things are, there cannot be a systematic body of ethical truths (Williams, 1985, p. 148). We have also argued that pluralism is at the heart of all things ethical. In particular, the justification for our actions is not unitary, as 'value has fundamentally different kinds of sources' (Nagel, 1979 [1977], p. 132). However, it does not follow that 'nothing can be either right or wrong and all decisions under conflict are arbitrary' (ibid., p. 134). This is the case because, where theory ends, practical judgement can begin. By practical judgement, Nagel has in mind what Aristotle referred to as *phronesis*, that is, practical wisdom: 'the position does not imply that we should abandon the search for more and better reasons and more critical insight in the domain of practical decision. It is just that our capacity to resolve conflicts in particular cases may extend beyond our capacity to enunciate general principles that explain those resolutions' (ibid., p. 135). The need for judgement arises from the limitations of theory. As there will never be a general and complete theory of right and wrong, 'the role of judgement in resolving conflicts and applying disparate claims and considerations to real life is indispensable' (ibid., p. 137).

On this account, when I engage in practical reasoning, when I reason towards a practical judgement, I do offer *reasons* in defence of my conclusion. I offer *generally* applicable reasons of the following kind: 'In situation S, we should do action A, because of reasons R (and, it follows, because of R, anyone in S should do A)'. Such generality is necessary if the reasons that I offer are to count as reasons for others when I account for, that is, justify, my actions. But it does not follow that, in giving such reasons to justify practical judgements, we also appeal to or apply a general rule for the resolution of moral conflicts. For example, if I argue that, in a given case, we should protect a child's liberty, and do so at the expense of efforts to protect the child's well-being, I am arguing that, in any sufficiently similar situation, I (and others) would be justified in acting as I did. It does *not* follow that I am also arguing that, as a general rule, the former value has priority over the latter.

In what way do we make such practical judgements? For example, how are we to decide whether the teenage daughter who wishes to participate in a research study for altruistic reasons should be allowed to do so? First, moral principles are central to such practical reasoning, for we must take on board the plurality of relevant moral considerations, weighing up their relative significance for our judgement. In this example, the girl's own well-being and liberty are central, but so too is the promotion of utility, the duty not to harm others, and also perfectionist ideas (such as the girl's altruism itself). Second, although empirical evidence may have little relevance to certain types of abstract theoretical reasoning, it is relevant when we make practical judgements. What type of fact is relevant? They include empirical evidence about the likely consequences of different courses of action, as well as detailed knowledge of the context in which the decision is made, including knowledge of relevant legislation, policy, and services. A careful examination of the facts can reveal what moral issues, problems, or questions are at stake. It can also highlight what alternative courses of action are open and should be considered. For example, joint decision making is one such option, and we can examine the evidence for its consequences. Third, often we can and should make these decisions with others and not in isolation. This is because very often moral questions are posed for a group of individuals rather than for the individual acting in isolation from others. Thus, in this example, once again we are brought back to joint decision making.

Elsewhere, I have explored these three facets of practical judgement in respect of the ethical review of research applications. I argue that, in making such practical judgements, committee members must not only 'marshal the relevant moral considerations', but also 'illustrate the current state of the research domain in question', and then 'work together towards resolving the moral conflicts that have arisen and do so with considerations that should be acceptable to others as participants in a public debate' (Fives, 2016d, p. 172). I took this approach when considering a specific study, an experimental design, whose purpose was to evaluate a reading programme for disadvantage first and second grade children. Although the study involved denying to some children a potentially beneficial programme, in that instance I argued that the study was permissible, in part at least because the duty of care was not as a general rule the fundamental consideration (Fives et al., 2015). This is a judgement made in consultation with others (researchers, programme providers, research ethics committee members, parents, and children) and on the basis of empirical evidence for the known benefits of such programmes. And it is a judgement that appeals to general reasons without claiming to have identified a general rule for resolving all moral conflicts. This type of approach to practical judgement is defended by others, in particular in the field of medical decision making. It is argued that physicians must not only 'consult as widely as possible' and create the conditions that foster 'decision making capacity' among patients, but also articulate the relevant ethical problems and identify the relevant facts and interests, and select the option that is then best supported by ethical principles (McCarthy et al., 2015, pp. 11, 13, 15; see also Steinkamp and Gordijn, 2003).

Although we have looked at the type of considerations appropriate to practical judgement, one important question remains. If judgement is necessary, but decisions between conflicting claims are not always based on general rules, what distinguishes judgement from mere arbitrary assertion? What gives judgement its justification? I want to first look at an approach to practical judgement that is, in the end, unacceptable, before looking in more detail at a better alternative.

The first approach I will look at is casuistry, which builds inductively from cases and intuitions to justified moral beliefs. An important illustration is found in the work of Albert Jonsen and Stephen Toulmin (1988), in their examination of the ethical permissibility of research with children. In what was to result in the Belmont Report, they were tasked by the National Commission for the Protection of Human Subjects in the US with developing 'recommendations to protect the rights and welfare of human subjects of research and to develop the ethical principles that should govern such research' (Jonsen, 1995, p. 239). They found that, while debate over general principles, 'such as "should children ever be subjects of research", ran on interminably, quick agreement greeted more specific cases in which the research aims, the estimates of risks, the condition of the child, and the competence of the parents were described' (ibid.). In addition, 'the development of ethical principles to govern research, was performed at the end [...] after it [the committee] had proposed recommendations for many specific cases of research' (ibid.). This suggests that, in debates on the ethical permissibility of research with children, including medical research, moral judgement proceeds by precedent cases, analogical reasoning, and attention to circumstances (ibid., p. 245). Great importance is thus given to the particular, both the particularities of the case and 'the nature of the practice or institution that gives rise to the case' (ibid., p. 246). We build up from attention to circumstances, the particularities of the case, and 'the nature of the practice or institution that gives rise to the case' (ibid.).

An inductive approach claims to arrive at general principles in a bottom-up fashion, that is, by working up from the specific cases to the general moral principle. This is a very significant, and controversial, claim to make. In particular, critics will question what implications there are for the critical function served by moral thought. If it is the case that we arrive at moral principles inductively, from the specifics of the case and its circumstances, can the moral point of view ever be a truly critical one in respect of the taken-for-granted assumptions and the practices of that very context? This is a question often directed against writers in the 'communitarian' tradition, who contend that moral reflection starts from the particular, but from that basis can arrive at objective moral judgements (MacIntyre, 1985; 1988).

A further objection to a bottom-up, inductive approach, like casuistry or communitarianism, is that it both conceals moral disagreements and prevents their resolution. If we are to build upwards from our specific context to general ethical principles, and if different individuals or groups build upwards from what are understood to be mutually exclusive starting points, they may well arrive at mutually incompatible conclusions and yet be unaware of any conflict of values. For example, in some contexts, individuals may be expected to give priority to children's well-being, in particular where professionals such as physicians and teachers have a duty of care towards children (Freedman, 1987; 1990; Freedman et al., 1996; Miller and Weijer, 2006; 2007). In other contexts, individuals may be expected to give priority to children's autonomy, for example, in the context of scientific research where primacy is given to securing fully informed consent from research participants (Veatch, 2007; Miller and Brody, 2003; 2007). And in the research ethics literature, there has been deep and on-going disagreement between representatives of these two points of view, and this can be represented as a conflict between the values and assumptions characteristic of two different practices or cases (Fives, 2016d). Therefore, rather than help resolve disagreements, the bottom-up, inductive approach can be responsible for the emergence of multiple, conflicting, and unresolved conclusions concerning the same moral issue.

Reasonableness and public justification

What type of practical reasoning is available to us if we are concerned about and wish to distance ourselves from communitarianism and casuist ethics? I want to consider whether we can address moral dilemmas concerning the legitimacy of parents' power through what Rawls referred to as *public* or *political* reasoning, that is, reasonableness (1999 [1997]) as well as Nagel's account of public justification in a context of actual disagreement (1990 [1987]). The problem with communitarianism and casuist ethics is that neither can provide a critical standpoint when engaged in practical reasoning and indeed each can result in the emergence of multiple, incompatible, and unresolved points of view tied to distinct practical contexts. How can an account of practical reasoning avoid such a fate?

Nagel offers an account of public justification in a context of actual disagreement. It requires a common ground made up, in the first instance, of a willingness to 'submit one's reasons to the criticism of others', to 'present to others the basis of your own beliefs, so that *they have what you have*, and can arrive at a judgement on the same basis'; and second, disagreement which falls on 'objective common ground must be open-ended in the possibility of its investigation and pursuit, and not come down to a bare confrontation between impersonal points of view' (Nagel, 1990 [1987], pp. 315–16; emphasis in original). In later chapters, in discussing the appropriate form of practical reason when evaluating the legitimacy of parents' power, I will return again to the work of Nagel (see Chapter 7). For now I merely wish to emphasise the overlap between what Nagel proposes here and what Rawls has argued for in response to the following question: What kind of consideration is permitted in 'public' reasoning?

Nagel distinguishes between 'what justifies individual belief and what justifies appealing to that belief in support of the exercise of political power' (1990 [1987], p. 312). Thus, the members of a particular community or the practitioners in a particular practice may adhere to a distinctive set of values as justifying their distinctive beliefs, and yet such beliefs by themselves cannot suffice to justify the exercise of political power over others. Similarly, for Rawls, reasonableness is the appropriate approach to reasoning in the public sphere, the 'political domain', as it requires that we do not insist on the truth of our philosophical or moral doctrine, whatever it happens to be. Instead, we are to rely on public reasons, or reasons it is reasonable to expect others, viewed as our moral equals, to accept. Reasonable citizens view one another as free and equal moral persons and are willing to offer each other fair terms of social cooperation (Rawls, 1999 [1997], p. 579). Moreover, they recognise and accept the 'consequences of the burdens of judgment', namely that differences between reasonable comprehensive doctrines have a morally innocent source. For that reason, they try to attain rational agreement without insisting on the truth of a single comprehensive moral doctrine (Rawls, 1993, p. 55).

One line of criticism highlights the 'liberal' moral and political commitments evident in Nagel's and Rawls's approach. Such an approach to reasoning, it is argued, is inappropriate when we address moral conflicts that arise within a community, or within a family, that is, among those who share certain moral commitments not shared more widely. For example, if we consider the situation of the parents and children of a family who belong to a religious minority, should we require that, when they deliberate on moral issues among themselves, they do so by offering public reasons and by recognising the burdens of judgement? It may be that if the family members do adopt such an approach to reasoning, they will be more likely to perceive moral conflicts where before there were none, precisely because such conflicts did not arise when they were not required to recognise the burdens of judgement in their reasoning. In addition, if we require family members to reason in this way, will this unjustifiably hamper parents' efforts to share a way of life with their children when that way of life is not recognisably 'liberal'? I return to this very significant set of questions again in detail in Chapter 7, but we should note that the critics of such an approach say that the 'reasonable' citizen is given the freedom to regard 'non-liberal' beliefs and values as false or invalid or flawed. Rawls does explicitly put to one side the question of their truth or falsity. However, it is precisely in doing so that, his critics argue, Rawls implicitly trivialises comprehensive non-liberal moral beliefs. Non-liberals contend that they *can* establish that their doctrine is true, and that it is for this reason that they should employ these ideas in crucial political debates (MacIntyre, 1988, p. 345ff.).

In addition, it is argued that Rawls's account of political reasoning actually presupposes certain truths it claims to bracket, in particular Kantian, liberal ideas that moral justification is based on consent or contract, and that a morally worthwhile life must be an autonomous life (Dryzek and Niemeyer, 2006; Thunder, 2006). Elsewhere I have argued in reply that a distinction should be made between justifications *of* morality and justifications *in* morality. It may well be that there are Kantian, liberal substantive moral commitments beneath and behind this approach to practical reason, while alternative philosophical doctrines provide competing justifications *of* morality. However, justification *in* morality is a common feature of all moral doctrines, as all assume we can be held to account and should be willing to give an intelligible account of ourselves. Reasonableness is offered as one such approach, and the case for it as a better approximation of justification *in* morality (a better approximation than alternative theoretical accounts of moral judgement in politics) is that it requires we view others as free and equal fellow citizens (Fives, 2010; 2013a; 2013b).

Nonetheless, the concern remains that, if we equate good practical reasoning with reasonableness, we will require that individuals give priority to certain moral considerations and therefore bias the resolution of moral conflicts. Will this approach to political reasoning bias us towards characteristically 'liberal' commitments when we resolve moral dilemmas? In particular, if we adopt a Rawlsian approach, will we be more likely to give priority to the duty to protect individual liberty when it comes into conflict with perfectionist and utilitarian aims? And will we give priority to general considerations, such as general rights and general duties, when they come into conflict with personal commitments? These are the conclusions that Rawls himself reached, in particular through seeking what he referred to as 'reflective equilibrium'. For Rawls, we must seek reflective equilibrium between, on the one hand, our 'considered judgements' and, on the other hand, the moral 'principles' that describe our sense of morality. In seeking reflective equilibrium, we may revise our considered judgements so that they are in line with our principles, or alternatively revise our principles so that they are in line with our considered judgements (Rawls, 1971, p. 48). The outcome of such a process is, for Rawls, to place our moral principles in an order of priority, and, as we saw, he concludes that we are not justified in violating an individual's right to liberty so as to pursue social and economic justice (or perfectionist goals or general utility). The underlying claim is that his principles of justice 'confirm judgements that were already fixed points in our thinking; for example, that they [...] do not permit individual civil and political liberties to be infringed for the sake of other goods' (Scanlon, 2003, pp. 156–7).

If the aim of reflective equilibrium is to place our moral principles in an order of priority, then such an approach is ill-suited for our purposes here. As Patricia Marino argues, moral dilemmas are a possibility because, first, we have a number of common but distinct moral cares, and second, 'different people direct those cares at different objects and prioritize among them in different ways' (Marino, 2015, p. 4). Our moral considerations cannot be systematised so as to show 'how the various principles and duties follow from something more basic' (ibid., p. 7). Therefore, while I employ Rawls's account of reasonableness and Nagel's account of public justification in a context of actual disagreement, my aim is not to look for reflective equilibrium of the kind that issues in a systematic ordering of our moral considerations. Yes, in particular cases, when we make judgements of what we should do, and if we are faced with conflicting moral claims, then we will have to give priority to one moral claim. That is what arriving at a judgement and making a decision involves. However, this process of reflection will not justify giving priority to one moral claim as a general rule. The point and purpose of reasonableness is not that it identifies the fundamental moral claim, but rather that it forces us to adopt the moral point of view in addressing others and in attempting to work through moral problems with them. We adopt the moral point of view in viewing others as our moral equals, in being willing to offer them fair terms of social cooperation, and in recognising and accepting the consequences of the burdens of judgement.

Conclusions

It is widely believed that moral dilemmas do not arise. It is argued that, all things considered, we cannot be required to do *both* X and Y¬X. Moral dilemmas are a logical impossibility, therefore, and so we should never feel regret at the item not acted on when moral claims are in conflict. This assumption also informs much of what is written on parents' power. Those who defend the liberal view on paternalism conclude that, when moral considerations come into conflict, we can identify the general rule that can resolve such conflicts. However, such an approach involves the problematic assumption that it is possible to identify the one fundamental moral claim. Such an approach diminishes the significance of competing moral claims, and involves a process of moral simplification and withdrawal of moral commitment.

I have argued that, in many situations, we can be faced with genuine dilemmas, that is, *moral conflicts for which we cannot identify a general rule for their resolution*. Also, we can resolve such moral conflicts through a type of practical reasoning or practical judgement that is in line with what Rawls calls reasonableness and what for Nagel is public justification in a context of actual disagreement. I shall return to the issue again in Chapter 7. There I shall once again address the danger we face in adopting Rawls's and Nagel's approach to practical reasoning, namely that we will impose a 'liberal' political solution on moral conflicts and in that way ourselves become guilty of moral simplification and withdrawal of moral commitment. I will also consider what the appropriate form of practical reasoning is when we address moral conflicts in respect of parent–child relations. If reasonableness is appropriate to the political domain, is it also appropriate to parent–child relations?

Notes

1 An 'all things considered' judgement is the moral judgement that has been arrived at, and that is morally justified when deciding between two or more moral courses of action. The phrase is used to refer to a judgement that takes on board the merits of the different considerations, and it is in that sense 'all things considered'. Of course, empirically, it is the case that some such judgements will be more comprehensive, and therefore more considered, than others. I cannot take up this point here. However, in the various case studies explored below, in the final three chapters, what we are attempting to do is to be comprehensive, in this way, in answering such moral questions.

2 It may be objected that Williams's argument relies on a view of science that is problematic, if he assumes that science is unitary, in the sense that all scientific methods will provide the same type of evidence about 'how things are'. In fact, it can be argued that the application of different methods will produce a plurality of types of data that is hard to reconcile. For example, I have argued elsewhere that we cannot organise evidence types into a hierarchy, and instead there is a plurality of methods suitable for answering a plurality of different questions (Fives et al., 2017). Nonetheless, it could be argued that Williams is right to distinguish between science and ethics in the way that he does, insofar as convergence under the umbrella of each scientific method can be explained by 'how things are', although this leaves open the possibility of irresolvable conflict between findings arrived at using different scientific methods.

3 I have changed slightly the content of Williams's example, which in his version related to the Conservative party and the British government in the mid-1960s.

4

Children's agency

Up to this point, our discussion has centred on the concept of paternalism and also the methodological challenge of how to resolve moral conflicts. In regard to methodological issues, I argued that paternalism involves moral conflicts, while, as we have seen, moral conflicts may arise in relation to other issues as well, including non-paternalistic power relations. Concerning the concept of paternalism, I defended Gert and Culver's pluralist definition, according to which paternalistic power involves moral conflict but also is exercised only over those capable of liberty of action. In this chapter, I continue our examination of paternalistic parental power exercised so as to promote the autonomy of the adult the child will one day be, and the moral conflicts this may generate.

As I acknowledged already, my line of argument is out of harmony with the prevailing, liberal view that parents are paternalistic caretakers. The leading figures taking this view have concluded that parents may exercise paternalistic power over children only insofar as children lack the qualities of an agent and only insofar as parental power makes up for the deficits that legitimate children's subordination (Scarre, 1980; O'Neill, 1989; Burtt, 2003; Archard, 2004; Brighouse and Swift, 2006; Archard, 2010; Brighouse and Swift, 2014). However, this position is not satisfactory, as we have seen. Parents cannot act paternalistically towards children incapable of liberty of action, while parents can exercise power over children that are fully competent, and for reasons other than to supply what their children lack in terms of agency. But there is a further reason to find the prevailing view unsatisfactory. Even when parents exercise their power in a paternalistic fashion so as to make up for children's deficits, parents can be faced with moral dilemmas, conflicts which call into question the legitimacy of parents' exercise of power even in these instances. This is the case, I shall argue in this chapter, because a number of different moral considerations are relevant when we consider children's agency, and they can pull in different directions and make incompatible demands when we evaluate parents' power.

I turn now, in the current chapter, to an analysis of children's agency itself. To use the terms introduced in Chapter 1, we are interested in both children's liberty of action, on the one hand, as well as the various possible qualities of children's agency, namely their competence, rationality, autonomy, and virtue, on the other hand. Or to use a related distinction, also introduced in Chapter 1, and discussed below in detail, we are interested in both children's negative freedom and their positive freedom. We are also interested in the relations, the interactions, between these aspects of children's agency. In particular, we address the following question: how do we evaluate situations where, while promoting children's positive freedom, parents violate the rights that protect children's negative freedom?

Before going further, it should be noted that the focus of this chapter is limited. It is restricted to those instances where parents' power *is* exercised so as to promote children's agency, and therefore it cannot be seen as an exhaustive account of the ends or aims of parental power. That is, while we are concerned here with those cases where my exercise of power over you empowers you (Haugaard, 2012; Fives, 2015), power can be exercised for other reasons, and legitimately so. Notwithstanding this limitation, in this chapter we have the opportunity to examine in detail many important considerations relevant to parents' power.

The psychology literature on children's agency

We start by looking at the empirically-based literature from the discipline of psychology. This claims to tell us *what is the case* concerning how parents' power affects children's agency, and how the different components of children's agency interact as children develop and mature. In the psychology literature, a positive association is hypothesised between, on the one hand, children's ever-increasing self-regulation, and on the other hand, children's effortful control and attention, competence, autonomy, and moral character. We will go on, in the next section, to see whether this hypothesis can be framed in the normative terminology of political philosophy, namely as a positive association between negative freedom and positive freedom.

I have already referred to Albert Bandura's definition of human agency (see Chapter 1). 'To be an agent', according to Bandura, 'is to influence intentionally one's functioning and life circumstances [...] People are self-organizing, proactive, self-regulating, and self-reflecting' (2006, p. 164). Nonetheless, as we saw, people's agency is but one part of a causal structure. Therefore, even if children are capable of agency, parents (along with other adults in positions of power over children) are, and will remain, key

Table 4.1   Four parenting styles (adapted from Shaffer, 2000)

	Demanding	Undemanding
Responsive	(1) Authoritative parenting style	(3) Permissive parenting style
Unresponsive	(2) Authoritarian parenting style	(4) Neglectful parenting style

determinants of children's lives. Given the importance of the power exercised by parents over children, in what ways can parents exercise this control?

To answer this question, Diana Baumrind (1971; 1991; 1996) categorises parenting styles based on the following two dimensions: responsiveness and demandingness. 'Demandingness' refers to the claims made by parents on children 'to become integrated into the family and community by their maturity expectations, supervision, disciplinary efforts, and willingness to confront a disputative child' (Baumrind, 1996, p. 411). 'Responsiveness' refers to the extent that 'parents intentionally foster individuality and self-assertion by being attuned, supportive, and acquiescent to children's needs and demands' (ibid., p. 410), and the extent to which the child 'experiences warmth, acceptance and nurturance from parents' (Nijhof and Engels, 2007, p. 710).

Based on these two dimensions, we can identify the following four parenting styles (see Table 4.1): (1) *Authoritative* parenting is the most child-centred. It is characterised by high levels of both parental interest and active participation in the child's life, open communication with the child, high levels of trust, encouragement of psychological autonomy, but also high levels of monitoring and high levels of awareness of what the child is doing, with whom, and where. In contrast (2) *authoritarian* parenting is more parent-centred. It is characterised by lower levels of both trust and open communication, and higher levels of psychological control. In contrast again, when parents are (3) *permissive* there is a lack of parental control, as they 'do not require mature behavior from their children', while (4) *neglectful* parents combine a lack of parental control with failure to monitor or support their children (Aunola et al., 2000, p. 207).

Our interest is with the ways in which parents' exercise of power impacts on the development of children's agency. And Lev Vygotsky's account of *proximal* and *distal* outcomes provides a way to conceptualise the role parenting style plays in children's emotional and social development generally, in particular in Baumrind's account. According to Vygotsky (1978), proximal outcomes refer to what a child is able to do in collaboration with a supportive adult, whereas distal outcomes refer to what a child will be able to do independently later as a result. Baumrind, applying Vygotsky's conceptual dichotomy, argues that the role of caregivers is to foster cognitive and social growth in 'the zone of proximal development', that is, the interval between the child's actual level of development and 'the level of potential development under adult guidance or collaboration with more capable peers' (Baumrind, 1996, p. 407).

For Baumrind, the control that authoritative parents exercise over their children is essential for the development of what she refers to as *autonomy*: 'Within the authoritative model, behavioral compliance and psychological autonomy are viewed not as mutually exclusive but rather as interdependent objectives: children are encouraged to respond habitually in prosocial ways and to reason autonomously about moral problems, and to respect adult authorities and learn how to think independently' (ibid., p. 405). For Baumrind, there should be an integrated balance between agentic and communal qualities: a balance between 'the need to be of service and to be included and connected' with the 'drive for independence, individuality, and self-aggrandizement' (ibid., p. 406). Both the communal and the agentic dimensions are evident as well in Baumrind's account of *moral character*, where moral agents are 'able to plan their actions and implement their plans; examine and choose among options; eschew certain actions in favor of others; and structure their lives by adopting congenial habits, attitudes, and rules of conduct' (ibid.). Therefore, children must become capable of regulating their behaviour and their emotions in line with social norms, while the role of parents is both to encourage children's independence and also to promote pro-social standards of behaviour and rules of conduct.

Let us look in a little more detail at specific studies examining the relation between children's self-regulation, on the one hand, and their socio-emotional skills and social and emotional growth, on the other. With respect to socio-emotional skills, evidence shows that pro- and anti-social behaviour in early childhood influence later social development and experiences. In particular, aggression towards peers at early stages of formal schooling is associated with social and emotional problems in later years, including delinquency, conduct problems, and dropping out of school; while exclusion by peers is associated with increased disengagement from school over time (Merritt et al., 2012). However, as there is both an agentic and communal dimension to children's development, socio-emotional skills cannot be reduced to mere *compliance* with adult requests and prohibitions. Baumrind concludes that both non-compliance and excessive compliance with adults are equally problematic: 'Although behavior problems accompany unskillful or excessive noncompliance, skillful noncompliance, which develops with age, is less aversive to parents and indexes age-appropriate autonomy' (Baumrind, 1996, p. 407).

It is also argued that the groundwork for building and maintaining strong social relationships originates in children's behavioural self-control, which enables children to interact in socially acceptable ways (Merritt et al., 2012). A neurological dimension to the development of behavioural self-control has been identified as well. The 'executive attention system' in the brain develops in the first year of life and allows the infant to deploy attention in the pursuit of goals and to plan and persist in the pursuit of goals. The child's development of 'executive functioning' involves a crucial transition from *external regulation* to *self-regulation*, and the development of executive functioning refers to 'higher order cognitive processes that underlie flexible goal-directed behaviors, such as inhibitory control, working memory, planning, and set shifting' (Bernier et al., 2010, p. 326).

The concepts of effortful control and attention are central in the transition to ever-greater self-regulation (Rothbart and Jones, 1998; Bernier et al., 2010). *Effortful control* (or behavioural control) is defined as the ability to voluntarily inhibit a dominant response to activate a subordinate response (Liew et al., 2010; Merritt et al., 2012). For example, the child who can refrain from playing with a desired but forbidden toy illustrates the capacity for effortful control. In addition, *attention* is defined as the ability to sustain and shift attention to tasks, a skill that is required in particular for engagement in classroom activities (Rudasill et al., 2010).

Bridging science and philosophy

What relevance do these findings from the psychology literature have for political philosophy? What can they tell us about children's agency and the normative evaluation of parents' power? The most important overall message is that parents can use their role, and the power it brings, to promote their children's agency. As children experience cognitive, emotional, and social development, in particular in the areas of effortful control, attention, competence, autonomy, and moral character, it is claimed, parents should move increasingly away from the external imposition of control on children and towards children's own self-regulation. This hypothesis can be expressed as well in the normative terminology of political philosophy. As we saw in Chapter 1, according to Isaiah Berlin, negative freedom refers to an 'area' in which a person 'is or should be left to do or be what he is able to do or be, without interference by other persons'. In contrast, positive freedom derives from the idea of being my own master (2004 [1958], pp. 169, 179). Therefore, to use the concepts of political philosophy, in the psychology literature, a positive association is hypothesised between children's negative freedom and positive freedom. The empirical findings from psychology would, in addition, seem to support the normative conclusions of the caretaker thesis. The former suggest not only that parents can exercise their power over their children in such a way as to promote their (children's) positive freedom but that in doing so there is no conflict with the protection of children's negative freedom. This is the case because opportunities for children's negative freedom follow on from children's development of their positive freedom: children's self-regulation 'indexes age-appropriate autonomy' (Baumrind, 1996, p. 407).

A word of caution is necessary before we proceed. We are here using terms and concepts from two different disciplines. Given the disciplinary differences, we can hope to do no more than indicate, in a rough and imprecise way, areas of convergence in the conceptualisation of agency. Nonetheless, what we have seen suggests it is possible to incorporate the insights of the different disciplines on children's agency, and to allow psychology to inform a philosophical analysis of children's agency.

In the next section, we will look at Joseph Raz's discussion of positive freedom, which refers to both 'the inner capacities required for the conduct of an autonomous life' and 'an adequate range of options' to choose from (Raz, 1986, p. 408). Raz offers a conceptualisation of positive freedom, and considers how negative freedom may be impacted when we attempt to promote positive freedom. Therefore, the conceptual terrain covered by his investigation would seem to be very much the same as the one psychologists pass through in considering 'self-regulation', 'external regulation', 'responsiveness', 'negotiated non-compliance', 'effortful control' and 'attention', 'autonomy' and 'optimal competence', and 'moral character' and 'congenial habits and attitudes'. That is, psychologists and political philosophers seem to be talking about the same things, given the similarities in subject matter and the concepts used. But we are still left with a methodological puzzle. As psychology is an empirical science and political philosophy a branch of normative theory, how can we incorporate insights from the former into the latter?

First, it should be noted, political philosophers do use empirical evidence in their arguments about parents' power. For example, empirical claims underlie Robert Noggle's distinction between adults, referred to as 'moral agents', and children, who are considered mere 'moral patients' capable only of what he calls 'simple agency' (2002, p. 100). Children are capable of the deliberate, intentional, and rational pursuit of goals, what we have referred to as liberty of action. However, according to Noggle, children lack what we have called competence, rationality, autonomy, and virtue: they lack the capacity for the kind of moral agency that allows adults to interact with other moral agents on equal terms (see also Freeman, 1997, p. 37; Brennan, 2002, p. 60). And so, to the extent children are incapable of such moral agency, it is the role of parents, acting as a 'bridge' between children and the community, to facilitate children meeting these requirements

(Noggle, 2002, p. 111). Second, the views expressed above by Noggle, and those of the caretaker thesis, seem to be supported by psychology findings. As we have seen, the psychology findings are in line with the assumption in the caretaker thesis that parents, acting paternalistically, are not faced with moral dilemmas in regard to children's right to liberty.

However, the way in which science and ethics have been brought together, above, is not completely satisfactory. As we saw in the last chapter, when we make practical judgements about the legitimacy of parents' power, we should incorporate empirical data of various kinds, including findings from scientific studies of the effects of parenting practice on children's development of agency. Empirical evidence can inform us about the different possible options available, for example, the four different parenting styles discussed above. At the same time, empirical data are by no means decisive in practical judgement. Indeed, and following on from what Bernard Williams has argued (see Chapter 3), even if there is convergence in *science* on the relationships between various components of children's agency, it is still possible to have reasonable *ethical* disagreements about this very topic. More precisely, even if it is generally the case that promoting children's positive freedom is compatible with protecting children's negative freedom, it is possible for the two values to come into conflict, as it is possible that I ought to protect my child's negative freedom and I ought to promote my child's positive freedom and that if I do one of these I cannot do the other. Indeed, as Berlin (2004 [1958]) argues explicitly, and as a critical reading of Raz shows, the requirements to protect negative freedom and promote positive freedom can leave us facing irresolvable moral conflicts.

Positive freedom: autonomy

We have been examining the arguments, in both psychology and political philosophy, claiming to show a positive association between children's negative freedom and their positive freedom. So as to continue our examination of this issue, in this section, I turn to Raz's perfectionist account of autonomy and positive freedom in *The Morality of Freedom*.

What is 'positive freedom'? Raz is interested in 'the capacity sense of autonomy', and he states the 'autonomous person has the capacity to control and create his own life' (1986, p. 408). For Raz, such capacities are of value insofar as they contribute to an autonomous life, and thus the capacity for autonomy is 'a secondary sense of "autonomy"' (ibid., p. 372). Positive freedom 'derives its value from its contribution to personal autonomy' (ibid., pp. 408–9). As I said, this is a *perfectionist* account of positive freedom and of autonomy. Raz's intention is to provide a 'moralistic doctrine of political freedom', 'understood as presupposing value-pluralism and as expressing itself in personal autonomy' (ibid., p. 367). In addition, for Raz, freedom is related to some notion of what types of life are valuable or worthwhile. While 'positive freedom is intrinsically valuable because it is an essential ingredient and a necessary capacity of the autonomous life', in turn 'autonomy is a constituent element of the good life' (ibid., pp. 408–9).

Despite talk of *the* good life, Raz insists there is a *plurality* of good ways of life, just as there is a plurality of virtues and moral values (ibid., p. 412). He also contends that what matters is whether the individual in question believes their life to be good, not whether it is judged good by someone else who claims the authority to do so. A person is autonomous 'only if he pursues the good as he sees it' and this 'is consistent with many of his options being bad ones' (ibid.). As the individual is the final judge of whether their life is good, society is not entitled to impose any one way of life on them in the hope of making them autonomous: 'It is the special character of autonomy that one cannot make another person autonomous', as one is 'autonomous if one determines the course of one's life by oneself'. Others can help, but such 'help is by and large confined to securing the background conditions which enable a person to be autonomous' (ibid., p. 407).

How are we to enable someone else to lead an autonomous life? How can we secure the background conditions of someone else's autonomous life? Raz identifies three ways in which we can do so: (1) In general we should 'stand off and refrain from coercing or manipulating him' (ibid., p. 407). That is, we should not use either coercion or manipulation so as to limit their negative freedom. However, we have obligations beyond this. (2) We should also 'help in creating the inner capacities required for the conduct of an autonomous life' (ibid.). These include 'cognitive capacities, such as the power to absorb, remember and use information, reasoning abilities and the like, [...] one's emotional and imaginative make-up, [...] health, and physical abilities and skills'; as well as the 'character traits essential or helpful for a life of autonomy': namely 'stability, loyalty and the ability to form personal attachments and to maintain intimate relationships' (ibid., p. 408). (3) Finally, we are responsible for creating 'an adequate range of options for him to choose from' (ibid.).

Note that, for Raz, one way in which to help someone become autonomous is to protect them from coercion or manipulation. However, he does also conclude that interference with others' liberty (through coercion or manipulation) *may not* harm their autonomy:

Coercing another may express contempt, or at any rate disrespect for his autonomy. Secondly, it reduces his options and therefore may be to his disadvantage. It may, in this way, also interfere with his autonomy. It may but it need not: some options one is better off not having. Others are denied one so that one will improve one's options in the future. (ibid., p. 410)

This passage makes clear the possibility for moral conflict. Although we ought to protect negative freedom, this may come into conflict with the requirement to create the inner capacities and the adequate range of options required by a moralistic, perfectionist account of positive freedom and autonomy. Raz's attempt to resolve the moral conflict he faces is, however, open to question. As I shall argue, although Raz concludes that, as a general rule, we may rightly interfere with someone's freedom of choice when we attempt to help that person develop autonomy, his work suggests that he lacks philosophical licence to justify this claim.

The first thing to note is Raz's 'ready embrace of various paternalistic measures' (ibid., p. 422). He accepts, for example, 'strict qualifications as a condition for advertising one's services in medicine, law, or other professions'. He believes such measures do not coerce those they are intended to benefit, but, 'Their net effect is to reduce people's choices on the ground that it is to their own good not to have those choices' (ibid.). It could just as easily be said that such measures need not reduce people's choices.[1] However, the point Raz wishes to make here is that, if there is a paternalistic interference with liberty, it is justified if it is compatible with the promotion of autonomy, 'the creation of the conditions of autonomy' (ibid., p. 423). Why is it that we may rightly interfere with others' negative freedom whenever we are doing so in order to promote their positive freedom?

He stresses that 'Perfectionist goals need not be pursued by the use of coercion. A government which subsidizes certain activities, rewards their pursuit, and advertises their availability encourages those activities without using coercion' (ibid., p. 417). However, he believes it is justifiable to use compulsory taxation to fund such policies. If the taxes are justified by our duty to provide others with options and opportunities, then any violation of the duty (that is, not funding those policies) will harm those it is meant to benefit. Therefore, he does accept that the coercive apparatuses of the State can be used so as to *encourage* 'good' options: 'The requirements of autonomy as well as other considerations may well call for governmental intervention in directing or initiating such processes' (ibid., p. 411). In what other circumstances may we interfere with someone's liberty so as to promote their positive freedom? Raz does not think that his position justifies coercive or manipulative paternalistic action that is intended to enforce one, preferred way of life. Because he accepts that values are plural and incommensurable, he will not countenance 'the state [...] forcing or manipulating people to do what it considers good for them against their will' (ibid., p. 412). However, he does not rule out the use of coercion or manipulation so as to remove 'bad options' from an individual.

He is critical of what he calls 'a blind obsession with the avoidance of coercion' (ibid., p. 410). His position is that freedom from coercion 'is valuable inasmuch as it serves positive freedom and autonomy' (ibid.). Therefore, the value of freedom from coercion and manipulation is conditional on its contribution to positive freedom. As we saw, he writes of denying people options so as to improve their options in the future. At the very least, this may entail coercing or manipulating others, for their own good, that is, for their own future autonomy. And surely this could be done by the State, or by others with power, including parents making decisions for their children. For example, his position may justify parents interfering with their children's liberty to eat what they want, including fatty foods, so that in later life they will have improved health and, as a result, more options will be open to them as adults. Alternatively, the State may be justified in interfering with parents' freedom to let their children eat fatty foods, and for the same reason, namely that this is a bad option that children are better off not having.

As Raz accepts that we may legitimately remove a harmful option from an individual if, in doing so, we promote the individual's autonomy, his position does not 'protect' the individual's freedom to choose those 'bad' options. But this is a significant moral loss, and one Raz does not acknowledge. As J. S. Mill points out, the social pressure towards conformity, the 'tyranny of the prevailing feeling and opinion', poses a significant threat to individual liberty, as I may be vulnerable to interference from other individuals or groups who believe I should not be free to take what they believe to be bad options (Mill, 1985 [1859], p. 63). The coercive apparatuses of the State in such situations *could* be used to protect me in my pursuit of my so-called bad options. However, Raz will not guarantee that the State will do so, and so, we must conclude, any other citizen may justifiably interfere with my choices, without fear of punishment from the State, if this is done so as to limit my so-called bad options.

We need to consider now whether Raz deals with these conflicting values in a satisfactory manner. There is a conflict here between two moral claims, namely, that we ought to protect individuals' negative freedom and that we ought to promote their positive freedom (or autonomy, in Raz's terms). Raz is fully aware of the possibility of real or genuine moral conflicts. Indeed, he insists that, when we resolve such conflicts, we do so by making the moral 'judgement' required of us by 'the situation':

> Those who recognize the reality of moral conflict hold that a judgment that an action is intrinsically bad can be, for example, compatible with a conclu-

sive judgment that all things considered it is justified. It may be both justified and intrinsically bad [...] Conclusive judgments merely adjudicate between prima facie judgments. They declare which of the prima facie judgments is of greater weight or urgency in the situation. (Raz, 1986, p. 405)

If the values of negative freedom and positive freedom can pull in different directions, demanding different and incompatible things, such conflicts can be real rather than merely apparent. So how are we to resolve such real, genuine moral conflicts?

For Raz, moral dilemmas can take one of two forms. In one type of moral dilemma, each of the options are wrong and the options are incommensurable and so it is not possible to make a judgement of better or worse between them: 'In it there is no right or best action. All the avenues which are open to one are wrong' (ibid., p. 359). However, whenever the promotion of autonomy is one of the options, we have a moral dilemma of a second kind, namely where it is possible to compare the value of options: 'Some [moral dilemmas] are said to be cases in which one of the agent's options is clearly the better one, or at least involves the lesser evil. In such a case there is a right course of action [...] Nevertheless, it is claimed, performing the right action does not mean that one does not do a wrong' (ibid.).

When one of the possible options is to promote autonomy, why is it 'clearly the better one'? For Raz, 'the ideal of personal autonomy', the autonomous person as 'part author of his life', is the 'particular conception of individual well-being' that has 'acquired considerable popularity' (ibid., pp. 369, 370). He rejects the counter-argument that autonomy is just one valuable style of life, that is, a style of life valuable to those who do choose it, and a style of life we are free not to choose: 'For those who live in an autonomy-supporting environment there is no choice but to be autonomous: there is no other way to prosper in such a society' (ibid., p. 391). Thus, when it comes into conflict with other moral claims, the requirement to promote autonomy is, as a general rule, 'clearly the better one': 'In judging the value of negative freedom one should never forget that it derives from its contribution to autonomy' (ibid., p. 410).

Although the psychology literature hypothesises a positive association between negative freedom and positive freedom, Raz accepts that the two may generate moral dilemmas for us. However, is Raz's attempt to resolve such conflicts acceptable? There is what seems to be a significant tension in his argument, illustrated by his claiming both that, in order to promote the autonomy of others we should protect their negative freedom, and also that, as a general rule, we may justifiably interfere with others' negative freedom so as to promote their autonomy. Raz acknowledges the plurality of moral considerations and the reality of moral conflicts, and he recognises that we resolve real moral conflicts by making moral judgements in particular situations. Therefore, when negative freedom and positive freedom come into conflict we should resolve those conflicts by making practical judgements. And yet he insists that autonomy is the fundamental value, that the value of negative freedom derives from its contribution to autonomy, and that whenever the two come into conflict, as a general rule, we may rightly sacrifice someone's freedom of choice when we attempt to help that person develop autonomy.

Positive freedom: conflict with negative freedom

At the outset of this chapter, we discussed the findings from the psychology literature on child development, where a positive association is hypothesised between children's positive freedom and children's ever-increasing independence from parental control. We have also looked at the work of a political philosopher who makes the related point that, as negative freedom is of value insofar as it contributes to positive freedom, we will experience no irresolvable moral conflict between the requirement to protect negative freedom and the requirement to promote positive freedom. Isaiah Berlin's work is of particular interest in this context. Like Raz, Berlin acknowledges that moral considerations can pull in different directions leading to moral conflicts. Unlike Raz, however, Berlin adheres consistently to this pluralist position, and does not attempt to avoid moral conflict through abstract theoretical arguments and conceptualisations. Although Berlin's 1958 essay, 'Two concepts of liberty', is the seminal account, and defence, of negative freedom, it is also a pluralist work, and acknowledges that, on occasion, we may have to sacrifice negative freedom so as to satisfy other moral commitments.

What is Berlin's argument in respect of negative and positive freedom? First, he concludes, it is a legitimate exercise of political power to defend negative freedom. We as a society may justifiably and legitimately exercise power, including coercive power, over those who would otherwise interfere with the negative freedom of any other individual(s). And Berlin believes that this follows from Mill's principle of liberty (see the Introduction and Chapter 1). Again based on Mill's principle of liberty, Berlin concludes that we may *not* coerce others so as to promote what some may believe to be their positive freedom:

> To threaten a man with persecution unless he submits to a life in which he exercises no choices of his goals; to block before him every door but one, no matter how noble the prospect upon which it opens, or how benevolent the

motives of those who arrange this, is to sin against the truth that he is a man, a being with a life of his own to live. (2004 [1958], pp. 174–5)

What does Berlin mean by positive freedom and why in his work is it treated differently from negative freedom?

The concept of positive freedom is derived from the idea of being one's own master, which, Berlin notes, seems of no great distance from the concept of negative freedom. Nonetheless, the two notions have 'developed in different directions' (ibid., p. 179). The idea of being one's own master can be equated with what we have called voluntary action, that is, being free from liberty-infringing external influence and excessive internal urges and compulsions. However, the idea has developed into what Berlin takes to be the intellectually and morally dubious notion of being true to my 'dominant self', which

> is then variously identified with reason, with my 'higher nature' [...] with my 'real', or 'ideal', or 'autonomous' self, or with my self 'at its best'; which is then contrasted with irrational impulse, uncontrolled desires, my 'lower' nature, the pursuit of immediate pleasures, my 'empirical' or 'heteronomous' self, swept by every gust of desire and passion, needing to be rigidly disciplined if it is ever to rise to the full height of its 'real' nature. (ibid.)

If positive freedom in its original meaning, namely being one's own master, is not considered problematic, why is this particular development of that idea unacceptable? It is objectionable, according to Berlin, as it brings with it the following danger: if others know, or claim to know, that I have a dominant self, and what that dominant self is, and that I am only truly free if I am striving to attain that state, then it is possible to formulate a theory according to which it is permissible for society to force me to be free: if 'it is my good, then I am not being coerced, for I have willed it' (ibid., p. 180). Although it is Rousseau who states explicitly that I may be forced to be free (1762, Book 1, Ch. 7), something like this idea of a dominant self is evident in some versions of socialism too. Most notably, for Marx, in capitalist societies, we are unable to appreciate what our true human potential is, our higher self, namely 'conscious life activity' or 'productive life' (Marx, 1973 [1844], p. 113). Thus, a revolutionary overthrow of capitalism, and also the use of force against all those who would resist it, is permissible and is justified in the name of the positive freedom of all, including those who are thus forced.

May we be forced to be free? For Berlin, it is an illegitimate exercise of power to coerce me so that I lead what is thought to be a good life, the life of my 'dominant' self. And this is the case even when theorists present this as the (forceful, coercive) promotion of my own (positive) freedom. This line of thought is clearly relevant to a critique of revolutionary movements. However, as we saw when discussing Raz's work, contemporary theorists are *not* arguing that coercive power may be exercised to force upon me one way of life. Raz's argument is that society may legitimately exercise power over me so as to secure the background conditions of my autonomy, which in turn is conceptualised in a perfectionist manner, as unavoidably tied up with 'good' ways of life. Nonetheless, as we saw, Raz concludes that society either may remove 'bad' options from me through the exercise of coercion or manipulation, or need not protect me when I wish to choose 'bad' options, that is, options not likely to promote my autonomy. What is more, Raz concludes that, as a general rule, society is justified in failing to defend my negative freedom in this way. As a general rule, negative freedom derives its value from its contribution to autonomy.

What I find problematic with Raz's position is a failure to acknowledge the independence of moral values. And it is the independence of moral values that Berlin does insist on. For example, Berlin accepts that we may rightly decide to limit liberty so as to promote social justice, among other values, and this may be morally justified (see Chapter 7). However, if we do so, we cannot claim that what we have done is, at the same time, to protect liberty:

> if I curtail or lose my freedom in order to lessen the shame of [...] inequality, and do not thereby materially increase the individual liberty of others, an absolute loss of liberty occurs [...] it is a confusion of values to say that although my 'liberal', individual freedom may go to the board, some other kind of freedom – 'social' or 'economic' – is increased. (Berlin, 2004 [1958], pp. 172–3)

Therefore, for Berlin, there may be occasions where the right thing to do is to make some sacrifices to individual negative freedom so as to promote some other value, such as social justice. But when we do so we must also acknowledge the moral loss for what it is, something that otherwise we should have done, or in Williams's terms, a moral item not acted upon. In contrast, as Raz insists that negative freedom derives its value from its contribution to autonomy, for him there is no moral loss when we interfere with negative freedom so as to promote positive freedom.

Berlin's is a pluralist approach, as he accepts there is a diversity of moral principles we should adhere to, even though he gives special weight and significance to the value of negative freedom. Why is this the case? We value negative freedom, he argues, because pluralism is unavoidable, and it is unavoidable because 'Out of the crooked timber of humanity no straight thing was ever made' (Kant, 1908 [1788], vol. 8, p. 23, line 22, in Berlin, 2004 [1958], p. 216). It is because 'we are faced with choices between ends equally ultimate, and claims equally absolute', because there will never be a condition where the 'agony of choice' disappears, it is because this is our situation that we 'place such immense value upon the freedom to choose' (Berlin, 2004 [1958], p. 214; see Galston, 2001b). Nonetheless, as we saw, freedom can be legitimately curtailed. Although Berlin believes that 'Some portion of human existence must remain independent of the sphere of social control', he accepts that freedom must be restricted for at least two reasons: because our aims do not always harmonise and because we want to promote other values (Berlin, 2004 [1958], p. 173).

If freedom may be limited for the sake of other values or other people's freedom, then, he asks, 'Upon what principle should this be done?' (ibid.). In what for our purposes is a crucial statement, Berlin contends that we will not resolve such conflicts in all instances by appeal to a general rule or principle. As Berlin does not accept that 'freedom is a sacred, untouchable value', then 'One or other of these conflicting rules or principles must, at any rate in practice, yield: not always for reasons that can be clearly stated, let alone generalised into rules or universal maxims. Still, a practical compromise has to be found' (ibid.). In the same vein, he argues that the proper scope of negative freedom is a matter that we will always debate and therefore cannot be decided upon as a general rule. Some, like John Locke and Adam Smith, are optimists and believe a great deal of freedom should be guaranteed; while others, like Thomas Hobbes, are pessimists. The question of what is the minimum that man cannot give up 'without offending against his essence as a human' is a 'matter of infinite debate' (ibid.).

Some may be dissatisfied with the contention that we will resolve moral conflicts only through practical reasoning, and that the proper scope of individual freedom is a matter of infinite debate. Is Berlin saying that rational analysis, deliberation, and debate have no role to play? Absolutely not. And, as we saw in Chapter 3, Nagel makes much the same point. It is not that we cannot rationally resolve moral dilemmas, according to Nagel, but that the 'capacity to resolve conflicts in particular cases may extend beyond our capacity to enunciate general principles that explain those resolutions' (Nagel, 1979 [1977], p. 135). At issue here is whether, in adopting Berlin's pluralist approach, there is some way in which to reconcile a defence of negative freedom with policies that secure the background conditions of autonomy. How can we do this and yet not rely on what we know to be the empty claim that we resolve moral conflicts by appeal to a general rule or principle? Let us look very briefly at two ways in which Berlin himself attempts to make such practical judgements.

First, Berlin sets out how to distinguish between greater and lesser degrees of freedom. The extent of my freedom, he argues, can be made greater or lesser depending on: (1) how many paths are open to me, (2) how easy or difficult each of these possibilities is to actualise, (3) how important these possibilities are in my plan of life, (4) how far they are closed and opened by human acts, and (5) what value I and the general sentiment of society places on them (2004 [1958], p. 177, n. 1). Turning to the case of parents and their children, these criteria help distinguish between contexts that are more or less supportive of children's freedom. Some of the criteria can refer to inner resources, such as the capacity to regulate one's behaviour, as well as to external conditions, such as opportunities. Potentially, therefore, this approach allows us to take account of what Raz calls the background conditions supportive of autonomy, without going on to claim, as Raz does, that negative freedom derives its value from its contribution to positive freedom. These are therefore conceptual resources available to us when, in a given situation, we are faced with a difficult decision in resolving conflicts between children's negative and positive freedom.

Second, just because this approach to decision making is practical rather than theoretical, it does not follow that it will be uncritical. In fact, Berlin is able to take a critical stand point and reflect back on taken-for-granted assumptions. For example, Berlin notes that the scope of my freedom is broader than the specific paths I am disposed to choose. That is, he distinguishes non-interference from non-frustration, as freedom is not the 'absence of frustration [...] but the absence of obstacles to possible choices and activities' (Berlin, 2004 [1969], p. 32). The distinction is important as one can overcome 'obstacles to the fulfilment of desire' by adapting one's preferences so as to desire whatever options happen to be available (ibid.) or by killing desire (Berlin, 2004 [1988], p. 326). This enables us to take a critical stand point with respect to what people do desire, and also to the forces that shape people's desires. This will be of particular importance when discussing parental power. Parents do shape the preferences of their children, often with the intention that their children will not desire certain 'bad' options and will feel no frustration in not pursuing those 'bad' options.

Conclusions

In this chapter, we have explored one aspect of parents' power over children. We confined ourselves to those instances where parents' power is exercised so as to promote children's agency. As a result, and as I said at the outset, this chapter cannot be seen as an exhaustive account of the ends or aims of parental power. Nonetheless, the findings are extremely important for our understanding of parents' power generally and paternalistic power more specifically. We have seen that, even when parents exercise their power so as to make up for children's deficits in agency, parents can

be faced with moral dilemmas, conflicts which call into question the legitimacy of parents' exercise of power. This is the case because a number of
different, independent moral considerations are relevant when we consider
parents' power and children's agency, and they can pull in different directions demanding incompatible actions from us.

I examined efforts by Raz to resolve moral conflicts of this sort, and I
argued that his attempt was unsuccessful. Raz is acutely aware of the
reality of moral conflicts, and does himself insist that we can resolve such
conflicts only when we make moral judgements in the given situation.
Nonetheless, he also believes that, as a general rule, autonomy is more
fundamental than negative freedom, as negative freedom derives its value
from its contribution to autonomy. So, when there is a conflict between
the moral claims associated with different aspects of human agency, it is
resolved by appeal to a general rule or principle.

However, we have argued elsewhere that the appeal to a general rule in
resolving moral conflicts lacks justification, and it was as a way out of this
impasse that I turned to Berlin. I have drawn attention to two aspects of
Berlin's argument: he is a pluralist and therefore sensitive to the diversity of
moral considerations, and he believes we can only resolve moral conflicts
through practical reasoning. And such an approach, combining pluralism
and practical reason, may be able to address the concerns that we raised
about Raz's work. Berlin does not claim that through abstract and general
philosophical reflection we will resolve moral conflicts. Nonetheless, he
indicates how practical reasoning can be critical and can take account of
the background conditions supportive of autonomy.

Note

1 As we know already, paternalism need not involve interference with liberty. If
the State prevents those without a medical licence from referring to themselves
as medical doctors in their advertisements, then, when I need someone to help
cure my chronic back pain, this may make it less likely that I will choose, for
instance, a faith healer over a qualified orthopaedic doctor. It may, but it need
not. I am still left free to search out practitioners of alternative medicine and
submit myself to their care.

5

Parental power

How should we conceptualise parental power and how can it be evaluated? In previous chapters, in the evaluation of parental power I made the case for an irreducible plurality of moral considerations and of morally relevant features. In this chapter, I will examine what is, I argue, an irreducible plurality of forms of power itself. I leave until the following chapter to explore the moral considerations appropriate for the evaluation of its legitimacy. However, in the current chapter, I do go some way towards addressing methodological issues relating to how we can best deal with moral conflict when we evaluate parental power. I look first at the empirical literature on parents' power, this time from sociologists influenced by Michel Foucault (1984), and examine what it can tell us as political philosophers. I then evaluate, and ultimately reject, a reductive approach to the conceptualisation of power and therefore also a reductive approach to the resolution of moral conflicts when evaluating parental power (Lukes, 2005 [1974]).

Psychology and Foucauldian sociology, as we shall see, are indicative of two distinct approaches to the conceptualisation of parental power. While psychologists emphasise plurality in analysing the different impacts of alternative parenting styles, Foucauldian sociologists adopt a reductive approach, emphasising what different parenting styles are said to have in common, namely the subjugation of children. Thus, the psychology literature supports our taking a pluralist, non-reductive approach to the conceptualisation of parental power in political philosophy. We can and should distinguish *power to* (power as capacity) from *power over* (power as affecting others and producing effects for others), and both of these from *power with* (power exercised together so as to achieve a shared objective). Within the 'power over' category, I also distinguish coercion, interference with liberty, control, authority, and paternalism.

In doing so, I argue against reductive approaches, according to which power can be reduced to, is nothing more than, coercion. According to the latter, if I as a parent have power it follows that I have power over my children, I am affecting them, *and also* interfering with their liberty and coercing them. For this line of thought, the mere presence of power requires normative justification for the reason that all power is affecting others in this way. In contrast, I argue that 'power to' and 'power with' are not in themselves morally objectionable; it is only when power is exercised over others that we may find reasons to object, although we may also rightly conclude that even coercive power has legitimacy. When it comes to normative evaluation, in the main, we should judge what parents do with their power, that is, the type of power they exercise and what impacts it has, not whether parents have more capacity than their children. Nonetheless, taking on board the critical insight of Foucauldian sociology, I accept that, in one of its guises, power in and of itself requires justification, independently of its being put into action. A relationship of authority, where one party commands and the other obeys, is an asymmetrical power relation, and such asymmetry, for instance between parents and children, requires normative justification.

Foucauldian views of parental power

In the last chapter, I expanded on an earlier argument concerning the differences between science and ethics. Based on the work of Bernard Williams, it was argued that, while in science *how things are* explains convergence or agreement, in ethics if we do obtain agreement it is not because of the way things are. I also looked at the psychology literature on children's agency, where the empirical evidence suggests positive associations between children's negative freedom and children's positive freedom. However, I argued, even if it is generally the case that children's negative freedom and children's positive freedom contribute in a positive way to each other, it is nonetheless possible for the two as normative values to come into conflict, as it is possible in some situations that I ought to protect my child's negative freedom and I ought to promote my child's positive freedom and that if I do one of these I cannot do the other.

What role can empirical evidence about the effects of parents' power on their children's lives have in our normative evaluation of parental power? As we saw in the last chapter, the empirical evidence from the psychology literature does strongly suggest that parents can use their position, and the power that it brings, in such a way as to promote and enhance their children's agency. Although Foucauldian sociologists agree with that factual claim, they reach a very different, in fact a diametrically opposed, normative judgement of the relationship between parents' power and children's lives. In Chapter 1, I examined the literature on parental paternalism. As we saw, many liberals have argued that parental power is paternalistic, but also that paternalism involves interference with the liberty of another. The sociological literature on childhood, in particular work under the 'socio-logical child' banner, characterises parental power in much the same way.

Allison James, Chris Jenks, and Alan Prout start from 'Foucault's discussion of the conditions of discipline', and on that basis examine the 'ways in which the child is constituted sociologically' (James et al., 1998, p. 26, p. 55). Efforts to educate and care for children, efforts to promote children's well-being, whether by parents or by professionals, are all forms of paternalistic control: 'All these conspire tactically for the child's own good and represent the culmination of a nineteenth century trajectory towards, finally, regulating the space within the child' (ibid., p. 57). Parental power represents a 'form of control, modest, suspicious, calculating'; and, as is the case with Foucault's re-interpretation of Jeremy Bentham's model for a 'panopticon' prison, modern parental power 'is refined, invisible, viscous and yet mobile' (ibid., p. 56). Although the inmates in the panopticon prison do not know when they are being observed by the guards, they do know that at any moment they *could* be observed, and for that reason begin to regulate their own behaviour in line with the expectations and demands of their guards. Similarly, the domestic space, the home, is the site of power relations, where children are policed and under surveillance, and as a result experience an 'absence of autonomy' (ibid., p. 54). Thus, on this account, parental power is a form of paternalistic interference with children's liberty and even coercion.

This is highly relevant to the psychology literature on parenting styles. On the basis of psychological accounts of authoritative parenting, many parenting programmes have been designed and delivered for the purpose of changing the ways parents interact with children so as to better promote the latter's well-being. Crucially, these parenting programmes are also designed so as to promote what we referred to in Chapter 4 as children's positive freedom. For example, parents are to encourage their children to become independent problem solvers, to regulate their own emotions and behaviour, to develop pro-social behaviours, and in these ways to develop their agency (Sanders, 1999). What do Foucauldian sociologists think of such programmes? They agree that parents play a crucial role in the development of children's agency, as, through various processes of social construction, children are empowered. However, for the Foucauldian sociologist, autonomy itself is a social construct, and therefore the 'autonomous' individual has been constructed through a process of 'subjugation': 'Individuals are constituted as autonomous individuals only in the sense that they are subjects, i.e. subjected to social power relations' (Göhler, 2009, p. 33). That is, what psychologists consider to be good parents, what Baumrind refers to as authoritative parents, are, according to the Foucauldian sociologist, those who merely subjugate their children.

One immediate objection suggests itself, as it has done for many readers of Foucault (Habermas, 1990; Fives, 2009). If autonomy is a mere social construction, if my efforts to promote my children's autonomy simply subjugate them, then how can we distinguish between good and bad parents, and between legitimate and illegitimate parental power? In other words, are Foucauldian sociologists guilty of moral relativism, in that they take what appear to be conflicting views, outlooks, and practices, and show that 'each of them turns out to be acceptable in its own place' (Williams, 1985, p. 156)? In fact, because they take a relativistic stance to morality, they make *no* normative distinction between different ways in which children are affected by the exercise of parental power. It is argued that, if childhood is a social construction, this 'erodes the conventional standards of judgement and truth', as our 'standards of judgement are relative to our world view' (James et al., 1998, p. 27). The implication of such a relativistic stance is that inverted commas are used in referring to child 'abuse', so that the authors can distance themselves from the presumption that there are non-relative moral standards available to condemn such treatment of children.

However, the authors do not adhere to relativism consistently. They do not use inverted commas when referring to the dichotomy between children's *autonomy* on the one hand and parental *subjugation* on the other. Although deeply inconsistent, this is an understandable consequence of a critical or radical stance they take concerning the subjugation of children, which requires a normative commitment to promote autonomy and minimise subjugation. What is it that Foucauldian sociologists propose as an alternative to children's subjugation? Although they argue that autonomy is a mere social construct, they also believe that the process of social construction can be made less 'vicious' and in that way individuals can enjoy greater autonomy. In much the same way, Foucault explores how it is possible to make less severe the process of subjugation, whether in the prison, hospital, army, or school, and concludes that we can do so by creating for ourselves what he terms 'games of liberty' and 'practices of the self', which can be described as strategies of aesthetic re-constitution of our identities out of the materials available to us in the discourses that would otherwise merely subjugate us (1984, p. 48). The aim, therefore, is to free ourselves, however partially and incompletely, from the processes of subjugation.

When we consider parents and children, what would such games of liberty look like? For the 'sociological child' thesis, it is the asymmetry between parents and children that is objectionable. It is because of this asymmetry that parenting, in particular the style of parenting encouraged by psychologists and manualised in parenting programmes, involves an objectionable paternalistic interference with children's liberty and even coercion:

> The individual child, it would appear, emerges via the disciplined, spatial implementation of the timetable which instils a regularity and a rhythm in all the activities and tasks of children, including control of the material body through the performance of duty and style of life. So for example, just as soldiers are drilled persistently even beyond basic training, so children are required to eat, sleep, wash and excrete at specific and regular times. Within the modern conditions for discipline there is a further, internal spatialization for each activity. Periodized and subdivided into steps or stages for the individual, the learning of tasks is subject to a spatial and temporal division of labour leading to a more specialized and efficient functioning. (James et al., 1998, pp. 55–6)

What can be said in summing up the 'sociological child' position? It is a clear limitation of such an approach that it does not allow a distinction to be made between normatively desirable and normatively undesirable outcomes of power. For example, if the exercise of power serves to create 'a self-disciplined social subject who is internally restrained', this may well be a good thing, namely a condition of possibility for individual liberty as well as a just society and legitimate power relations (Haugaard, 2015, p. 155). Nonetheless, the great insight of the Foucauldian sociologist, one that we must not lose, is that, in the main, it is parents who monitor, judge, regulate, and, at times, coerce children. Arguably, this critical insight and sensitivity is missing when psychologists evaluate parenting power, and such an absence is a significant deficit. Psychologists are happy if parental power leads to good consequences for children's development, and, it could be said, show insufficient concern for what is sacrificed along the way in terms of children's liberty. Nonetheless, the Foucauldian approach is a reductive one. It reduces the variety of parenting activities to what is thought to be their common feature, namely the subjugation of children, the paternalistic interference with children's liberty and even coercion.

The implication of the Foucauldian sociologist's argument is that there is a conflict of interests between parents and children, as every increase in parents' power entails further subjugation of children. However, if we wish for clarity and precision in our analysis, this is clearly not satisfactory. In Chapter 1, we set out a pluralist position according to which not all forms of power will interfere with another's liberty. In this chapter, I will endeavour to defend this pluralist position, and in so doing reject the reductive approach of Foucauldian sociologists and others. Interestingly, the psychologist is a pluralist conceptually, with Baumrind distinguishing between four main parenting styles, as we saw in Chapter 4. Thus, for

psychologists, in some instances parental power can have beneficial consequences, and we can and should distinguish good parenting from parental
power that does not have such good consequences.

We can, once again, say that the empirical literature has important
implications for political philosophy. As we have seen, Foucauldian sociology indicates one area where further normative evaluation is needed,
namely concerning the asymmetry between parents and children. In addition, it provides us with a key question: *Should we adopt a reductive or a pluralist approach to the conceptualisation of parents' power?* With this question
in mind, in the remainder of this chapter I try to clarify as precisely as possible the meaning of the concepts 'power to', 'power over', and 'power with'.
And I start by distinguishing a number of forms of 'power over'. We shall
see that, as power takes various forms, we cannot simply reduce parental
power to interference with children's liberty and coercion.

'Power over'

What is the meaning of power? How should we define it? Is power plural
or can the different types of power be reduced to one of its forms? In order
to answer these questions, I start by examining what it is to have power
over someone. As we saw in Chapter 1, Peter Morriss makes a distinction
between *affecting* something or someone, which is to alter or impinge on it
in some way, and *effecting* something, which is to bring about or accomplish something. He argues that 'simply affecting something or somebody
is not an exercise of power unless the actor thereby effects something'
(Morriss, 2002, p. 300). Similarly, for Dennis Wrong, 'Power is the capacity of some persons to produce intended and foreseen effects on others'
(Wrong, 1995 [1979], p. 2). Therefore, 'power over' refers to *the power of*
A *to influence* B *and to bring about or effect something for* B. But 'power over'
itself has a variety of forms, as we shall see. As some authors equate power
with coercive power, as we see in more detail later, it is important to begin
by examining what coercion means, before moving on to show that not all
'power over' is coercive.

Coercion

One way in which A can exercise power over B is when A coerces B. As
we saw in Chapter 1, when A coerces B, A affects B in such a way that B
is compelled to comply with A. Indeed, the pressure that B is placed under
by the exercise of coercive power is so great that we do not hold B responsible for what B subsequently does, because, we say, B has no choice but
to comply with A. Thus, coercion is 'defined as the threat of force', and
'the use of [...] negative sanctions to obtain compliance' (Wrong, 1995

[1979], pp. 26, 31). As Wrong points out, 'For A to obtain B's compliance by threatening him with force, B must be convinced of both A's *capability* and *willingness* to use force against him', and so it follows, 'a coercer may succeed without possessing either the capability or the intention of using force, so long as the power subjects believe he possesses both' (ibid., pp. 41, 42; emphasis in original). And the threatened force, the threatened sanction, must be an 'irresistible incentive'. That is, insofar as B is coerced, B is forced to act in a specific way and therefore is not morally responsible for doing so: 'Coercion provides an adequate excuse and absolves one of responsibility for the consequences of one's actions' (Kligman and Culver, 1992, p. 187). Therefore, A *coerces* B *insofar as* B *believes that* A *has the capability and the willingness to impose a sanction on* B *and this belief is sufficient to explain* B's *behaviour whether in whole or in part*.

What do we mean when we say that people are not responsible for the consequences of their actions because they have been coerced? According to one position, people are coerced when they are *psychologically* compelled to comply: 'In all cases of coercion, the coercer attempts to make the will of the victim conform to an other-regarding desire of his or her own' (Arnold, 2001, p. 56). The person, B, who is coerced by A has an irresistible desire to comply with A, and therefore is psychologically compelled to comply. For example, this is the case when A is a robber pointing a gun at B, and B hands over a wallet because B is 'unable to bring himself not to perform [the action]' (ibid., p. 55). However, I think this is too narrow and restrictive as a definition of coercion. For instance, on this definition, B is not coerced by the armed robber if B has had time to think through the options and has decided that, all things considered, handing over the wallet is the only rational thing to do. Rather, following Michael Kligman and Charles Culver (1992), it is surely correct to say that, when B is threatened by A with significant evils, B is coerced because we assume it is reasonable for B to do as A wishes, even when B retains the capacity to reflect on the options, and does so.

Therefore, when I am coerced, I am not responsible for acting as I do for the reason that the incentives to do so are sufficiently strong, but I may rationally evaluate the alternatives and act based on such a rational evaluation. What should count as 'sufficiently strong incentives'? For Kligman and Culver, 'Such irresistible incentives generally involve the threat of significant evils, such as death or serious disability' (1992, p. 187). However, the list of possible threatened sanctions must be longer than this, for, as Wrong argues, we cannot equate force with physical force (1995 [1979], pp. 27–8). This is the case because what matters is that B's belief that A is capable of, and willing to, impose a sanction is sufficient to explain B's behaviour. For example, the possibility of a prison term may be a credible threat that will explain my behaviour when I refrain from breaking the law (or attempt to flee when caught in the act of breaking the law). Similarly, children's belief that their parents will remove some privilege (the right to watch television, for instance) may be sufficient to explain their subsequently complying with their parents' wishes. In neither case is there a threat of serious disability or death, but because the threatened sanction is sufficient to explain the behaviour in question we can say that coercion is exercised.

Interference with liberty

Having briefly examined coercion, we are now in a position to consider whether power can take other forms. Can I have power over you and nonetheless not coerce you? The position I outlined in Chapter 1 is that, although all cases of coercion involve interfering with another's liberty, it is possible to interfere with someone's liberty without using coercion. Therefore, my argument so far has been that coercion is a sub-category of interference with liberty.

What then do we mean by 'interference with liberty'? As we saw in Chapter 4, for Isaiah Berlin, freedom is broader than the mere 'absence of frustration' in pursuing one's current aims, and extends to encompass 'the absence of obstacles to possible choices and activities' (2004 [1969], p. 32; 2004 [1958], p. 177, n. 1). In what way can I exercise power over someone else and in so doing interfere with that person's liberty but not resort to coercion? In Chapter 1, I spoke of a civic education programme composed of a classroom-based component and a community service component. Imagine a situation where parents decide that their children should not participate in the community service component, let us say out of a concern for their children's physical safety when off school grounds, and without waiting to discern whether their children do in fact wish to participate in this component, remove this option by refusing to provide the required parental consent. The parents interfere with their children's liberty insofar as they do indeed close off an option for them. (If the children nonetheless somehow manage to participate in the community service component, there has been no interference.) However, if they have not threatened the children with any sanction for non-compliance, this does not fall under the heading of coercion. It follows, *obstacles to possible choices and activities count as interference with liberty, whether or not those obstacles are or entail the threat or use of sanctions.*

There is one sense in which the person whose liberty is interfered with but who is not coerced nonetheless is not responsible. If the controlling unit removes one of the responsive unit's options, the responsive unit cannot be held responsible for not choosing that option. For example, if parents ensure that their children do not have the option of enrolling in community service work (as above), the children cannot be held responsible for subsequently not enrolling. This is different from situations where the responsive unit is coerced into performing an action. Let us imagine another scenario where the children in question are coerced by their parents into joining a public protest against the civic education programme. Then, the children are not responsible for doing so. They simply have no choice. In contrast, if the parents merely remove the option of enrolling in the community service work without coercing the children into acting one way or another, the children are morally responsible for what they *then* do. They are responsible for the use they make of their time and what option they do then choose of those that are available. And as I said, this is the case even if it does not make sense to hold the children responsible for not enrolling in the community service work.

Control

So far we have seen that coercion is a sub-category of interference with liberty. I also claimed in Chapter 1 that I can have power over you and still not interfere with your liberty. Given the tendency, already discussed above, to equate power with coercion, it is a highly significant issue whether one can control others without even interfering with their liberty. My argument here is that interference with liberty is a sub-category of control. Therefore, all instances of interference with liberty also entail control, but I can control someone, and even control someone's behaviour, without thereby interfering with that person's liberty. In addition, I need not even attempt to control the other person's behaviour, for instead the object of my attention may be the other person's experiences, beliefs, or emotions and feelings.

It has been argued that attempts to control another's behaviour need not interfere with that person's liberty. This is the case with so-called 'libertarian paternalism', which is represented by, among other things, procedures whereby employees are automatically enrolled in savings plans that they (the employees) are free to opt out of. This position is libertarian as 'choices are not blocked or fenced off'. Yet power is exercised to 'steer people's choices', namely 'to influence the choices of affected parties in a way that will make choosers better off' (Sunstein and Thaler, 2003, p. 1162). The libertarian paternalistic proposals of Sunstein and Thaler are such that options are not closed off, but rather the background for making choices is altered, making it easier and therefore more likely that individuals will make choices that are (it is thought) to their benefit, for example by remaining in rather than opting out of a savings scheme. Crucially, in this proposal, workers retain the freedom to opt out. That option has not been 'blocked or fenced off'. Of course, our judgement and categorisation of the situation will rightly vary depending on the extent to which obstacles are placed in their way when workers attempt to opt out of the saving scheme.

Manipulation, persuasion, inducement, and deprivation

So far we have spoken in very general terms about the forms of control exercised when one person has power over another, and again in very general terms, made the argument that there is a diversity of forms of 'power over'. In this section, I will look at some of the specific ways in which A can attempt to control B's behaviour, including efforts to manipulate, to convince through rational persuasion, to induce, or to deprive of some needed resource. In which instances of such power relations, and for what reasons, is it the case that A does interfere with B's liberty?

I start with the power exercised over someone through persuasion. According to one definition, if A wants to 'persuade' B to act as A desires, then in good faith A must try to convince B that acting in the way that A desires is in B's interests (Kligman and Culver, 1992, p. 186). As it stands, this definition of persuasion is too narrow, as it is restricted to those cases where A wishes to convince B to act in B's own interests. However, I can convince you, and do so through rational persuasion alone, to act in a way that is altruistic, that is, without appealing to your own interests. For example, in the 1930s many socialists, anarchists, and other anti-Fascists were persuaded that they should go and fight in the Spanish civil war, not so as to promote their own interests, but so as to help halt the spread of Fascism in Europe (Orwell, 1989 [1938]). It is more than a mere possibility that, as in the case of George Orwell, many were persuaded to do so through rational persuasion, and yet by appealing to considerations other than their own interests.

Therefore, a revised definition of persuasion would read as follows: *if A wants to persuade B to act as A desires, then in good faith A must try to convince B that acting in the way that A desires is rationally defensible.* For example, if a mother (A), through rational argumentation alone, convinces her child (B) that she (B) should show extra consideration and kindness towards a new child in her class (C), then A has persuaded B. In this example, B is persuaded to act in a way that is primarily designed to benefit someone else (C). Note also that, in this example, A affects B in the sense of controlling B's behaviour. However, we do not say that A interferes with B's liberty, as B freely choses to act on the basis of A's persuasive argument. Persuasion, it follows, does not entail interference with liberty.

Persuasion is distinct from 'manipulation', but manipulation need not entail interference with liberty either. According to one definition, through manipulation, A attempts to procure or engineer B's assent by bringing pressure to bear on what A presumes to be the 'manipulable features of B's motivational system' (Kligman and Culver, 1992, p. 187). For example, if parents offer an incentive to their children so as to procure their children's assent to attend school, then the children are manipulated rather than persuaded. However, the children's liberty is not interfered with insofar as they (the children) weigh up the options and freely decide in favour of the option that included the incentive. However, according to another definition, manipulation occurs when the manipulators conceal their purpose from the manipulated: 'When the power holder conceals his intent from the subject – that is, the intended effect he wishes to produce, he is attempting to manipulate the latter' (Wrong, 1995 [1979], p. 28). And when manipulation takes this second form, when the manipulator's intentions are concealed, is it more likely to entail interference with another's liberty?

This is the case if the manipulation of the information results in B being unaware of some options, thus closing off those options for B. For example, this may be the case in a situation where parents ensure their daughter does not receive a blood transfusion because of their (the parents') religious beliefs. If the child requires a blood transfusion in order to survive a medical emergency, and the child's parents convince her that such a procedure will be extremely painful for her, and in doing so manipulate her motivations and so bring about their undisclosed intention, namely to adhere to the religious ban on blood transfusions, then the parents have indeed interfered with their daughter's liberty. But it should be noted, it is not the concealing of intentions but the closing off of options that makes this an interference with liberty.

Finally, let us examine 'inducements' and 'deprivation'. If a parent offers an inducement to a child, the child may be manipulated on the basis of that inducement. Will an inducement interfere with the liberty of the induced party, if, in offering the inducement, A takes advantage of B's ignorance or vulnerability to secure B's compliance (Beetham, 1991, p. 44)? If A takes advantage of B, and in doing so closes off some option for B, then A interferes with B's liberty. Similarly, if A threatens B 'with the deprivation of some resource or service that is necessary' to B, and in doing so closes off an option for B, then again we speak of interference with liberty (ibid.). And if 'deprivation' takes the form of a credible threat, then it will entail coercion as well. This is the case if there is a credible threat that certain of B's actions will lead to the imposition of a sanction on B and as a result a diminution of some valuable good for B, for example, a monetary fine. But once again, we talk of interference with liberty only when options are in fact closed off.

Authority

The argument so far is that I have power over you when I affect you and produce effects for you, whether or not I coerce you, interfere with your liberty, or merely control you. Therefore, the forms of 'power over' are diverse; and we cannot reduce 'power over' to one of its forms. The next two sections expand on this argument for the irreducible plurality of forms of 'power over', but in a manner different from what has gone before. In this section, I discuss authority, and what I want to show is that authority (like paternalism, discussed again briefly below) can take any one of the forms of 'power over' already discussed. Therefore, for each form of 'power over' we have to consider whether or not it is also at the same time an exercise of authority.

Authority refers to a right to rule and a corresponding duty to obey; it is 'voluntary obedience' (Wrong, 1995 [1979], p. 22). Therefore, A *has authority over* B *when* B *willingly obeys* A *and/or when* A *successfully claims a right to rule* B. Let us return to an earlier example, where I am out walking with my fifteen-year-old son and I prevent him from walking on a slippery plank across a deep gorge. In this example, let us assume that I exercise coercion over my son, as I prevent him from walking on the slippery plank by threatening him with a severe sanction. But in doing so I *may* act with authority, and this is the case *if* I claim a right to command my son and/or *if* my son willingly complies with such commands. So it is possible for me to coerce my child and do so with authority. Indeed, there is a clear distinction to be made between coercive authority and coercion *simpliciter*. What is at issue here is not just that coercion may lack legitimacy. Rather, an exercise of coercive power may be legitimate but lack authority, and this is the case if those who are coerced are not duty bound to willingly comply with the (legitimate) coercer: 'Indeed, they may be justified in trying to escape coercion. This could be the case in a military occupation of a country that is justified on the grounds that it is necessary to stop a third country from engaging in morally indefensible aggression' (Christiano, 2012).

Thus, we must distinguish coercion from legitimate coercion, and we must distinguish legitimate coercion from coercive authority. In addition, those who claim a right to rule may or may not be justified in doing so. Therefore, a further distinction is needed between *de facto* authority, on the one hand, and *de jure* or legitimate authority, on the other. According to Joseph Raz, governments are 'de facto authorities because they claim a right to rule and because they succeed in establishing and maintaining their rule. They have legitimate authority only if and to the extent that their claim is justified and they are owed a duty of obedience' (1985, p. 5). In his discussion of authority, Raz concentrates on the problem of coordinating our common efforts so as to attain some shared good (see Chapter 6). Those who claim obedience are owed obedience, they have legitimate authority, he argues, insofar as such obedience secures the social coordination 'which everyone desires for independent reasons' (1990, pp. 7–8).

Before moving on, I want to draw attention to a further important distinction, namely between being *an authority* and being *in authority*. The former is sometimes referred to as theoretical authority and the latter as practical authority. I am 'an authority' if my 'views or utterances are entitled to be believed'; whereas I am 'in authority' when I am entitled 'to make decisions about how other people should behave' (Friedman, 1990 [1973], p. 57). It would therefore seem as if only the latter is relevant to our discussion of power. However, one approach conflates the two forms of authority. For conservatives, political institutions have legitimate authority only insofar as they reflect or embody or promote the 'authoritative beliefs' of a society (ibid., p. 58). However, although it is the case that citizens may have a duty to obey because they share certain 'authoritative beliefs', it is another thing altogether to insist that the duty to obey must be based on authoritative beliefs. Indeed the aim of conceptual precision is furthered by distinguishing between theoretical and practical authority, while acknowledging that on occasion the latter may be based on the former.

Although I want to distinguish between the two meanings of authority, the distinction is at times blurred, and justifiably so. One reason for this is that both involve the surrender of one's private judgement. Concerning practical authority, it is argued that one should surrender one's private judgement and instead act as the person in authority commands, and do so because such obedience secures the social coordination necessary for the attainment of some shared good. Therefore, the justification for your duty of obedience is based, in part at least, on the claim that it is right and proper you surrender your private judgement. And, as Richard Friedman argues, this is what is common to both theoretical authority and practical authority: 'it is the contrast between authority and persuasion through rational argument (rather than the contrast between authority and coercive power) that is essential to the delineation of the distinctive kind of dependence on the will or the judgement of another person involved in an authority relationship' (1990 [1973], p. 67).

Paternalism

So the distinction between being 'an authority' and being 'in authority' is at times justifiably blurred, as both require surrender of one's private judgement. There is a second reason why this may be the case. Paternalism has been discussed at some length already in the earlier chapters of this book. I return to paternalism now, and very briefly, solely to highlight the overlap and the differences between it and the concept of authority, as just discussed.

Two necessary features of paternalism are A's belief that A is qualified to act on B's behalf, and A's belief that B believes (perhaps falsely) that B generally knows what is for B's own good. In everyday usage of the term, it is said that, as a parent, I am justified in acting paternalistically towards my child because *I know what is best* for my child (and, at times, that my child does not). So the right to exercise paternalistic power rests, in part, on the claim that my views and utterances are entitled to be believed: that is, I claim I am 'an authority'. Nonetheless, it does not follow that we can equate paternalism with authority. While each paternalist must be (or believe themselves to be) 'an authority', it does not follow that they are 'in authority'. That is, although paternalists must believe they know what is best, it does not follow that they have legitimate practical authority: it does not follow that those over whom they exercise paternalistic power owe a duty of obedience to them.

The reverse is true of practical authority. Namely, those 'in authority', those with legitimate practical authority, need not be, or claim to be, 'an authority'. It is not the case that I am owed a duty of obedience (I am 'in authority') only insofar as I also claim (rightly or wrongly) that my views or utterances are entitled to be believed (I am 'an authority'). Indeed, if I am 'in authority', I am owed a duty of obedience even when I make a mistake, even if I am mistaken about how to solve the coordination problem and to secure the good we have independent reasons to pursue. This is the case because what is at issue is the justification of behaviour rather than of belief; and your compliance with my commands may be justified even if, on occasion, I am mistaken.

To sum up, 'power over' can take various forms. When I exercise power over you, I affect you and bring about effects for you. I can control you through persuasion, manipulation, inducements, deprivations, and efforts to affect your experiences and emotions. (See Table 5.1, and the left hand column of Table 5.2.) However, my 'power over' restricts your liberty only when it places obstacles in the way of your options, and my 'power over' coerces you only when, because of my threat or use of sanctions, there are irresistible incentives to comply and in consequence you are absolved from moral responsibility. My 'power over' in addition may be exercised in any one of these ways with authority. That is, I may have a right to command you and you may have a duty to obey me. And finally, any of the forms of 'power over' may be exercised paternalistically, when I exercise power over you, for your own good, and without your consent.

Up to this point, therefore, I have distinguished the various forms of 'power over'. In doing so, I have laid the conceptual foundations for a broader objective, which is to investigate whether, when we evaluate the

Table 5.1   Glossary of power concepts

Forms of power

Power with: to exercise powers together so as to achieve a shared objective

Power to: power as an ability, capacity, or dispositional property

Power over: to affect others and bring about effects for others

Forms of 'power over'

- *Coercion*: A coerces B insofar as B believes that A has the capability and the willingness to impose a sanction on A and this belief is sufficient to explain B's behaviour whether in whole or in part (all instances of coercion also entail interference with liberty and control)
- *Interfere with liberty*: obstacles to possible choices and activities (interference with liberty need not entail coercion and will always entail control)
- *Control*: an exercise of power so as to control someone's experiences, behaviour, beliefs, or emotions (control may but need not entail either coercion or interference with liberty)

The following can be manifested as various forms of 'power over'

- *Persuasion*: if A wants to persuade B to act as A desires, then in good faith A must try to convince B that acting in the way that A desires is rationally defensible
- *Manipulation*: A attempts to engineer the needed assent by bringing pressure to bear on what A presumes to be the manipulable features of B's motivational system and/ or A conceals their intent from B
- *Inducement*: A attempts to secure B's compliance through the offer of an inducement, whether or not A thereby interferes with B's liberty or takes advantage of B's ignorance or vulnerability
- *Deprivation*: A threatens B with the deprivation of some resource or service that is necessary to B
- *Paternalism*: A exercises power over B, for B's own good, and without B's consent
- *Authority*: A has authority over B when B willingly complies with or obeys A and/or when A successfully claims a right to rule B

legitimacy of parental power, we are faced with an irreducible plurality of relevant moral considerations and of morally significant features. To continue that work, in the next section I examine whether it is possible to distinguish 'power to' and 'power with', on the one hand, from 'power over', on the other.

'Power to' and 'power with'

Let us start with the distinction between 'power to' and 'power over'. According to one line of argument, the one put forward here, 'Power [...] is

Table 5.2 The forms of power

'Power to': capacity				
'Power over': controlling	**Not controlling**			
Affecting others and bringing about effects for others	Not affecting others and/or Not bringing about effects for others			
Interference with liberty — Control AND Remove options	**Potential not acted upon**	**Effecting without affecting**	**Affecting without effecting**	
Coercion — Control AND Remove options AND Credible threat of sanction	e.g. when parents do not act on their capacity to enforce a rule	e.g. when I paint my house a bright colour but this does not affect my neighbours as I had intended	e.g. when I display my wallet to a thief and, without my intending it, as a result am robbed	

Persuasion — Control only

Manipulation — Control only or Interfere with liberty

Inducement — Control only or Interfere with liberty

Force — Coercion

Deprivation — Control only or Interfere with liberty or Coercion

Authority — Control only or Interfere with liberty or Coercion

Paternalism — Control only or Interfere with liberty or Coercion

'Power with'
Controlling   or   Not controlling

always a concept referring to an ability, capacity, or dispositional property' (Morriss, 2002, p. 13). My 'power to' is my capacity, and I cannot affect you and bring about effects for you unless I have sufficient capacity to do so. At the same time, the argument goes, not every instance of 'power to' involves or entails 'power over'. I can have capacity, and even exercise capacity, without thereby of necessity controlling your experiences, behaviour, beliefs, or emotions. Although my having power may entail that I *could* control others, and even do so to their detriment, it does not

follow that my having power *does* control others or does so to their detriment (see also Allen, 1998). This line of thought stands opposed to those
who conclude that 'power over' has logical priority over 'power to', as the
latter is based on the former: 'the social relations on which *power to* is based
are, specifically, relations of *power over*' (Pansardi, 2012, p. 86; emphasis
in original). Rather, as Morriss illustrates, there are at least three ways in
which one can be said to have 'power to' and yet not have 'power over' (see
the right hand column of Table 5.2).

First, when I exercise power over you, I affect you and bring about effects
for you. However, *it is possible to effect something without affecting someone*
(ibid., p. 30). If I have capacity ('power to'), I have the capacity to bring
about (effect) some state of affairs; and I may successfully bring about that
state of affairs and yet not affect anyone. For instance, if I have the power
to paint my house, I have the capacity to effect a state of affairs. I may do
so in the hope of thus controlling the behaviour of others, and yet fail in
that objective. Let us assume I inform my next door neighbours that I will
paint my house with bright red, luminous paint unless they pay me a large
sum of money once every year, but let us assume also that they refuse to
pay me the money. The fact that I have the capacity to bring about this
state of affair for my neighbours (a state of affairs where they will be living
next door to a crimson coloured house) does not mean or entail that, when
I do so, I thereby also control someone else. That is, my having the power
(capacity) to bring about a state of affairs for others does not in any way
entail that I have power over those others.

Second, *it is possible to affect someone without thereby effecting something
for that person.* For example, if I 'incautiously' display 'a well-filled wallet'
it does not follow that I exercise power over the thief who subsequently
robs me (ibid., p. 29). The thief may have been affected by my behaviour
(when I displayed my wallet) but it does not follow that I have succeeded
in bringing about some state of affairs for the thief. The attempt to steal my
wallet may be as a direct consequence of my incautiously displaying that
wallet, and the thief may be caught and punished as a result. However,
again, I did not effect this state of affairs; I did not bring this about through
my exercise of power over the thief. Situations such as this illustrate that
'Power is identical with *intended* and effective influence' and for that reason
power is distinguished from 'acts of *unintended* influence' (Wrong, 1995
[1979], p. 4; emphasis in original). We can see this point if we think instead
of a situation where my *intention* is to lure the thief into attempting to steal
my wallet. If I display my wallet in order to encourage a thief to attempt to
steal it so that the thief will then be caught in the act and punished, then
I am attempting to both affect the thief and bring about or effect a state of
affairs for the thief.

Finally, third, it is important to distinguish between power and its exercise. *Power can be a potential not acted upon.* 'For if A could, *but does not*, "limit" B in some way, then there is nothing in B's conduct or situation for which A can be held responsible: ex hypothesi, A has not contributed to the situation that B faces' (Morriss, 2002, p. 21). For instance, in the main, parents will have access to a far greater compliment of capacity ('power to') than their children. However, parents do not always act on this power; and some parents will do so more than others; and some parents will use coercion more than others, and so on. Therefore, we should analyse parental power not in terms of parents' capacity, or 'power to', but in terms of whether this power is exercised by parents over their children and if so in what way.

Therefore, it is possible to have 'power to', and even exercise 'power to', without also exercising 'power over'. I now turn to consider whether it is also possible to exercise 'power with' without exercising 'power over'.

'Power with' is the human ability to act in concert. According to Hannah Arendt: 'Power corresponds to the human ability not just to act but to act in concert. Power is never the property of an individual; it belongs to the group and remains in existence only so long as the group keeps together' (Arendt, 1969, p. 44). Arendt believed that *all* power fitted this description, and *only* such relations were power relations, but that claim does not hold up when we consider the numerous ways in which individual parents have the capacity to affect others and to bring about effects for others. However, what is of interest to us here is the possibility that 'power with' is a form of power, and that it cannot be reduced to or equated with 'power over'. As we shall see, some, such as Lukes, do not accept that what is referred to as 'power with' is really power at all. I shall try to show that the concept 'power with' is appropriate for relations where individuals are exercising power together so as to achieve a shared objective, and that, in doing so, they may exercise 'power over', but also they may not.

Let us imagine a scenario where parents with shared musical interests come together to create an informal parenting support group. They come together, employing their capacities jointly, so as to put on a performance of Puccini's *Tosca*. In doing so, they exercise their powers together so as to achieve a shared objective. The successful performance of *Tosca* represents their exercise of 'power with'. However, we can distinguish such an exercise of 'power with' from any exercise of 'power over'. As we saw when discussing 'power to', one's behaviour can influence without controlling others, and the same is possible concerning 'power with'. For example, contrary to her parents' intentions, the performance of the opera may inspire the daughter of one of the performers to give up all aspirations of herself one day becoming an opera singer. After seeing the lengths to which her mother must go to perfect her performance, she (the daughter) draws the conclusion that such effort is beyond her. The parents' exercise of their 'power with' has influenced the young girl (she has been affected) but not as they intended. It would be incorrect to say they have exercised power over her as they have not controlled her: they have not brought about effects for her.

In other cases, it may be that those who exercise 'power with' *will* also exercise 'power over'. And they may exercise power over themselves or others. Regarding the former, the group who have come together to perform their favourite opera may also enforce regulations upon the individual singers in their group. For example, if singers do not turn up on time for rehearsals they may be fined, and the group may select one of their own singers to enforce this sanction on behalf of the whole group. Alternatively, the group of singers can have power over others. For example, the singers may exercise control over who attends the performances, and specifically in their role as parents, they may oblige their own children to attend. So it is possible for those who exercise 'power with' to also, and on that basis, exercise 'power over'. It is a possibility, but it need never happen.

We are asking whether we can distinguish 'power to', 'power with', and 'power over'. At the start of this section we saw that one can have 'power to', and even exercise 'power to', and yet still not control others. Therefore, although I cannot exercise 'power over' unless I have the requisite 'power to', 'power to' does not entail or involve 'power over'. Similarly, now we have seen that there are cases where individuals exercise their powers together to achieve a shared objective. As we have seen, exercising 'power with' may also involve or entail 'power over', but it need not. In acting together, it may be that we do not affect others, or we may merely influence others without controlling them. Therefore, 'power with' does not necessarily entail or involve 'power over'.

The irreducible plurality of power concepts

As I emphasised at the outset of this chapter, I am addressing two very different approaches to the conceptualisation of power. One approach is reductive, as it equates all power with 'power over', and, in particular, interference with liberty and even coercion. We have already seen that the Foucauldian sociology literature on parental power takes such an approach, and as we shall see presently, so too does Steven Lukes when he presents his third 'dimension' of power. I will call this the reductive position. Another approach distinguishes 'power to' and 'power with' on the one hand from 'power over' in all its various forms on the other hand. I will call this the pluralist position. This is the approach adopted here.

Let us start with the reductive approach. Steven Lukes reduces power in all its forms to 'power over', and specifically coercive power, and contends that power is exercised only where there is a conflict of interests. This is what Lukes refers to as the third dimension of power, building as it does on a critique of the work of Robert Dahl (the first dimension) as well as Peter Bachrach and Morton Baratz (the second dimension). In Dahl's formulation, as we saw in Chapter 1, power entails control of behaviour through decision making. I have power over you if your behaviour depends 'in some circumstances' on my behaviour as a 'controlling unit' (Dahl, 2002 [1968], pp. 10–11). In Chapter 1, I said that I thought Dahl's approach was compatible with pluralism in the conceptualisation of power. Dahl does not equate power with coercion, but rather sees relations where 'severe sanctions' are expected or applied as a 'smaller subset' of all power relations (ibid., p. 11).

Bachrach and Baratz accept that power is exercised through decision making, but also argue that through agenda setting power of a different type, or face, is exercised:

> Of course power is exercised in the making of decisions that affect B. But power is also exercised when A devotes his energies to creating of reinforcing social and political values and institutional practices that limit the scope of the political process to public consideration of only those issues which are comparatively innocuous to A. (Bachrach and Baratz, 2002 [1962], p. 30)

As noted earlier, the second dimension of power narrows the focus of analysis to those situations where the controlling unit interferes with the liberty of the responsive unit by ensuring that certain choices are not even options available for the latter. The focus of analysis narrows even further with Lukes's third dimension of power, which equates power with coercion.

Lukes's position is based on a two-fold critique of the theories of both Dahl and Bachrach and Baratz. Instead of a concern with the actions and intentions of individuals, Lukes emphasises the social structural dimension of power, and rather than a concern with observable conflicts of subjective (perceived) interest, he emphasises its ideological function whereby the powerless do not recognise their real interests (Haugaard, 2002, p. 38).

I will start with the latter point. For Lukes, when I exercise power, I impose sanctions on those with whom I have a conflict of (real) interests. Not only that, there is the 'third-dimensional capacity to frame public issues in a way that distorts or suppresses people's perceptions of their interests' (Hayward and Lukes, 2008, p. 7). As Stewart Clegg has observed, this is both a radical and humanist approach: 'It theorizes and evaluates actual behaviour by reference to a model of what people would do if they knew what their real interests were' (1989, p. 92). So power is always a matter of conflicting (real) interests. For that reason, Lukes is critical of the 'power to' concept because it refers only to an ability and not a relationship, and 'accordingly, the conflictual aspect of power – the fact that it is exercised *over* people – disappears altogether from view' (Lukes, 2005 [1974], p. 31; emphasis in original). Lukes also rejects the concept of 'power with', and defines all such consensual behaviour as influence rather than power. However, to accept Lukes's distinction between power and influence requires that we also accept his view that power is by definition conflictual, that power is, as a matter of 'fact', coercive and exercised over others.

Relatedly, Lukes distinguishes between power and authority. Where there is a conflict of (real) interests between ruler and ruled, and sanctions are threatened or imposed, then power and power alone is exercised; but where there is a relationship of authority, and no conflict of interests, influence alone is exercised, through inducement, encouragement, or persuasion (ibid., p. 36).[1] For Lukes, power and authority overlap only in one instance, namely when there is a conflict of interests between ruler and ruled, but such power/authority takes the form of *manipulation* rather than *coercion* or *force*. But the central point is that power properly understood, power that is not combined with authority, is coercive. Therefore, we can say that Lukes reduces power to coercive power exercised in situations of conflicting interests. I want to question this approach on a number of grounds.

First, we have already argued against distinguishing coercion and authority in the way Lukes proposes (see earlier in this chapter). Indeed, those who exercise coercive power may (or may not) do so with authority. For instance, a democratically elected government, exercising power within the law, based on the consent of the governed, and in accordance with accepted normative principles, nonetheless does have access to coercive measures. If we argue that the citizens of such a society should willingly obey this government then we are saying the government has authority, and yet the government may legitimately have access to, and use, coercive force. It is also the case that a governing party may abuse and misuse its power. In such a situation, the governing party may still exercise coercive power, and we may judge that such an exercise of power has legitimacy, for example, if it is the only plausible alternative either to chaos or to an even more illegitimate regime. Nonetheless, it may be that, in this situation, citizens are not duty bound to obey the government, that the government has lost its authority, for example, when the government's forces threaten innocent civilians with physical violence. Here we can see the necessity of a plurality of 'power over' concepts. They are needed in order to take account of situations where coercive power has (or has not) legitimacy, but also, and more to the point here, when legitimate coercive power has (or has not) authority.

Second, it seems a mistake to conclude that power requires a conflict of interests. As we have seen, parents do act paternalistically, and when they do so they act in the interests of their children. If, as it is widely accepted, paternalism is a form of power, it follows that a conflict of interests is not a necessary feature of power relations. Interestingly, Lukes is 'inclined to adopt' the proposal that when A's preferences are in B's 'real interests' but B is unaware of B's real interests, then A may act paternalistically towards B up to the point where B does recognise B's real interests (ibid., p. 37; see Hayward and Lukes, 2008, p. 7). What this shows is that even Lukes accepts that power can be exercised when there is no 'real' conflict of interests, although it is revealing that the responsive unit experiences the situation as if it were marked by a conflict of interests. This is the case because Lukes reduces power to coercion, and so, if there is no need for A to threaten sanctions against B to secure B's compliance, then, for Lukes, A is not exercising power over B.

Again, we can question Lukes's argument. The first and most obvious issue is that it requires some account of 'real interests', which in turn requires access to objective knowledge about human interests that the individuals in question themselves do not have access to (Haugaard, 2002, pp. 39–40; see Clegg, 2010, p. 6). As we have already seen in analysing the concept of agency (see Chapter 4), many authors have attempted to establish that one feature of agency is more fundamental than others, and all have failed to do so. All such attempts at reduction are bound to fail because of the irreducible plurality of the morally relevant features of human agency. The same will be true of 'real interests', however we define them. For Lukes, B, and B alone, can identify B's real interests, and only under 'conditions of relative autonomy' (2005 [1974], p. 37). But this too involves a questionable process of reduction, here a reduction of the morally relevant considerations in the evaluation of paternalistic power to what an agent (the responsive unit) will choose under conditions of relative autonomy. This equates human interests with autonomy. As Berlin points out, the concept of 'positive freedom' becomes problematic when we have it refer to the mastery of one's dominant self, which in turn is equated with just one of our qualities or strengths, whether it be rationality or virtue, or, as in this case, autonomy. Indeed, Lukes acknowledges there is more than one way to think of real interests, accepting as he does that liberals and reformists will not conceptualise 'real interests' in the way that he, as a radical, does (Lukes, 2005 [1974], pp. 37–8; see Clegg, 1989, p. 91).

For Lukes, power is only exercised when there is the threat or use of sanctions. It is true that only coercive power is exercised in this way. However, we have also seen that there are ways in which to affect others and bring about effects for others without using or threatening sanctions. Lukes would define all such non-coercive interactions as 'influence' rather than power. Yet, as we have seen, we need to distinguish types of influence that do control (i.e. 'power over') from those that do not control: the government's introduction of an 'opt out' savings scheme does control workers without coercing them; but my incautiously displaying a full wallet merely influences the thief without controlling the thief. This justifies our using 'power over' to refer to the former and not the latter, even though in the former case there is no coercive power exercised. Indeed, Lukes now concedes that he 'plainly erred' when originally arguing that power involved conflicting interests, accepting now the need for a pluralist stance. He is now critical of 'a conflict model in which the power of actors consists in prevailing over other actors, to the neglect of the innumerable ways in which power can be beneficial, collaborative, and empowering' (Lukes, 2015, p. 266).

Let us turn finally to the second feature of Lukes's position. Lukes believes that power is not something that *individuals* possess or exercise. He 'regrets' the 'everyday usage' of the term 'exercise of power', on the grounds that it has the following connotation: 'it is sometimes assumed to be both individualistic and intentional, that is, it seems to carry the suggestion that the exercise of power is a matter of individuals consciously acting to affect others' (ibid., p. 41). However, as we saw in the last section, the idea of intention *is* needed so as to distinguish situations where one merely affects others in unintended ways from situations where one controls others, that is, where one influences others as one intends. As we shall see below, it can be argued that many unintended outcomes (for example, that person B has much less capacity than person A) are morally objectionable, but we need not apply the term 'power over' to such situations in order to make this evaluative judgement. In addition, we should note that, for Lukes's radical view of power, what is morally objectionable is any concentration of power, for instance, within organisations or social groups, for this entails 'power over' and conflictual relations. However, I have tried to show that it is possible to distinguish 'power to', 'power over', and 'power with'. Therefore, a concentration of power does not entail or involve a concentration of 'power over', never mind coercive power. If that is the case, how are we to evaluate power?

To try to answer that question, let us turn to the alternative, 'pluralist' view. A person's 'power to' must be distinguished from the specific sorts of acts that person then performs thanks to that power. Just as not every exercise of 'power to' is also an exercise of 'power over', so those with 'power to' can use that capacity to pursue a variety of objectives. For instance, power can be used by parents to help empower or liberate their children, or it can be used to exploit or dis-empower their children: 'When it comes to holding people morally responsible – praising and blaming them – it is invariably their actions (and omissions) that we look at, not their powers' (Morriss, 2002, pp. 21–2). Thus, when we judge parents, according to this line of thought, we judge what parents do with their power, rather than what power parents possess. If parents use their power so as to control their children, we can analyse whether these controlling acts are justified. If parents also interfere with their children's liberty, we can ask whether these obstacles to children's choices are legitimate.

The inequality in 'power to' between parents and children is a separate matter. If children enjoy a far smaller amount of capacity than their parents, then, taken by itself, we have no reason to analyse this in terms of the legitimacy of 'power over', for we are considering 'power to': 'What is wrong with being powerless is that you *are* powerless – that is lacking in power. And if people are powerless because they live in a certain sort of society – then that, itself, is a condemnation of that society' (ibid., p. 41). It may be that you as a child do not have enough 'power to'. It does not follow either that you are thereby in someone else's power or that you only have a valid complaint if someone else is responsible for your powerlessness. We can and should deal with these two issues separately, until the point where they are not separate, the point where, for example, it is parents' 'power over' that is keeping children powerless.

We are distinguishing between 'power to', 'power over', and 'power with'. This three-fold distinction has important political implications, as has been shown with respect to feminist theory and feminist politics. It is argued that while feminists are, by rights, interested in 'understanding the ways men dominate women' (one form of 'power over'), they must also consider women's 'power to' and 'power over' (Allen, 1998, p. 32). Feminists are interested in women's 'power to', that is, 'feminine empowerment [...] the power that women retain in spite of masculine domination', as well as women's 'power with', that is, 'the kind of power that diverse women can exercise collectively when we work together to define, and strive to achieve, feminist aims' (ibid.). Therefore, as Amy Allen concludes, an analysis of male domination is not sufficient, as a feminist analysis of power needs both a conception of 'power to' as well as a conception of 'power with' (ibid., pp. 34–5). This pluralism is required for conceptual clarity and precision of analysis, but also for making sense of the political possibilities and priorities of feminists.

As we know, not everyone accepts this line of thought. In particular, those who take a reductive, radical approach argue that inequalities in capacity just by themselves equate with, or entail, 'power over'. I return to that argument again in more detail in Chapter 6, in particular when examining republican arguments about legitimacy. I have already argued against this radical approach, on the grounds that 'power to' does not necessarily entail, it need not involve, 'power over'. Nonetheless, there is one sense in which power as such is a matter that requires normative legitimation, whether or not that power is exercised, and that is when 'power over' takes the form of authority.

Authority is a form of 'power over' that entails a right to command and a duty to obey. Parents have authority over children insofar as they have a right to command their children and their children have a duty to obey. The morally relevant feature of such a relationship is its asymmetry, as one party, and one party alone, has a duty to obey the other (see Levin, 1997). Despite what I have said so far in defence of the pluralist position, it *does* make sense to say that such asymmetry requires normative justification, and this is required independently of our evaluation of any specific acts of authority and even whether or not parents act on their authority. We can ask whether it is right, whether it is legitimate, that some should be *in a position* of authority with respect to others, and specifically, whether parents' position of authority is legitimate.

Conclusions

I have brought this chapter to a close by drawing attention to cases where power as such requires justification, namely where it takes the form of authority. However, we are not led as a result to embrace a radical view of power, for the reason that it involves an unjustified reduction of moral considerations. We have seen, in the previous chapter, the plurality of morally relevant considerations and morally significant features relating to agency. We have also seen how such moral considerations can pull in different directions, leading to moral conflict. This can happen when we ought to protect children's negative freedom, and promote children's positive freedom, and if we do one of these we cannot do the other. In the current chapter I have made the argument that there is an irreducible plurality of power concepts, including 'power to', 'power with', and the various forms of 'power over'. It follows that a wide variety of moral considerations are relevant when we evaluate parental power.

Therefore, we are led to ask the following questions when we consider the various aspects of the parent–child power relationship: Do parents have a rightful claim to *authority* and do children have a duty of obedience to their parents? May parents make use of *coercively* imposed sanctions (whether or not they also have authority)? May parents infringe their children's *liberty* (whether or not they coerce their children in doing so)? May parents *control* their children (whether or not they restrict their children's liberty in doing so)? May parents act *paternalistically* towards their children (whether or not they have authority, coerce their children, or infringe their children's liberty in doing so)? And finally, is it justifiable that there is an asymmetry in the power relations between parents and children such that children have a duty to obey and parents have a right to command?

The next chapter takes up the conceptual issues that arise when we evaluate the legitimacy of parental power. I look at legitimacy as an issue in normative justification. Each of the forms of 'power over' are analysed in turn, and it is here that the possibility for moral conflict is clear when we evaluate parental power. That this is so is explained by the fact that, when we evaluate the normative legitimacy of parental power, we are not just asking the one question, we are not just applying the one normative concept, and we are not just concerned with one dimension or aspect of parent–child relations.

Note

1 Hannah Arendt approached authority in much the same way: 'A father can lose his authority either by beating his child or by starting to argue with him, that is, either by behaving to him like a tyrant or by treating him as an equal' (1963, p. 93).

6

Normative legitimacy

In what way can we evaluate the normative legitimacy of parents' power? What makes some power relations and some exercises of power legitimate and others illegitimate? Throughout the earlier chapters of this book I drew attention to the possibility of moral conflict. I argued that there is no sufficiently strong reason to accept, as a general rule or principle, that one moral claim is more fundamental than all others, and that, when they are in conflict, should be given priority over those other claims. The same holds for the normative justification of parental power. Insisting that, as a general rule, we should give priority to one moral claim, for example that parents' coercive power must be based on children's hypothetical consent, is inadequate to the plurality of moral considerations that are appropriate for the evaluation of parental power. I have also argued that there is no sufficiently strong reason to concern ourselves with only one feature of parental 'power over', for example, parental coercion. As I will try to show here, such an approach would be inadequate to the various morally relevant features of the parent–child power relationship.

Without in any way claiming to be exhaustive, in this chapter, I offer a critical overview of numerous ways in which philosophers have evaluated the legitimacy of power. My exegesis will take a particular form as I have a specific purpose in mind. Although I will discuss numerous theoretical positions (in particular, republicanism, anarchism, various forms of liberalism, and social contract theory), I do not pretend to offer a comprehensive judgement of their value as political theories. I do not have the space required to do justice to such a task, but in any case it would not meet our current needs. I am not concerned here with which theoretical position is the best 'fit' with the reality of parental power, although in the main it is in those terms that they have been presented to us. Rather, I will analyse these various opposing theoretical arguments in order to illustrate how moral values may come into conflict when we evaluate the legitimacy of parents' power in concrete situations.

Specifically, I hope to show the inadequacy of efforts made to equate power with one of its forms and, in that way, to reduce moral complexity concerning the legitimacy of power, namely arguments about liberty, coercion, control, authority, and paternalism. Even among those who concern themselves with, say, coercion, seemingly intractable moral disagreements arise, and these theoretical disagreements are, I shall argue, evidence of underlying conflicts between independent moral values. In any case, as I shall try to show, there is no sufficient justification for equating 'power over' with just one of its forms, as there will always be more than one morally relevant feature of the case, and for that reason we find ourselves compelled to examine the case from the perspective offered by some other form of power.

Republicanism and liberalism: interference with liberty

Some believe we should give priority to the protection of liberty when we evaluate the legitimacy of power. I will return to a liberal version of this position presently, but I start with Philip Pettit's republicanism. His argument is that we are not free if we do not have a certain standing relative to our fellow citizens. If our social position is such that others *could* interfere with our choices, whenever they wished, then we are dominated.

For the republican, the antonym of freedom is domination, and Pettit defines domination as the *capacity* to interfere, with impunity and at will, in certain choices of another. The 'interference' must involve a more or less intentional attempt to worsen another agent's situation of choice; the 'with impunity' requirement means there is no penalty or loss for individuals who interfere; while the 'at-will' condition entails that individuals can initiate interference at their own pleasure (Pettit, 1996, pp. 578–80). These three conditions are sufficient for domination to occur. A further condition is likely: it will be a matter of common knowledge that these three conditions are fulfilled (ibid., p. 582). But crucially, Pettit believes that individuals have arbitrary power if they have the *capacity* to interfere, with impunity and at will, in someone else's freedom of choice.

Subjugation is defined as defenceless *susceptibility* to interference, and children (Fives, 2015) can be susceptible in this way:

> The powerful employer, husband, or parent who can interfere arbitrarily in certain ways subjugates the employee, wife, or child. Even if no interference actually occurs, even if no interference is particularly likely – say, because the employee, wife, or child happens to be very charming – the existence of that relationship and that power means that freedom fails. The employee, wife,

or child is at the mercy of the employer, husband, or parent, at least in some respects, at least in some measure, and to that extent they live in a condition of servitude. (Pettit, 1996, p. 598)

Note, to enjoy high degrees of arbitrary power over those subject to them, the husband, the employer, and the parent need only have the *capacity* to interfere, with impunity, and at will; they enjoy arbitrary power whether or not they do so interfere. Or to use the terms presented in the last chapter, if I have the 'power to' needed to interfere with your choices then I also have power over you.

It is important to note that Pettit is not objecting to the negative conception of freedom here, defined as freedom from interference, but rather a liberal interpretation of it. For the 'liberal' view of negative freedom, associated with Mill and Berlin, there is no loss of liberty in just being susceptible to interference, and also there is no actual interference without some loss of liberty (Pettit, 1996, pp. 576–7). In contrast, for Pettit's republicanism: (1) even if the exercise of political power restricts liberty it may not dominate, (2) whereas the mere presence of vastly unequal amounts of capacity does dominate. Let us look at both of these points in more detail.

First, according to the republican, actual interference *need not* dominate. This is the case when reforms are introduced by democratically elected representatives, even when they lead to restrictions of individual liberty. For the liberal, in contrast, any interference with liberty is a *prima facie* bad, as something is lost regardless of what may be gained. Even when the interference occurs as result of the policies and laws created by a body of citizens acting in concert, once again, something is lost, namely liberty (Berlin, 2004 [1958], pp. 172–3). But for republicans, if the laws are passed by citizens acting together and free from domination, then any resulting interference is non-dominating: 'But to the extent that people share equally in the exercise of such power over government, [...] they are going to determine at least the broad shape of the laws under which they live. And to that extent those laws are not going to represent an alien will or *arbitrium* in their affairs' (Pettit, 2016, p. 190). When our democratic government intervenes in my life, including when it removes some of my options, it does not dominate me, because it is merely 'channelling' my own 'will':

> When Ulysses was held to the mast by his sailors, on this way of thinking, he was not dominated by their interference, because they were acting only on terms that he laid down. They were not imposing an alien will in the practice of such interference but merely channeling his own will, as that had been expressed in his instructions to them. (ibid., pp. 189–90)

Second, for the republican, the mere presence of vastly unequal amounts of capacity *does* dominate. If others retain the capacity to interfere with my choices, I will be dominated even if they never do interfere. For example, if I ensure they never interfere by ingratiating myself with them, I will not be free if it remains a matter of will, taste, or favour that others leave open my options (Pettit, 2011, p. 705). The solution, he argues, is for institutions to promote 'antipower', namely, to 'get rid of a certain amount of domination without putting any new forms of domination in their place' (Pettit, 1996, p. 588). And to promote 'antipower', we give the powerless *protection* against the resources of the powerful; we *regulate* the use the powerful make of their resources; and finally we give the powerless new, *empowering* resources of their own (ibid., p. 590). Therefore, when our democratic government does intervene it should promote 'antipower', and when it does so, once again, it does not dominate.

Returning again to the language used in Chapter 3, we can say that, in this way, the republican distinguishes between the types of interference that are a *prima facie* bad and those that are justified all things considered. When options are removed from me by the activities of a democratic government, this is a *prima facie* bad, but as it is non-dominating it is justified all things considered; and when options are removed from me so as to promote my 'antipower', again this is justified all things considered as a means to reduce domination.

What are the implications of the opposing liberal and republican positions for the evaluation of parents' power? The liberal view is that, even if I have fewer resources than my parents, I as a child am free insofar as no one (including my parents) *does* interfere with my freedom of choice, thereby limiting my options. Although Berlin acknowledges strong normative grounds to oppose deep social and economic inequalities, as they are 'unjust and immoral', nonetheless he believes such inequalities in and of themselves are not infringements of liberty: 'Mere incapacity to attain a goal is not lack of political freedom' (2004 [1958], pp. 169, 172–3). In contrast, for the republican, if I, as a child, must ingratiate myself to my parent to ensure continued protection against my parent's interference, then by definition I am un-free, for my parent *could* interfere with impunity and at will in my freedom, and I am un-free even if my parent *never does* interfere. Therefore, if we make efforts to reduce social and economic inequalities between parents and children, and in doing so interfere with liberty (whether of parents or children), this will not count as domination. Rather, it will reduce illegitimate forms of power, or in Pettit's terms, it will promote children's 'antipower', by protecting and empowering children, and by regulating parents' power.

Let us apply these theoretical arguments to a concrete example. We shall discuss civic education in greater detail below (see Chapter 10), but for now we can distinguish characteristically liberal and republican approaches to this issue. As liberalism is concerned with whether or not options are in fact closed off to individuals, a liberal would place great importance on both parents and children being free to choose whether or not children attend civic education classes, as well as whether the aim of such a programme is to increase the options of the adults the children will one day be (Feinberg, 1980). In contrast, as it is concerned with the capacity to interfere, a republican approach would place great importance on whether a civic education programme genuinely promotes children's 'antipower', even if options are removed from children or parents in the process.

One approach is for the design and delivery of civic education programmes to be increasingly child-centred and/or voluntary, which takes power from parents and teachers and places it, increasingly, in the hands of children. And when we consider such developments we see how the values on which the liberal and republican approaches to civic education are based can come into conflict. On the one hand, a child-centred civic education programme may promise to promote what republicans call 'antipower', but if we make participation compulsory, then this will interfere with the liberty of children and/or parents, and thus set off liberal concerns. On the other hand, if we permit children/parents to opt out of such a civic education programme, as liberals may wish, children may not receive the supports necessary to overcome domination, the aim of republicanism.

It seems clear that liberal and republican approaches can have markedly different implications for both children and their parents. The liberal and the republican both acknowledge the importance of freedom as non-interference. However, the liberal gives priority to the extent to which we are protected from actual interference. For the republican, in contrast, what matters most is the capacity to interfere, as actual instances of interference will not be dominating if they are based on genuine democratic participation and/or if their aim is to counteract unjustified differences in status and capacity. As I said at the outset of this chapter, my aim is not to evaluate each of these as theoretical systems. Rather, I want to use these opposing arguments to illustrate how we can be faced with conflicting values in concrete situations of actual choice. As we saw very briefly when considering civic education, we have here two values that pull us in different directions: the value of reducing actual interference with liberty, on the one hand, and the value of minimising differences in capacity to interfere, on the other hand. If participation in civic education classes is necessary for children's republican freedom, is it legitimate to make children's attendance compulsory? In whatever way we answer this question we are deciding between these two values.

If we are faced with conflicting moral claims, what method may be used for their resolution? Arguably, Pettit takes a reductionist approach to moral conflict. His position is that, if we cannot promote children's 'antipower' without at the same time restricting children's options, then, as a general rule, the latter is justified. Indeed, just as his shipmates did not dominate Ulysses when they held him to the mast, we are 'channelling' children's own 'will' when we promote their 'antipower', even when we coerce them in order to do so.[1] As we saw in Chapter 4, Berlin (unlike many fellow liberals, it must be said) does not take such a reductionist approach to moral conflict. Berlin acknowledges that values will come into conflict and that we will not resolve such conflicts by appealing to general principles but rather by what he called a process of practical compromise. Taking Berlin's approach, we can say that, although we value the empowerment of children, if we bring this about by limiting children's options, then we have obtained one goal by making sacrifices in respect of another.

My final point is that, in this section, we have focused on those who give priority to the protection of liberty when evaluating power. However, when we evaluate power it is simply not possible either to exclude or to diminish in significance other normative features in this way. For example, although both the republican and the liberal contend that protection of liberty is the most fundamental consideration, nonetheless, both accept that, for example, coercion is justified at some point. Without coercion, the liberal cannot guarantee that individuals will be protected against unjustified interference, and the republican cannot guarantee that individuals will be able to enjoy the 'antipower' required to overcome domination. We cannot avoid talking about coercion because, when we try to put in place what we take to be a justified policy designed to protect liberty, we may have to overcome unjustified opposition to our proposals and to do so we may need to threaten, and use, sanctions.

Social contract theory and coercion

Indeed, others have argued that whether or not power is legitimate turns on the question of the exercise of coercion. That is, the central or fundamental issue, they claim, is whether or not those who do exercise coercive power do so with legitimacy, and as we shall see, this question has been pivotal for social contract theory in particular. However, this apparent consensus is belied by deep divisions within social contract theory itself. Most notably, there is a significant difference in normative outlook between those who, like Hobbes, contend that coercive power can be legitimate only if it is also *absolute* and those who, like Robert Nozick, believe that coercive power can be legitimate only if it is *limited*. In any case, as we shall see later in this section, there are good reasons to doubt that coercion in fact is the central or fundamental consideration when evaluating legitimacy.

Let us begin with Max Weber, as he places coercion at the centre of his definition of the modern State. He defines the State with reference to the 'monopoly' it enjoys on 'the legitimate use of physical force within a given territory':

> Specifically, at the present time, the right to use physical force is ascribed to other institutions or to individuals only to the extent to which the state permits it. The state is considered the sole source of the 'right' to use violence. Hence, 'politics' for us means striving to share power or striving to influence the distribution of power, either among states or among groups within a state. (1946 [1919], p. 78)

While Weber is concerned here with legitimate violence, we should, as Dennis Wrong has argued, conceptualise 'force' more broadly. The exercise of coercive force includes both physical and non-physical sanctions: that is, we can coerce others without using or threatening the use of violence against them (Wrong, 1995 [1979], pp. 27–8). I will focus here on the 'right' to use such coercive force. And I am interested in parents as one of those 'groups' who strive to 'share power'.

What is it that confers the right to exercise coercive power? Social contract theory attempts to answer this question by considering what the subordinate party does, or could, consent to. Thus, for social contract theory, legitimacy can be conferred by tacit, actual, or hypothetical consent. We discuss tacit and actual consent in some detail in the next chapter. For now, let us note that, for John Locke, *tacit* consent is evident when each 'free man ... comes to be of age' (1993 [1679–83], Book 2, Ch. VIII, para. 116), while the *actual* consent of elected representatives in the legislature, the consent of the majority, is needed to impose taxes (ibid., Book 2, Ch. X, para. 140). At the same time, all social contract theorists employ some notion of *hypothetical* consent, such as Rawls's account of the 'original position' (1971). In considering hypothetical consent, we ask *would* rational and autonomous persons have agreed to create a society like this, and in some cases we ask whether those individuals *would* leave a state of nature to do so. And a society is legitimate if rational and autonomous individuals *would* give it their consent in this way, that is, if '(a) it can be generalized and (b) none of the actors involved constitutes a means to an end' (Haugaard, 2012, p. 37; see Scanlon, 1998).

Although social contract theorists agree on the importance of consent for legitimacy, as I said, social contract theory itself represents a broad spectrum of opinion, with the arguments of Hobbes at one extreme. For Hobbes, a near contemporary of Locke's, the State must be able to call on the force necessary to guarantee each subject's 'security' and 'preservation', and if the State cannot do so, its subjects should not accept 'that restraint upon themselves' (1996 [1651], Ch. 17, para. 1). That is, the State has legitimacy, it has a right of 'dominion', or 'sovereignty', only if it can successfully exercise coercive power so as to carry out its essential functions (ibid., Ch. 20, para. 1). Those essential State functions include protecting subjects from each other, that is, when individual subjects otherwise would harm or interfere with the liberty of others. For example, the State protects its subjects when it ensures parents are free to 'institute their children as they themselves think fit' (ibid., Ch. 21, para. 6). This would require protecting parents from interference when they attempt to share a way of life with their children.

Hobbes places the coercive power of the State (or 'Leviathan') at the centre of his normative evaluation of power. The reason for this can be found in what he takes to be the terrible consequences of our living without legitimate coercive power. In what he refers to as a 'state of nature', there is a 'perpetual and restless desire of power after power, that ceaseth only in death' (ibid., Ch. 21, para. 2), that is, a struggle that leads to civil war, and in consequence the loss of 'industry', 'culture', and all other benefits of civilisation (ibid., Ch. 13, para. 9). Even in this 'state of war' all persons can appeal to the following 'right of nature': '[the] liberty each man hath, to use his own power, as he will himself, for the preservation of his own nature; [...] and consequently, of doing any thing, which in his own judgement, and reason, he shall conceive to be the aptest means thereunto' (ibid., Ch. 14, para. 1). Although in the state of nature I have a 'right to all things', my enjoyment of this right is continually impeded by other individuals pursuing their enjoyment of their own right to all things. The coercive power of the State is legitimate if, through the restrictions it imposes upon each of us, it guarantees each individual's security, the basis for all the benefits of life in a civilised society. At the same time, only a State with *absolute* power could have legitimacy as only it could provide sufficient protection of each individual's security. As a solution to the threat of civil war, therefore, sovereign power must be irresistible, indivisible, and self-perpetuating, and its rightful powers include the government of opinion (ibid., Ch. 18, para. 5 and 16; Ch. 19, para. 12; Ch. 29, para. 6).

Not all social contract theorists accept that the State must or even may have absolute power. In fact, according to Nozick, only a minimal State can have legitimacy. And this limitation placed on legitimate coercive power can be traced back to a Kantian commitment to individual autonomy. For Nozick, our fundamental moral duty is to respect each person's rights of inviolability. These rights are justified by 'the underlying Kantian principle that individuals are ends and not merely means; they may not be sacrificed or used for the achieving of other ends without their consent. Individuals are inviolable' (Nozick, 1974, p. 31). Whereas Hobbes concluded that each individual has a right to all things in the state of nature, for Nozick, in contrast, in the state of nature each individual has a duty not to use others merely as a means. So, for Nozick, as was the case for Locke before him, morality more generally, and in particular the moral requirement to respect individual autonomy, is 'the source of whatever legitimacy the state's fundamental coercive power has' (ibid., p. 6).

Nonetheless, Nozick accepts that, even in the best possible anarchic situation, people *only generally* 'satisfy moral constraints' and 'act as they ought' (ibid., p. 5) As there is the continual danger of individuals *not* forbearing as they should, the need arises for a minimal State to overcome this situation of insecurity and enforce each individual's duty of forbearance. This is the ideal of the State as 'night watchman', the State that restricts its activities to protecting each individual's rights of inviolability (ibid., pp. 24–5). With that goes an 'historical' notion of justice. That is, a society is just insofar as each individual's present holdings are not the outcome of some unjust actions in the past, such as theft or deception or fraud. Therefore, the State should only employ its coercive power to protect individuals against such violations and also to punish those who have committed such crimes in the past (ibid., p. 154). The State is not justified in going further, either so as to preserve all the benefits of civilisation (in Hobbes's terms) or so as to bring about a more equal society (as republicans propose). To do either would require treating some merely as a means, those whose rights are infringed (Nozick, 1974, p. 206).

As I have said already, our purpose here is not to determine which theory is a better fit with reality. Rather, it is that in examining their respective accounts of coercive power we can better see that there are distinct and independent moral values relevant to our evaluation of parents' coercive power and that they can come into conflict. This is the case when we consider whether and for what reasons adults can be said to have a 'right to parent'. As we shall see in Chapter 8, it is argued by many that, if parents are not able to protect their children from harm, they should lose their right to parent. Priority is given here to ensuring the safety and well-being of children, as is the case in the caretaker thesis, as well as Hobbes's account of legitimate coercive power. However, so as to better protect their children in this way, parents often will be required to prevent their children from engaging in risky behaviour. In doing so, in protecting their children from harm and thus meeting the conditions that attach to the 'right to parent', parents may thus violate the moral requirement to protect children's liberty, the fundamental value for Nozick and also for the liberation thesis.

How do we explain the differences between Hobbes and Nozick in their account of legitimate coercive power? It comes down to what they believe to be the morally relevant counterfactual, that is, their respective accounts of the 'state of nature'. For Nozick, coercive power is justified if it can be shown to be better than the best possible anarchic condition: a non-State situation in which people generally do treat others as ends in themselves. In contrast, Hobbes contends that we each have a fundamental right of nature, the liberty to do 'any thing' that we consider necessary for our 'self-preservation', including treating others merely as a means. Only coercive power that is absolute can keep in check the conflicts that would otherwise arise from each person's unfettered exercise of their natural right of self-preservation, conflicts that would tear to the ground all the benefits of civilisation.

What does this disagreement show us? It is that when we evaluate the normative legitimacy of coercive power we may be faced with a conflict of values. The value of prudence and even the common good (i.e. the benefits of civilisation) pulls in one direction while the value of individual inviolability (i.e. the right to freedom from interference) can pull in the opposite direction. However, it is arguable that neither of these philosophers perceives this as a 'real' moral dilemma. We have here two reductionist positions, as Hobbes is willing to accept wide-ranging infringements of individual inviolability for the sake of maintaining a society that brings with it all the benefits of civilisation, while Nozick does not concede that any increase in utility or social justice itself justifies infringements, however minor, of individual inviolability.

In any event, what we have so far seen strongly suggests that we will be forced to look beyond coercion itself when evaluating the legitimacy of parental power. For example, according to the caretaker thesis, paternalistic parenting is justified because of children's deficits in agency and so as to make up for those deficits. Not only are parents to make decisions for children that children would make had they the ability to do so, they are also to foster children's capacities, and so parents take responsibility for the development of children's 'social, emotional, and cognitive capacities' (Burtt, 2003, p. 258). Parents must not only discipline their children when necessary, therefore, but also, through a variety of means, both coercive and non-coercive, promote what are considered valuable traits and skills. The implication is that we are no longer just interested in coercion, but rather must take account of non-coercive forms of control as well. The concept of coercion is necessary but not sufficient when evaluating parental power.

Liberal perfectionism, liberal neutrality, and control

In this section, I focus on liberal[2] arguments about the legitimate use of control. I do so for two reasons. Liberals in particular are sensitive to the possibility that those exercising control may violate fundamental liberal commitments, such as liberal neutrality, without using coercion and without interfering with liberty. Liberals are also keenly aware that, through the exercise of control, we may promote liberal ideals, such as an autonomous life, and again, without using coercion and without interfering with liberty. Therefore, liberals are particularly alive to the importance of power that takes the form of *mere* control. And, as we shall see for a variety of reasons, we also need to take seriously the control exercised by parents over their children.

I will start with liberal perfectionism and the argument that control can and should be exercised so as to promote autonomy. Perfectionism as a political philosophy has at least two features. The first is an argument that certain forms of life are *good*, or ethically valuable, and this information should be appealed to and utilised in political debates and in political decisions. As we saw in Chapter 4, in this way Raz argues that positive freedom is necessary for autonomy, and also that 'autonomy is a constituent element of the good life' (1986, p. 408–9). The second feature of perfectionism is an argument that, through the exercise of power, we should *promote* good ways of life. For example, Raz concluded that we should promote the background conditions of autonomy, and we can do so with or without exercising coercion or interfering with liberty (ibid., p. 417). It follows, the State should promote the autonomy of the adults children will one day be, and often can do so without interfering with liberty, whether the liberty of parents or their children.

Not all liberals accept this perfectionist position. Indeed, other liberals argue that the exercise of control so as to *promote* what is believed to be good ways of life breaches the liberal requirement that, in order to respect diversity, we must remain *neutral* between competing and often conflicting conceptions of the meaning and value of life. This is the case even when the way of life to be promoted is characteristically liberal, in Raz's terms, giving priority as it does to individual autonomy generally and critical thinking in particular. For that reason, Thomas Nagel argues, it is not legitimate to exercise control so as to promote children's autonomy by, *inter alia*, introducing children to evolutionary theory as part of their scientific education, while at the same time excluding 'intelligent design' from their curriculum (Nagel, 2008; see Dworkin, 1978).

Nagel's argument rests on the following two claims. First, intelligent design, unlike creationism, is offered as an explanation of the empirical evidence, while there are grounds to doubt evolutionary theory as an explanation of the same evidence. To the extent that the opposition between intelligent design and evolutionary theory represents a scientific disagreement, we are not justified in excluding intelligent design from our children's science curriculum. However, second, whether or not one adopts the position of intelligent design or evolutionary theory in fact depends on religious beliefs that are not themselves decided by the evidence. Therefore, according to Nagel, to ban the teaching of intelligent design would contravene the 'requirement of religious neutrality [...] because it too would depend on a view, atheism or theistic noninterventionism, that falls clearly in the domain of religious belief' (2008, p. 201).

How do we account for the differences between Raz and Nagel concerning the legitimate exercise of control? Both are liberal theorists committed to liberal values. However, while Raz gives priority to the promotion of autonomy as an intrinsically valuable way of life, for Nagel, because of the requirement of neutrality in the public sphere, we must be impartial when we confer benefits and burdens. They both recognise that power can be exercised through efforts to control that do not coerce or interfere with liberty. However, when we evaluate the normative legitimacy of efforts to control, we can arrive at conflicting conclusions by arguing either from the value of neutrality or from the value of autonomy.

In Chapter 9, we shall examine the topic of children's informed consent, and this will require consideration of both the types of parental influence that limit children's voluntariness as well as the type of decision making by children that can be considered competent. Therefore, this topic is highly relevant to the question of whether society should require parents to promote the autonomy of the adults their children will one day be. For example, Raz's position is such that parents would be required to foster and promote their children's capacity for autonomous decisions, including autonomous informed consent decisions. In addition, parents themselves can exercise power over their children so as to promote their children's autonomy without interfering with their children's liberty. This is the case in particular with some forms of joint or collaborative decision making, namely where parents and children make decisions together and do so on the basis of persuasion alone. However, autonomy is not the only relevant moral value when we consider informed consent. For example, some equate competence not with autonomy but instead with decisions that promote one's well-being (Buchanan and Brock, 1986). And the implication of the latter is that parents are not required to promote their children's autonomous decision making.

As already made clear, I have some sympathy with Nagel's position. If we acknowledge a plurality of independent moral claims, and if we accept that there can be real conflicts between the values of autonomy and well-being, then we will also conclude that we cannot simply equate competence with autonomy. Nagel's approach will be of particular interest to us in attempting to work through such conflicts, although, as we shall see in the next chapter, there are reasons to be concerned about the overriding liberal tenor of his position of impartiality. That is, we need to find a way to work through conflicting moral values that acknowledges the reality of moral conflicts, as Nagel does, but without insisting on a distinctively liberal outcome to all such situations.

Liberalism, anarchy, and authority

We know that 'power over' is the ability to affect others and produce effects for others. The controlling unit, A, may coerce B, interfere with B's liberty, or merely control B. In any one of these forms, the exercise of power may or may not have legitimacy, and so far in this chapter we have focused on just some of the arguments attempting to determine what it is that makes 'power over', in each of its forms, legitimate. What we have yet to ask is whether those who exercise power legitimately also do so with authority. Do those subject to legitimate power also have a duty of obedience, and do those who exercise legitimate power have a right to command? For instance, we may conclude that a mother can legitimately control her son so as to promote his autonomy, but it is quite another matter to conclude that the boy has a duty to comply with her when she does so. Therefore, once again, we are required to address the situation from the perspective offered by a different form of power. What is more, as above, we shall find that, when we evaluate the exercise of authority, we can be faced with values that pull in different directions leading to moral conflicts.

How is the claim to authority justified? According to Raz, while governments are 'de facto authorities' because they claim a right to rule and because they succeed in establishing and maintaining their rule, to have legitimate or *de jure* authority the government's claim must be justified and as a result they are 'owed a duty of obedience' (1985, p. 5). If the State successfully exercises coercive power so as to protect me as a citizen, it may but it need not follow that I have a duty of obedience to the State: 'It seems plain that the justified use of coercive power is one thing and authority is another. I do not exercise authority over people afflicted with dangerous diseases if I knock them out and lock them up to protect the public, even though I am, in the assumed circumstances, justified in doing so' (ibid.). Legitimate authorities do also issue directives and some (but not all) do also use or threaten to use force to back up these directives, but legitimate authority cannot be reduced to mere coercion.

It must be acknowledged that the very idea of authority is forcefully rejected by some. In particular, it is argued, a duty to obey is incompatible with personal autonomy. This is the anarchist counter-argument, and according to Raz much of the debate on authority is in response to that challenge (Raz, 1990). Anarchists start from the premise that, as rational and autonomous human beings, we each have the right and even the duty to govern ourselves. Robert Wolff's defence of anarchism rests on a Kantian view of humans as self-legislating beings, 'not subject to the will of another', whose 'moral autonomy is a combination of freedom and responsibility; it is a submission to laws which one has made for oneself' (Wolff, 1990 [1970], p. 26). Authority, or 'the right to rule', is in conflict with autonomy, 'the refusal to be ruled': 'so long as we recognize our responsibility for our actions [...] we must acknowledge as well the continuing obligation to make ourselves the authors of such commands as we obey' (ibid., p. 29). Authority may be appropriate for 'children and madmen', Wolff believes, and with respect to children this is the case as they 'do not yet possess the power of reason in a developed form' (ibid., p. 26).[3]

Can it be shown, in response to the anarchist challenge, that authority is compatible with moral autonomy? Let us examine why Raz thinks it is. First, Raz contends that 'responsibility for one's life is consistent with handing power over to someone else, to be better able to concentrate on those aspects of one's life for which one has better aptitude' (1990, p. 12). Raz's example is that of letting one's doctor decide whether or not one should undergo surgery. He believes that this is compatible with moral autonomy, which must not 'require continuously deciding for oneself on every aspect of one's affairs' (ibid.). This is true, as far as it goes. However, surely the point is that some decisions are more significant than others, including a decision about whether to consent to surgery, and it is reasonable to question the propriety of handing over such a decision to someone else. Raz foresees such an objection, for he clarifies his position, stating that 'no unlimited authority can be legitimate. If an autonomous person must keep continuous responsibility for his life he cannot abandon responsibility altogether' (ibid.).

Nonetheless, even limited authority involves 'deference', a 'surrender of private judgement'. We obey the command of the person with authority 'simply because it comes from someone accorded the right to rule' (Friedman, 1990 [1973], p. 64). Our obedience is *not* justified by asking for reasons that we can grasp or that satisfy us. 'Authority is a "theirs is not to reason why" affair, even if the subordinate is convinced, as in Tennyson's poem, that "someone has blundered" in giving a particular command' (Wrong, 1995 [1979], p. 35). Why should we obey, even in cases when the person in authority has, or may have, 'blundered'? According to Raz's 'service' conception, authorities are justified because they better ensure we achieve what we already have reason to and, in particular, they promote and protect our autonomy (1986, p. 21). Authority is justified only 'when this is necessary to enable people better to conduct themselves in the light of considerations which apply to them anyway' (1990, p. 13). More generally, we should surrender our private judgement because such obedience secures the 'social coordination' 'which everyone desires for independent reasons', and this is the case because, without it, some good will be lost or can be secured only by an unjust burden on a smaller number of people (ibid., pp. 7–8). There are goods we can achieve only through social coordination, and we can achieve social coordination only 'if one does not try to act on one's independent judgement but subjects oneself to the judgement of the authority' (ibid., p. 11).

More precisely, authorities are justified because their commands are based on *dependent* and *preemptive* reasons. The example Raz gives of an authoritative decision is an Act of Parliament that imposes 'on parents a duty to maintain their young children' (1986, p. 11). The authority's decision is based on dependent reasons, as parents have such a duty of care already. Based on the service conception, it is argued that 'authorities do not have the right to impose completely independent duties on people, because their directives should reflect dependent reasons which are binding on people in any case' (Raz, 1985, p. 24). However, the authority's decision also provides a preemptive reason for action, as it 'is also meant to replace the reasons on which it depends' (Raz, 1986, p. 10). We should obey the commands because they issue from someone in authority and this replaces the dependent reasons as reasons for compliance. Therefore, the authority's decrees will be binding even if mistaken about pre-existing obligations in a given case. This is necessary, as if every time a directive 'failed to reflect reason correctly, it were open to challenge as mistaken, the advantage gained by accepting the authority as a more reliable and successful guide to right reason would disappear' (Raz, 1990, p. 25).

Raz's argument is that we should defer, we owe a duty of obedience, to those in power who secure the social coordination everyone desires for independent reasons, in particular so as to secure the background conditions of autonomy, but also that legitimate authority is always limited, and therefore this is only ever a partial surrender of one's private judgement. So it could be said that a duty to obey others is *de jure* or legitimate when such deference is necessary for everyone's good, and in particular everyone's autonomy. However, if we recall, the anarchist objects to any arrangement whereby some are in the position of rulers and others are ruled. Why is this difference in roles important in itself (see Chapter 5)? For the anarchist, it matters because the ruled are thereby unable to make themselves the authors of their own acts.

So, on the one hand, liberals argue that we should defer to authority in order to better promote the autonomy of all, while, on the other hand, anarchists conclude that any deference to authority of itself is incompatible with one's autonomy. Again, as I said above, I cannot hope to show which of these theoretical arguments is a better fit with reality. Rather, I merely want to point out that these opposing theoretical arguments illustrate a potential conflict of moral values when we evaluate parental power. Once again we can see the possibility for such moral conflict when we consider civic education programmes whose aims include the promotion of autonomy (see Chapter 10). If parents act with authority when enrolling their children in such a civic education programme, even when they do so in order to promote the autonomy of the adults their children will one day be, they cannot at the same time ensure their children are the authors of the commands they obey. Such parents are making some sacrifice to their children's autonomy as self-legislators so as to promote their autonomy as future adults. And if this also goes against their children's wishes then, in Raz's terms, such parents are giving preemptive reasons priority over dependent reasons.

Now it is important to stress the significant limitations of the anarchist position. An argument that rejects *all* imposed order is incompatible with both the State's guarantee of rights to children as well as parents' enjoyment of their own rights, both of which can be responsible for significant gains in individual autonomy. Raz's own position seems to show how the autonomy that anarchists seek can be promoted by the authority that anarchists object to. And what is more, even if the value of autonomy supported the anarchist conclusions, there is reason to doubt that it overrides all other values (Horton, 2010, p. 129). Nonetheless, giving consideration to their position, at the very least, has a salutary effect. For it is arguable that Raz fails to recognise the importance of the fact that, in a relation of authority, one party, and one party alone, has a duty to obey the other. It *does* make sense to say that such an asymmetry requires normative justification, and that this is required independently of our evaluation of the beneficial consequences of deferring to the authority of another. This is the same issue of asymmetry that arises when we consider whether adults have a 'right to parent', independent of whether adults also are in authority (see Chapter 8).

In this section we are examining the idea of authority and applying it to the situation of parents and children. The question of whether there is a duty to obey those in authority has exposed deep disagreement. The anarchist contends that authority is incompatible with personal autonomy, while liberals believe that partial surrender of our private judgement is necessary to secure the social coordination that in turn guarantees individual autonomy. This demonstrates how, when considering parental power, two values can pull in different directions when evaluating authority, the value of submitting only to laws which one has made for oneself, and the value of submitting to authority so as to promote the autonomy of all persons. Once again, we are faced with conflicting moral values when evaluating the legitimacy of parents' power.

Paternalism for liberals and pluralists

In this the final section of this chapter, I return to paternalism as a form of 'power over'. In the first two chapters of this book we explored the justification of parental paternalism. Not only did we raise questions about whether paternalism can be justified. We also questioned whether all forms of parental power are paternalistic. While there is no need to go over this material again in any great detail, there are three issues that I want to stress, briefly, before concluding this chapter.

As we know, if I exercise paternalistic power over my daughter, I do so for her own good, and without her consent. In Chapter 1, we looked in detail at the differences between liberal and pluralist views on paternalism. For the liberal, when I act paternalistically towards my daughter, I interfere with her liberty. Against this common assumption, at that point I made the claim that there is a plurality of forms of paternalistic power. I have tried, in this and the preceding chapter, to support the general position that there is an irreducible plurality of forms of power, and the extent to which that attempt has been successful provides added support for the pluralist view on paternalism. This is the first point I want to make. That is, in acting paternalistically, I may use coercion, I may interfere with my child's liberty without resorting to coercion, I may merely control my child, and I may do any of these with or without authority. And, when we examine a number of case studies later in this book, we shall see many instances where paternalism, in these different forms, can be legitimate.

Second, in the debate on the legitimacy of paternalism, the issue of moral conflict is central to the distinction between liberal and pluralist positions. For the liberal, there are no moral conflicts when I exercise paternalistic power legitimately: I merely do what I believe to be in my child's best interests. For the pluralist, in contrast, even a legitimate exercise of paternalistic power involves moral conflict. That some rule is violated when I act paternalistically explains why I, as a paternalist, have something to answer for and something to explain. Since we introduced this issue in Chapter 1, we have had ample time to consider whether we can be faced with moral dilemmas when we exercise power over children and if so whether such conflicts are 'real'.

So far I have argued that we can be faced with real moral dilemmas even when we evaluate the legitimacy of non-paternalistic parental power, never mind paternalism. Moral conflicts are at the very least a possibility when we evaluate parents' power. Note, I have not argued that we will always be faced with conflicting moral claims when we evaluate parental power. In many cases, parents will control their children without having to reconcile a conflict of values. Therefore, the general position in this book is less extreme than what may be assumed to follow from the pluralist view on paternalism. For the pluralist, paternalism, as a matter of definition, involves moral conflict. It is not just that moral conflicts may arise, but that they are a necessary feature of paternalism. The position I have adopted here is that this may well be true regarding paternalism, without its being true for all forms of power relations.

Finally, we have already seen that paternalism is not sufficient to account for parents' power over their children. There are numerous ways in which the parent–child power relation is not paternalistic: I can exercise power over my daughter for my own good rather than her good; I can do so with her consent; I can do so in order to protect her liberty *qua* child rather than promote her well-being; I can exercise power over very young children who lack the qualities of an agent; and, finally, I as a parent may be the responsive unit and my child may exercise power over me. It follows, we cannot equate parental power with parental paternalism. This fits with what we have seen so far concerning each of the forms of 'power over'. There is no one form of power that is predominant or fundamental when we evaluate the legitimacy of power. And with respect to paternalism, we may find that, even if there are good reasons to believe that parental paternalism is justified in a given situation, nonetheless we may be required also to consider the legitimacy of non-paternalistic parental power. And finally, and just as we have seen when considering the legitimacy of each of these forms of power, these distinct moral considerations may at times come into conflict leading to real moral dilemmas. So, in conclusion, not only does paternalism involve moral conflict, paternalism itself may come into conflict with the requirement to exercise another form or forms of power.

Conclusions

In this chapter, I have been exploring the irreducible plurality of appropriate moral considerations and of morally relevant features when evaluating the legitimacy of parental power. Once again, I have argued against reductionist accounts, to begin with those that equate power with just one of its forms. We have seen that, even when we examine the legitimacy of just one form of power, we can be faced with incompatible moral requirements pulling us in different directions. In any case, questions are raised about legitimacy that cannot be answered by considering one form of power only.

For example, when analysing the legitimacy of power employed to protect liberty we were forced to consider what would make legitimate the use of coercion against those who refused to accept these efforts. Nor is the concept of coercion by itself sufficient. If we want to distinguish between legitimate and illegitimate parent–child power relations, we must consider a wide range of factors, including the use made of non-coercive control. In all of these cases, there was a further issue left unresolved, namely whether parents also had a right to command and whether children also had a duty of obedience. And finally, as we have just seen, the requirement to act paternalistically towards children generates moral conflict, but also itself may come into conflict with the requirement to exercise other forms of power.

Although others will argue that we are not here faced with an irreducible plurality of independent moral considerations, what we have seen in this chapter has not given any sustenance to such a view. Indeed, in this chapter we have seen how conflicts may arise between the requirements to limit interference with liberty and to restrict the capacity to interfere, to promote autonomy and to remain neutral, to preserve the benefits of civilisation and to protect individual inviolability, to respect each person's autonomy and to defer to authority so as to secure social coordination, and finally the requirement to promote another's good and any one of a number of moral items this may come into conflict with. As we shall explore in greater depth in the final chapters of this book, in various case studies, we can be faced with moral conflicts here, and it is not true that, as a general rule, in such conflicts one moral claim trumps all other considerations.

Notes

1 I leave to one side the further issue that it is not possible to equate the situation of Ulysses with that of a power relation between the State and (in this case) children whose 'antipower' is promoted against their will. In the former, individuals receive help to ensure that they do not give into temptation and act in ways that would be contrary to their current wishes. In the latter, a third party decides what the children need, and (if deemed necessary) acts against their will to ensure that those needs are met.

2 I appreciate that I could easily have looked at non-liberal arguments in exploring this issue, in particular as put forward by those working in the tradition of Aristotelian thought, such as Alasdair MacIntyre (1985; 1999), Philippa Foot (2001), and Charles Taylor (1989). I just want to remind the reader that this chapter is not offered as an exhaustive overview, or survey, of the literature but rather a selective examination of some of the contributions most relevant for our purposes here.

3 Wolff's position is an extreme one admittedly. A more moderate version of anar-

chism, one that does not call for the abolition of States but does reject the duty to obey the State, is that authority has legitimacy only for those who have explicitly committed to obey the law, and very few of us have done so (Simmons, 1987).

Part III

The moral legitimacy of parental power

In this the final part of the book, I examine some of the moral questions that arise when evaluating parental power. A great deal has been said already about the conceptual and methodological challenges faced when we do evaluate parental power. How then are we to proceed? To start with, we should acknowledge the growing interest among political philosophers in the debate between so-called *ideal theory* and *non-ideal theory*. This debate is concerned with whether and to what extent normative political philosophy should be informed and constrained by issues of practical feasibility. For ideal theory, the role of political philosophy is to work out an ideal vision of society, or some aspect of society, and then apply the theory in a top-down fashion so as to have social life altered to fit with the theory (Cohen, 2003; Mason, 2004). The liberation thesis is perhaps most obviously an example, but so too is the more moderate caretaker thesis. In both cases, it is assumed that we should make reality conform to theory, for example, in the caretaker thesis there is an underlying assumption that, despite the plurality of relevant moral considerations and morally relevant features, we should transform parent–child relations so that priority is given to parents' duty to care for their children.

The alternative approach is problem-driven rather than theory-driven. Problem-driven political philosophy, or non-ideal theory, starts from practice and the problems that it throws up. According to this line of thought, political philosophers must first have a clear understanding of the practical reality of people's lives, and only then can they go on to consider both what aims should be pursued and what we may do to effect such changes (Dunn, 1990; Williams, 2005; Wolff, 2011; Fives, 2016c). It follows, if we are to solve real-world problems, or work towards their resolution, then empirical findings are needed alongside moral deliberation. We have already discussed the relevance of empirical findings to normative judgement. It is not that empirical research will make moral dilemmas disappear, we saw (see

Chapter 3). Rather, empirical findings, for example concerning the types of agency children are capable of and the impact of parenting styles on the development of children's capacity for agency, help to clarify what moral questions need to be asked concerning parental power.

In the following chapters, I will evaluate parental power within the boundaries provided by a number of case studies: the right to parent and whether parents should be licensed, monitored, and trained (Chapter 8); children's capacity and competence to provide informed consent (Chapter 9); and sharing lives with children and shaping children's values through civic education (Chapter 10). Each case study explores both empirical evidence as well as the relevant legal, policy, and service context. Each outlines the conceptual issues requiring clarification as well as the ethical questions that arise. I also try to answer those ethical questions, but always with the following proviso: these are moral decisions to be made in practical contexts, and so any answers given here will be limited in their application, in the sense that they will be offered only as responses to the problems of specific cases. Because philosophy has its limits, we can only answer such questions through practical reasoning and practical judgement.

Nonetheless, such practical judgements must be made with methodological rigour, and it is in relation to this issue that an important counter argument must be addressed before we proceed to deal with specific cases (see Chapter 7). For others will object that the concepts and methods we use when evaluating the power relations of adults, those appropriate to the 'political domain', are simply not appropriate to the normative evaluation of the relations between parents and children. I turn to this objection next.

7

Legitimacy in the political domain and in the family

In previous chapters we have, in various ways, considered the legitimacy of power relations within the family. Beginning with an analysis of paternalism, before then examining the diversity of forms of power, we explored the plurality of appropriate moral considerations and morally relevant features of parent–child power relations. And finally, in the last chapter, we examined the plurality of legitimacy concepts themselves. However, I want to pause and reflect on the approach we have adopted so far and its underlying assumptions. For it would not be unreasonable to harbour doubts about the appropriateness of this whole enterprise. It could be argued that, up to this point, we have evaluated parent–child relations in the same way that we evaluate the power relations of adults in the wider society, that is, the power relations of the 'political domain', whereas the concepts and methods used when evaluating the power relations of the political domain are simply not appropriate to the normative evaluation of the relations between parents and children. I want to address and respond to two aspects of this criticism.

First, it could be argued that the question of legitimacy is posed in respect of what liberals call the political domain, and not the relations of parents and children. According to John Rawls, when we analyse power relations for their legitimacy, in effect we are asking whether it is morally justified, when we implement a particular social structure, to use coercion against those who are both equal in status and capable of giving or withholding their consent, but who reject that social structure, or the reasons used to justify it, whether in whole or in part (2003 [1989], p. 242). While institutions in the public sphere are imposed in this way, in contrast, it is argued, parent–child relations are situated in the private sphere of the family, and they do not involve the exercise of coercive power over those whose consent is normally required for legitimacy. The second objection follows from the first. In the political domain, it is argued, we must appeal to the most objective moral standards, and this is because of the moral seriousness of what is at stake, namely the use of coercion against our moral equals who happen to reject the basic institutions of our society or the justifications offered for them. As a social contract theorist, Rawls believes we do so by entering the 'original position' and reasoning from behind a 'veil of ignorance' (1971, p. 136ff). In contrast, it is argued that the issues at stake in family relations are not of the same order, for the reasons already outlined, and so when we reflect on the power parents exercise over their children, we are not required to appeal to the most objective moral standards in this way.

In this chapter, I respond to each of these criticisms in turn. First, I show that parent–child relations are not antithetical to the political domain, as the latter has been defined by Rawls and other liberals. When we evaluate the legitimacy of parent–child power relations, questions of children's consent do arise, and what is more we are concerned with the coercive imposition of the family as a basic social institution. It also follows, second, if the highest standards of moral objectivity are required for the evaluation of power in the political domain, as it is defined by Rawls and others, they are required in regard to the family as well. However, I also want to say more about the requirement of moral objectivity where competing moral claims are in conflict. In Chapter 3, I argued that we should resolve dilemmas through a form of practical reasoning and practical judgement owing much to liberal thinkers such as Rawls and Thomas Nagel. In this chapter, I explore whether such a 'liberal' approach to practical judgement is appropriate when we consider moral dilemmas in situations liberals themselves do not consider to be political.

Power and basic social institutions

As we have seen, some believe that, while the question of legitimacy *is* posed in relation to the coercive imposition of society's basic institutions, it is *not* posed in relation to parents and children. This is a characteristically liberal approach to power, which rests on a dichotomy between areas of life governed by the State's coercive power, that is, the political domain, and areas of life where individuals are rightly free from such coercive power, that is, the private realm, including voluntary associations and the family. As we have already seen, coercion is only one possible type of power (see Chapters 1 and 5). Nonetheless, in this section, I want to show that, when we evaluate the legitimacy of parent–child power relations, we are involved, *inter alia*, in an evaluation of the coercive imposition of the family as a basic social institution.

First, let us consider the liberal rationale for keeping the family separate from the political domain in this way. Rawls distinguishes the political domain from the voluntary and familial domains of the private sphere in the following two ways.

First, [...] Political society is closed, as it were; and we do not, and indeed cannot, enter or leave it voluntarily [...] Second, the political power exercised within the political relationship is always coercive power backed by the state's machinery for enforcing its laws. In a constitutional regime political power is also the power of equal citizens as a collective body. It is regularly imposed on citizens as individuals, some of whom may not accept the reasons widely thought to justify the general structure of political authority (the constitution), some of whom accept that structure, but do not regard as well grounded many of the statutes and other laws to which they are subject. (2003 [1989], p. 242)

Thus, the political domain is non-voluntary, and it involves the exercise of coercive power, a power exercised when its basic institutions are imposed, and a power exercised over individual citizens equal in status.

For these reasons, it is argued, the political domain is unlike the domain of voluntary associations, and unlike the 'affectional' domain of the 'familial', relations that do *not* involve the exercise of coercive power and need *not* be based on the consent of equals. Based on this clear distinction of domains, Rawls believes that principles of justice, which are to be applied to basic institutions, are *not* to be applied directly to the family. For example, while he believes we should ensure that all those who are equally endowed and equally motivated have the same opportunities, Rawls accepts that the family as an institution is a barrier to justice, in particular as 'the family will lead to unequal chances between individuals' (1971, p. 511). Within families, advantages (and disadvantages) are passed on from one generation to the next, and, the argument goes, we cannot prevent this from happening without abolishing the family itself. However, he sees this as an acceptable limitation of justice: it is, he says, vital to 'reconcile us to the dispositions of the natural order and the conditions of human life' (ibid., p. 512).

For the liberal, the political domain and the domain of the family are to be kept separate. However, the distinction between the two becomes blurred. This is recognised, in part at least, by Nagel, when he considers what he calls the 'problematic intermediate case' of the family. He concludes that liberalism 'leaves individuals free to regulate their own personal lives (and to a lesser extent, though this is a problematic intermediate case, the lives of their children) according to their full personal conceptions of how life should be lived' (1990 [1987], p. 322). Why is this a 'problematic intermediate case' for liberals? It is because there is evidence for power relations, sometimes coercive power relations, in a sphere of life thought of, in Rawls's terms, as 'affectional'. And it is not only the power of parents we must consider but the power of the State as well, as parents themselves are left free here by the State only 'to a lesser extent'.

The idea that the family is a site of power relations, and that such power stands in need of normative justification, is by no means novel. Feminists, in highlighting the 'neglect of gender in mainstream political theory', have focused on 'the politics of what had previously been regarded as paradigmatically non-political – the personal sphere of sexuality, of housework, of the family' (Okin, 1998, pp. 122, 123). Indeed, liberal feminists have attempted to remedy this deficit, arguing that Rawls's principles of justice *should* be applied to the private sphere, and in that way satisfy the feminist demand for reciprocity and autonomy in the family (Okin, 1989, p. 249). Some have begun to criticise the prevailing feminist approach to the family on the grounds that it is 'woman-centered, rather than child-centered' (Cassidy, 2006, p. 44), and in this book, it is the power relationship between parents and children that we consider. While this affords us the possibility of concentrating on a power relation all too often neglected, it is equally true that this book, because it evaluates parent–child relations independent of any evaluation of the (gendered) relations between parents, could be criticised for its 'neglect of gender'. Nonetheless, what this book has in common with feminism is a commitment to interrogate the legitimacy of power relations where they arise, whether in the family or the political domain as traditionally understood.

If we acknowledge that power relations in the family require justification, how are we to proceed? In structuring what follows, I rely on David Beetham's distinction between the following three domains of legitimacy: legal validity, consent, and normative justification. I return to the latter two below. In respect of the first of these, as Beetham makes clear, one dimension of the legitimacy of power relations is their legal validity, and I shall argue that we can and should consider the legal validity of family relations. That is, the State's coercive imposition of legal rules is one dimension of the legitimacy of parents' power. For those concerned with the law, the State's power is legitimate insofar as the rules in accordance with which it is acquired and exercised themselves have legal validity. Legal scholars address whether power 'is validly acquired, who is entitled to exercise it, within what limits, and so on' (Beetham, 1991, p. 4). We can evaluate the legal validity of the State and its various activities by examining whether its offices are filled in accordance with legally valid procedures and also whether its activities conform to legal safeguards and restrictions, such as the independence of the Judiciary or constitutionally-guaranteed rights. Why is law so important for legitimacy? It is because the 'main method whereby the State carries out its functions is the system of law, that is, rules backed by coercive power' (Raphael, 1970, p. 49).

However, it is not only in the political domain that such power is exercised. Indeed, I shall argue, legal validity is a requirement for the legitimacy of parental power as well. That this is so is explained by the State's sovereignty: 'To say that the State is sovereign is to say that the State has supreme or final authority in a community, that its rules override the rules of any other association' (ibid., p. 51). The examples of *associations* Raphael employs here include a borough, a factory, a trade union, and a university. He argues that all associations within a political society are subject to the authority of the State, and so whatever legal powers such associations have 'are granted to them by the legal authority of the State' (ibid., p. 52). It is the case that parent–child relations are not those of a *voluntary* association. Nonetheless, the family is a component of the social structure that the State's rules 'override'. Is it the case that the legal powers of families, whatever they are, are granted to them by the State? Parents and children may claim to have entitlements on some other basis, in particular, a moral one. However, for now, what are at issue are the legal rights that parents and children may claim.

The legal validity of parents' power

We can evaluate the legal validity of parental power by exploring the legal rights granted by the State to parents and children, as well as their legal duties. These legal rights and duties can be discerned from an examination of constitutions and legislation, as well as obligations arising from international, binding covenants and treaties. My discussion of these legal powers below is based on the following questions: Is there a sphere of privacy for parents and children where legal power has its limit? Do parents have rights that the State recognises and enforces? Are the rights of parents regulated by the State? Are children protected by the State against their parents? And finally, are children empowered by the State?

Is there a sphere of privacy for parents and children where legal power has its limit?

Some may well believe that, insofar as the family is a sphere of privacy, it is cut off from issues of political power. In fact, it is more accurate to say that the right to privacy is one of the legal entitlements that the State will or will not guarantee, to a lesser or greater extent. I want to examine the guarantee of privacy for parents, before considering children's privacy. But first, what is privacy?

It is argued that privacy refers to 'our ability to control who has access to us, and who knows about us' (Rachels, 1975, p. 329). There is a sense in which to enjoy privacy is also to enjoy liberty, as the sphere of privacy is one in which the State (or other agents) does not prescribe what is done. However, the two are not equivalent. On the one hand, you can reduce my privacy without of necessity interfering with my liberty of action. For example, the State may know all about what I am doing, let us say by monitoring all my written communications, and yet refrain from interfering with my actions by removing any of my options. On the other hand, you can interfere with my liberty without invading my privacy. For example, a father may refuse to provide the authorising consent required for his adolescent daughter to enrol in a medical trial, but scrupulously refrain from monitoring her social interactions generally and specifically her communications with the researchers conducting the study.

Also it is not strictly correct to characterise privacy as the *absence* of legal regulation or legal interference. Privacy is something the State can protect by providing individuals with the resources to prevent others (including State agencies) from having access to them and from knowing about them: 'the typical privacy claim is not a claim for noninterference by the state at all. It is a claim for state interference in the form of legal protection against other individuals' (Gavison, 1980, p. 438). Indeed, it is in this respect that there is a parallel between liberty and privacy. For Isaiah Berlin, negative freedom refers to an 'area' in which a person 'is or should be left to do or be what he is able to do or be, without interference by other persons' (2004 [1958], p. 169). As Berlin recognises, the 'function of law' is the 'protection' of this sphere of liberty from invasion, whether it is invasion by fellow citizens, non-citizens, or by the State's own agencies (ibid., p. 174).

Although the law may promote a sphere of privacy in the family, nevertheless privacy is never absolute. For example, State agencies may act in ways that limit privacy so as to gather the information needed to remedy perceived injustices within and between families. Within the private sphere, parents confer advantages on their children that children in other families do not enjoy. It may be decided that, while parents are entitled to confer some of those advantages (for example, the advantage of spending time with their children, or the advantage of using effective parenting styles), they are not entitled to confer other advantages (for example, the advantage of attendance at a private, fee-paying school) and the State may redistribute resources to limit parents' capacity to confer these 'unjustified' advantages (MacLeod, 2004b; Brighouse and Swift, 2014, p. 123ff). Also, parents in some families impose burdens on their children that parents in other families do not impose. Once again, some of these burdens may be deemed permissible (for example, requiring children to do a certain number of household chores) while others may be judged impermissible and punishable by law (for example, the neglect and abuse of children) (LaFollette, 1980; Archard, 2004; LaFollette, 2010).

Not only is privacy never absolute, some go on to question whether parents are justified in claiming in the first instance that they have an 'intimate' relationship with their children that is covered by a right to privacy. For example, David Archard has argued that intimate relations are those formed between equals, where each person has chosen that relationship, and where the sharing of knowledge is what is important about the relationship. In contrast, he contends, parents are in a position of superiority to their children, children do not get to choose the relationship, and much of what a parent does, such as comforting, caring, educating, disciplining, and so on, is *not* 'about the uncovering of the parent's self' (2004, p. 169). However, as we have already seen (Chapter 2), at other points Archard acknowledges that privacy and exclusivity are essential if parents are to perform their roles adequately. I return to this debate when we consider whether the State may justifiably monitor parents (see Chapter 8).

Despite this recognition that we may justifiably restrict privacy for the sake of social justice and the protection of children, and despite the differences between adult relations and parent–child relations, nonetheless liberal democratic thought retains a distinction between the public and the private spheres, along with a commitment to privacy in the latter. This is the case, for example, concerning the right to privacy when parents make decisions about their children's education. And liberals are concerned both to protect parents' rights of privacy here but also to protect parents from interference in their freely made choices: 'If the liberal democratic state were to legislate a conception of child or governmental interests that in effect nullified parental education choice, it would exceed the legitimate bounds of its authority' (Galston, 2003, p. 213).

We tend to think of privacy as a sphere in which *adult* citizens control who has access to them and who knows about them. It may be argued that when the State protects the privacy of parents, it follows that, as children are members of the same family, their privacy is protected as well. Thus, for Barbara Bennett Woodhouse, 'children's privacy is defined by the circle of care. Rather than privacy in the adult sense, children need privacy in the sense of protection from unwarranted intrusion in relationships with those who nurture them' (2003, pp. 280–1). And such an approach to children's privacy fits well with the idea that privacy, more generally, is valuable as a necessary component of the caring aspect of intimate relationships (Reiman, 1976). Although that may be true much of the time, nonetheless the State's guarantee of privacy to parents may equally well serve to undermine children's privacy as individuals. If the State protects my privacy as a parent, it protects me against others having access to and knowing about the ways in which I exercise power over my children. As a parent, I may or may not exploit this opportunity to restrict my children's privacy. Crucially, if I do so, I am protected from others having knowledge of and access to this intrusion in my children's privacy.

An alternative approach is to look at ways in which the State can protect *children's* privacy. Should children have the right to control their parents' access to and knowledge of them? As the First Amendment of the US Constitution guarantees freedom of speech, among other things, it is seen as securing privacy as well, as individuals have rights to limit who may collect information about them and to restrict what is to happen with that information, as is the case, for example, in the Privacy Act of 1974.[1] From the US Constitution, let us turn to the international Convention on the Rights of the Child (CRC) (United Nations, 1989). It guarantees *children's* right 'to freedom of expression' including the 'freedom to seek, receive and impart information and ideas of all kinds' (Article 13). One way to interpret Article 13 of the CRC is that it does for children's privacy what the First Amendment of the US Constitution promises for the privacy of adults. Children should not be impeded, whether by their parents or by others, when they 'seek, receive and impart' information. This is in line with liberationist arguments that children may claim the right to privacy if and when they wish to (Holt, 1975, pp. 143–4).

However, a different interpretation of the CRC is possible, one more in line with Woodhouse's view of children's privacy as 'defined by the circle of care'. Thus, the CRC recognises the 'rights and duties of the parents [...] to provide direction to the child in the exercise of his or her right [to freedom of thought, conscience and religion] in a manner consistent with the evolving capacities of the child' (Article 14). The CRC in fact calls on parents to have access to and knowledge of their children when their children exercise their rights to freedom of expression. As we shall see, parents have rights as parents, rights that are recognised and protected by the State, and those rights can limit and restrict children's rights. In particular, parents' legal rights can be a significant barrier to children's rights to privacy. How we are to resolve these tensions and even conflicts between the privacy rights of parents and children, when they arise, is the important matter (see Woodhouse, 2003, p. 279). Before looking at how to resolve such conflicts, I want to first say more about parents' rights.

Do parents have rights that the State recognises and enforces?

The State also can guarantee the rights of adults *qua* parents. I will not focus here on the right to bear children, which can also be referred to as the right to become a parent. My concern here is with (1) the 'right to parent', (2) parents' rights 'over' their children, and (3) parents' right to engage in activities independently of their children's interests.

(1) What I refer to here as the 'right to parent' is, for Archard, the right to act as a parent, by which is meant 'the right to occupy a custodial role in respect of a child' (2010, p. 29). More generally, it is the right to raise children (Brighouse and Swift, 2014, pp. 93–4). It is argued by some that the State should establish a licensing system and refuse to grant the 'right to parent' to those unable to prove they will not be bad parents (LaFollette, 1980). Even if this particular proposal is problematic, it is the case that the State's guarantee of the 'right to parent' is always conditional. This is most clearly evident in situations where the State and its agencies intervene to remove that right from certain adults, in particular when those adults do not satisfy basic conditions for its enjoyment, including when it is decided they do not satisfactorily protect their children from abuse and neglect. This point is accepted even by those who reject the liberation thesis and defend parents' 'authority' over their children: 'the state properly intervenes in family decision making only when ... [the child's] developmental needs are demonstrably in jeopardy' (Burtt, 2003, p. 248).

(2) Parents also have rights 'over' their children, in particular, the right to make certain choices on behalf of their children. There are various ways in which parents exercise power over their children, as we have seen, and any one of these can be put into effect with respect to issues of children's education, health care, religious practice, social life, and so on. Moreover, the State's actions, and the legal rights and duties it institutes, can restrict or expand such parental power. This is the case when, for example, the State guarantees parents' legal right to choose where and in what way to educate their children, and the State can protect this right by guaranteeing that parents may choose the schools their children attend, by taking steps to increase the options available to parents when choosing schools, and so on. According to one line of thought, although the State should require all parents to educate their children, beyond that point we should strongly favour parental discretion and choice concerning their children's education (Galston, 2003, pp. 231–2).

(3) The State also can guarantee parents' right to remain free to pursue their own interests independently of their children's interests. For instance, parents remain free to engage in activities that their children in the main are not free to engage in, including driving automobiles, engaging in sexual activity, drinking alcohol, working in paid employment, voting in elections, forming contracts, buying and selling property, getting married, and so on. In addition, even though parents have responsibilities to their children that other adults do not have, they remain free to engage in the same activities as those adults who

are not parents, even if this comes 'at some cost to their children's interests' (Brighouse and Swift, 2006, p. 81). The qualification or limit placed on this right is that parents are not entitled to engage in any of these activities in such a way that they are, as a result, no longer able to perform their duties as parents to a satisfactory level.

Are the rights of parents regulated by the State?

As the final point illustrates, although the State guarantees parents' rights in their various forms, it also regulates parents in the exercise of those rights. The State can and does prescribe the ways in which parental power is to be exercised. For instance, this is the case when the State decrees that, in specific situations, parents may not make decisions on behalf of their children either without the consent or assent of their children or without the agreement of an appropriate third party. When decisions are made about what medical care children will receive, children may have the right to reject the care proposed by parents and physicians, as is the case in the UK for children younger than sixteen (Cornock, 2007). Also, physicians may have the right to challenge parents' decisions about the medical care they want their children to receive, while the courts may intervene when 'good reasons exist to appoint guardians or to disqualify the family or health care professionals to protect an incompetent patient's interests' (Beauchamp and Childress, 2009, p. 189).

In addition, the State may require parents demonstrate their capacity to carry out their responsibilities towards their children. While some have argued for the licensing of parents, as we have seen, others have argued for more effective preventative interventions to support families, including the monitoring of parents (Archard, 2004). For example, if social workers have concerns that parenting practices are putting children at risk, they have a legal right and even a duty to investigate the way in which parents perform their responsibilities towards their children (see Chapter 8). However, although the State is entitled to regulate the rights of parents in these ways, we should note this is not the only relevant consideration. The State is required to recognise parents' rights, there are limits to the State's legitimate exercise of power, and the right to privacy also requires protection. As we shall see in the coming chapters, when we make moral judgements about legitimate power we are required to balance precisely these sorts of competing claims.

Are children protected by the State against their parents?

I have already spoken of the State regulating parents' rights, and one rationale for doing so is to protect children against parents' misuse of their power. The State can and does go further than this with statutes that guarantee children's rights or when children's rights are included in the State's constitution. This is the case with the Thirty-first Amendment of the Irish Constitution (2012), Article 42A, which states as follows: 'The State recognises and affirms the natural and imprescriptible rights of all children and shall, as far as practicable, by its laws protect and vindicate those rights' (Houses of the Oireachtas, 2012). In some conventions and constitutions, individual children are guaranteed rights that are to be enjoyed with the help and guidance of their parents, as we have seen already in respect of children's right to freedom of expression in the CRC. However, the Thirty-first Amendment of the Irish Constitution makes clear that children's rights can be claimed by children *against* their parents.

In extreme cases, according to the amendment, the State shall 'endeavour to supply the place of the parents', where 'the parents, regardless of their marital status, fail in their duty towards their children to such extent that the safety or welfare of any of their children is likely to be prejudicially affected' (ibid.). Therefore, the State's agencies can initiate proceedings to determine whether adults retain their 'right to parent'. In resolving such proceedings, 'concerning the adoption, guardianship or custody of, or access to, any child, the best interests of the child shall be the paramount consideration'; and in making such a decision, children's own views will be taken on board: 'in respect of any child who is capable of forming his or her own views, the views of the child shall be ascertained and given due weight having regard to the age and maturity of the child' (ibid.). This makes clear that legal rights can come into conflict and that decisions will be required to resolve those conflicts, in this case, the 'right to parent' and the rights of the child. The wording of the amendment outlines the process that should be followed to resolve the conflicts, including ascertaining the views of the child. It also stipulates the relative significance of the competing considerations, as children's welfare is given priority: it is 'the paramount consideration'. What I want to consider are the implications of the amendment for the moral and legal status of children.

First, it reflects an acknowledgement that, in some cases, parents will not act in the best interests of their children. Therefore, when parents exercise their power, on occasion this may result in harm to children; and the privacy of the family, again, on occasion, may be used so as to conceal the harm done to children. So it is *not* assumed that in protecting the rights of parents we therefore also always protect the rights of children. There is a second implication of the amendment. Not only is it the case that, on occasion, the rights of parents must give way to the rights of the State, namely when the behaviour of parents will be harmful to the wider society. In addition, the rights and interests of children, and their views on those rights and interests, should be a consideration independent of the rights and interests of both the State and parents. While the State has an interest in producing 'an informed and disciplined citizenry able to create and maintain necessary social institutions'; and parents have an interest in 'teaching children responsibility with regard to the family, the community, and civic institutions'; separate from both of these are children's own interests, and these too should be to the fore (Fineman, 2003, pp. 235–6).

Are children empowered by the State?

Let us therefore consider what interests and what rights children do have. To that end, I want to examine ways in which the State can *empower* children. In the previous chapter, we spoke of Philip Pettit's republican account of 'antipower', which involved *inter alia* the empowerment of the powerless. And we have already mentioned the CRC in this chapter. This convention includes articles relating to children's liberty and their welfare. To the extent that a State implements these articles, to the extent that children enjoy the rights listed, it is arguable that the State will in effect be working to empower children in the republican sense of that term.

One category of children's rights is concerned with children's welfare rather than their liberty. Such rights are in line with the idea that 'the primary responsibility of parenting' is 'to meet their children's developmental needs' (Burtt, 2003, pp. 248, 249). And the CRC includes rights to basic resources required to achieve well-being: the right to the highest attainable standard of health (Article 24), to a standard of living adequate for the child's physical, mental, spiritual, moral, and social development (Article 27), to education (Articles 28, 29), to rest and leisure, to engage in play and recreational activities (Article 31), and 'to be protected from economic exploitation' (Article 32.1). And independently of any specific area of children's welfare, Article 3 guarantees the 'best interests of the child' principle. However, given our interest here in moral dilemmas and their resolution, we should note that, while in the Irish Constitution children's welfare is 'the paramount consideration', the CRC, adopting a more pluralist position, states that the best interests of the child must be 'a primary consideration' in all actions concerning children.

Another category of children's rights is concerned with liberty rather than welfare. Children's liberty rights can be thought of in terms of the requirement to ensure an 'open future' for the adults children will one day be (Feinberg, 1980), or, in contrast, the duty to protect children's liberty *qua* children (Harris, 1996). While both considerations are evident in the CRC, it is the latter that is of particular interest to us here. The CRC guarantees the right to have one's say in decisions that affect one's interests as a child (Article 12). It also includes rights to access information and material especially those aimed at the promotion of children's well-being and health

(Article 17), 'to freedom of expression', as we have seen (Article 13), and 'the right ... to freedom of thought, conscience and religion' (Article 14). However, consideration of children's liberty rights, in particular, raises a number of important questions.

The first is whether those who have rights of liberty also have responsibilities. For example, if we guarantee children's legal rights to freedom of expression and to freedom of thought, conscience, and religion, does it follow that children have legal responsibilities concerning how they exercise those rights? Should we hold children responsible for illegal activity carried out as part of religious practice, such as acts of intimidation or hate speech directed at members of an alternative faith? The debate on criminal responsibility would suggest a qualified 'yes' in answer to this question. It is widely acknowledged that, although children below a certain age (say, seven years old) may be considered *dola incapax*, or incapable of committing a crime, for children between that age and some higher threshold (say, twelve years old), that presumption 'may be defeasible' if it can be shown 'that the child committed an act he knew to be wrong' (Archard, 2004, pp. 129–30). At the same time, there are reasons not to expose a child in the latter category to court procedures and penalties that an adult would face in a similar situation. Not only may such proceedings and penalties be harmful to the child, children's participation may also be contrary to the interests of others involved in the case.

A second issue concerns the absoluteness or otherwise of children's right to liberty. If the law guarantees children's right to have their views 'given due weight in accordance with the age and maturity of the child', as Article 12 of the CRC requires, to what extent does it follow that children have a right to make decisions for themselves? For example, if children are considered competent to make a decision about participation in a medical trial, does it follow they have the right to authorise their participation and to do so independently of their parents' wishes (see Chapter 9)? In trying to answer this question, the relevant considerations include the children's level of competence and the likelihood and the seriousness of the risks involved to the children if they act as they wish (Buchanan and Brock, 1986; Beauchamp and Childress, 2009). Yet, regardless of how competent the children are, other considerations must be taken on board, not least parents' right to make decisions for their children and their duty to care for their children, and as a result, children's liberty rights will be limited rather than absolute.

So far we have considered various ways in which parents' power is or can be exercised in accordance with legal rules. The first thing to note is that we have come some distance from the liberal position, which separates the political domain from the domain of the family. Rather, what we have seen is that the family is a site of power relations regulated by the State. Therefore, when we evaluate parental power we are also evaluating the coercive imposition of a basic social institution, the family. There are various ways in which the State can and does guarantee parents' rights, including the right to privacy, the 'right to parent', the right to exercise power over children, and the right to make decisions independently of children's interests. However, the State also places limits on the rights of parents, so as to either protect children's rights or promote children's interests. And in some cases, based on the interests of the State and the interests of children, the State will intervene and remove adults' parenting rights. As Weber argues, the right to exercise power 'is ascribed to [...] individuals only to the extent to which the state permits it'. What we have seen is that the State guarantees legal powers to parents and children, and also regulates the enjoyment of their rights. It follows, when we evaluate the legitimacy of parents' power, we must take into account the coercively imposed legal rules in accordance with which such power is exercised.

Legitimation through consent

Now, in this section, I examine the role played by consent in the legitimation of power generally and parents' power in particular. Liberals, in their evaluation of the legitimacy of power relations, examine whether and to what extent they are based on the consent of the subjugated party. Liberals also conclude that such issues arise in the political domain and not the family. I will try to show that, as parents can exercise their power with greater or lesser degrees of child consent, we can and should take this on board when evaluating parent–child relations.

Why turn to consent when we evaluate legitimacy? According to Beetham, legal validity is not sufficient for legitimacy. Rather, legitimacy requires 'evidence of consent by the subordinate to the particular power relation', and, crucially, 'evidence of consent expressed through actions which are understood as demonstrating consent within the conventions of the particular society' (1991, pp. 12, 16). For example, in a representative democracy, a governing party may acquire power in a manner that has legal validity and nonetheless have the legitimacy of its power put in question if it fails to secure the consent of the governed. This could be the case if a minority of very wealthy citizens have disproportionate influence over policy, a situation that, even when it is not illegal, is incompatible with the 'conventions' for 'demonstrating consent'. Although in one sense consent has been secured here, namely through the electoral process, nonetheless it is arguable that, given the disproportionate influence of a wealthy minority, the manner in which decisions are being made by the government is no longer based on the consent of the governed.

As we shall see below, there are, broadly speaking, two different ways to think of consent here. While social contract theorists talk of a hypothetical contract as conferring legitimacy on a political society, it is modelled on those instances where individuals, in forming a contract, give explicit consent to a relationship and its attendant obligations. This is *explicit or contractual* consent. However, we can often be said to have consented to a relationship and its obligations without having formed a contract. This is sometimes referred to as *tacit or expressive* consent. Should we think of political responsibilities in this way, as is also the case with associative obligations, then we will see them as analogous to the responsibilities we have in family relations that cannot be traced back to contractual agreements.

Contractual consent

Let us start with explicit, contractual consent. As mentioned already, for now, our interest is in *actual* as opposed to *hypothetical* consent. Admittedly, the latter is a central feature of many normative approaches to justification. However, at this point, our concern is to examine what role actual consent has in legitimation. The first thing to note is that explicit, contractual consent does matter when we evaluate the legitimacy of political power. A widely shared belief is that, in a representative democracy, political power is considered legitimate if, *inter alia*, it is acquired through elections, where 'the act of taking part in elections [...] secures the obligation of citizens in principle to obey it [the government]' (Beetham, 1991, p. 92). The government's power has legitimacy for me *not* insofar as I voted for its leaders, but because I was free to take part in the election that brought them to power. This is why 'unanimity' voting systems, which give each voter a 'veto', are objectionable (Pettit, 2012, p. 168). At some point, we expect the looser to accept the outcome of the election as decisive. Crucially, it is the existence of choice that confers legitimacy on the result, whatever the result turns out to be: there must be a choice between candidates, and parties, for elections to confer legitimacy on the resulting government, again regardless of whether I voted for those who were successful.

Nonetheless, even when these criteria are met, choice is always limited. Some object that there is 'much less of a choice about [...] whether to make that choice in the first place', because the interests of those who take part, and therefore their choices, 'are already pre-structured' (Beetham, 1991, p. 96). Not only that, in the main, I have little or no choice over what options are presented to me, such as the choice between candidates from party *A* and party *B* in a regime's general election. Nonetheless, arguably we can remedy such shortcomings only by creating ever-greater opportunities for choice itself. For republicans, there is a close association between, on the one hand, limiting democratic participation to the periodic election of a ruling party, and on the other hand, widening and deepening apathy among citizens (Pettit, 2012, p. 227).

Let us turn now to the parent–child relation. Is it a power relation whose legitimacy is determined in some ways by the explicit, contractual consent of children? As already discussed, those who defend 'the caretaker thesis' reject the argument that children's subordination to parental power 'must be, and can only be, justified by their prior free grant of permission to the exercise of power'. This is the case because it is said that children 'lack the mature capacities of reason and independent volition that are needed for the giving and withholding of permission to be possible' (Archard, 2010, p. 46). Rawls's account of the three stages of moral development has been extremely influential in shaping such views on children's moral and political status (1971, pp. 462–79). Rawls situates young children in the 'morality of authority', which involves following rules because they have been issued by authority figures, including parents. Older children may be capable of engaging in the 'morality of association', but even here the family is 'normally characterized by a definite hierarchy', where the content of morality 'is given by the moral standards appropriate to the individual's role' in the association (ibid., p. 467). In contrast to both of these is the 'morality of principle', where consent is necessary for legitimacy, as the acceptance of rules is founded on each individual's own capacity to construct and comprehend the general principles from which the rules derive (see Coleman, 2002, pp. 167–8). However, to operate at the level of the morality of principle requires fully developed moral autonomy, in Rawls's terms (1971, p. 516), or, as Archard expresses it, the 'mature' capacities of reason and independent volition (2010, p. 46). As children lack such moral capacities, it is argued, their consent does not confer legitimacy on parents' power.

However, it is not universally accepted that children's moral capacities are such that their willing concurrence can have no bearing on the legitimacy of their parents' power. Even if very young children do not have the capacity to provide authorising consent, they do have the capacity to *assent* to, that is agree to or concur with, what someone else (usually a parent) has authorised. For example, in the literature on the ethics of conducting research with very young children, best practice requires on-going, close engagement with and observation of children by researchers, to ascertain whether the children do or do not assent to their participation (Veale, 2005; Hill, 2006; Mason and Hood, 2011). That is, even if we should seek parents' authorising consent for the participation of very young children in research, it is accepted that parents' decisions lack legitimacy, they should be overridden, when their children are no longer in agreement. In contrast, many adolescents *do* have the capacity to give fully informed consent, and this is the case regarding decisions to participate in research and decisions about medical care (see Chapter 9). If children do have the capacity to give authorising consent, should their consent be not only necessary but also sufficient for the legitimacy of parental power?

Some will object that, regardless of children's capacities, it is counter-intuitive to talk of children's consent to the rule of their parents. Nonetheless, there are in fact important parallels between parent–child relations and the situation of citizens consenting to political rule. Children do not elect to join a particular family, but most adults do not elect to join their political community either: it is a non-voluntary relation, as Rawls observed. (I return to this point later in this chapter, when we consider the associative model of legitimacy.) In addition, even though citizens may be legitimately subject to the power of their (un-chosen) political community, it is thought that consent should be a central feature of a legitimate political community. Political regimes also can either encourage or discourage citizen involvement in decision making, for example through referenda, citizen consultations, party caucuses, various forms of contestation, and so on (Pettit, 2012). Similarly, some styles of parenting, in particular what Baumrind refers to as 'authoritative' parenting, are more conducive to children's freedom even while setting standards for children's behaviour (see Chapter 4).

So it is possible to talk about the meaningful assent of very young children and the consent of adolescents, and the role and nature of consent in the political domain has significant similarities to the situation of parent–child power relations. What follows from this? First, consent should figure in our evaluation of the legitimacy of parents' power. However, second, it does *not* follow that, in Archard's terms, children's subordination to parental power 'must be, and can only be' justified by their consent. This is the case for a number of reasons. The first is that consent is not the only relevant moral consideration when we evaluate the legitimacy of parental power, and, in some cases, other moral considerations may be given greater weight. That is, even when children do consent to their parents' power, it may lack legitimacy for other reasons. For example, parents who pose a significant threat to their children's well-being may lose their 'right to parent' and their right to exercise power over their children, even if their children consent to their power.

The second reason is that a person's actual consent may be deeply flawed, and thus by itself it may carry relatively little moral significance. For that reason, it has been argued that political power is legitimate only if it is based on a hypothetical, fictional social contract, i.e. what we *would* have consented to as rational and reasonable persons (Rawls, 1971). If we take this second approach, we would be concerned with what children would consent to, when reasonable, and therefore we would move from actual to hypothetical consent. As we shall see in later chapters, there are strong grounds for adopting this approach, at least in part, for the legitimation of parental power, for instance, when children wish to make decisions about their medical care or research participation (see Chapter 9). However, in considering parental power from this point of view, as is the case with associative obligations discussed below, we are moving away from the position that children's actual consent is a prerequisite of its legitimacy. But we have not finished with consent just yet, as we must also consider it in its tacit, expressive mode.

Non-contractual obligations

Many thinkers object to the idea that legitimacy is based on explicit, contractual consent, not least David Hume. In his seminal argument rejecting social contract theory, Hume argues both that no such original act of promising ever occurred, but also that such a promise is not necessary for legitimacy, which instead is based on the good consequences of political power, namely that it serves to promote what he calls our 'general and obvious interests' (1993 [1748], p. 287). However, while I do want to move away from the social contract approach in this section, nonetheless, unlike Hume, what I want to consider here is the possibility that consent in its non-contractual form *is* a source of legitimacy. Do we have 'noncontractual role obligations' (Hardimon, 1994, p. 347) in politics and should we adopt an 'associative theory' of political obligation (Dworkin, 1990 [1986]; Horton, 2010)? According to this line of thought, my political obligations need not be traced back to a contract that I have explicitly agreed to, for my continued membership of an association itself gives rise to the obligations.

There is some similarity between the argument for non-contractual obligations, on the one hand, and, on the other hand, both Hume's own argument (1969 [1739–40], Book 3, Pt. 2, S. 1, p. 535) as well as the Hume-inspired argument that morality itself is 'something like an institution' (Mackie, 1977, pp. 79–80). For the latter, I have reasons to act as morality requires only insofar as I am within the institution. However, John (J. L.) Mackie's is an extreme position, as it considers morality as such to be an institution. In contrast, what Ronald Dworkin and others like him wish to show is merely that we cannot trace back all our moral obligations to a contractual commitment. We have many 'associative obligations just by belonging to groups defined by social practice' (Dworkin, 1990 [1986], p. 222). And he illustrates this point by emphasising that we owe obligations to family and friends due to a shared history of 'events and acts that *attract* obligations, and we are rarely even aware that we are entering upon any special status as the story unfolds' (ibid., p. 224; emphasis in original).

The argument under consideration is that we should think of political legitimacy in the same terms as we think of the moral legitimacy of associations, and the latter may refer to friends, colleagues, but also families. This brings us back again to the public–private distinction in liberal thought. Just as we have called into question the argument that coercion arises only in the public sphere, others have argued that the non-voluntary obligations of the family should be our model when we consider legitimacy in the political domain. It should be noted, again, my aim is not to identify the one value on which to base the legitimacy of parents' power, but rather to explore the various appropriate moral considerations and morally relevant features of these situations. In particular, in highlighting the importance of associative obligations we are not led to abandon the value of contractual consent. Nonetheless, as Beetham has argued, it is worth considering ways other than through contractual agreements that we can be said to have consented to power. With that in mind, let us proceed to examine what tacit consent does look like.

One example given by Beetham is that of consultations resulting in agreements. When we take part in consultations or negotiations with the powerful, which culminate in agreement, such engagement carries with it 'not only a commitment on the part of the subordinate to support the policy or observe the terms agreed, but an implication that they acknowledge the authority of the powerful more generally' (Beetham, 1991, p. 93). In modern, Western societies, such consultations and negotiations are evident in the collective bargaining engaged in by trade unions, management, and government. Up to a point, it is possible to draw an analogy with parent–child relations. For example, parents can engage in joint decision making with their children, which culminates in agreement on a 'policy', for example a decision on what types of social activity an adolescent may engage in (Partridge, 2014). Although it could also be argued that joint decision making confers legitimacy on parents' power, in the same way that consultations or negotiations confer legitimacy on powerful groups in the political domain, in fact there are important differences between the two.

As the psychology literature highlights, adolescents have competence in a formative state, and also adolescent competence can be nurtured and developed by parents and other adults acting supportively. Making decisions jointly with their parents is thought valuable *insofar* as it helps nurture the decision making capacities of adolescents (Xiao et al., 2011; Partridge, 2014). Power relations between adult citizens are different, as it is the consultation itself that confers legitimacy, and does so regardless of whether it also nurtures the decision making capacity of those involved. In contrast, if parents' power is conferred with legitimacy insofar as it nurtures children's decision making capacity, then there is no necessary relationship between joint decision making and legitimacy. This is the case, in particular, if parents can better promote the competence of their children through other means. It follows that tacit consent of this kind may be irrelevant for the legitimacy of parents' power in many situations.

However, tacit consent need not require consultation or discussion. For example, 'demonstrations of popular support or mass mobilization confer a distinctive legitimacy in the age of popular sovereignty', and movements that can generate or harness such enthusiasm or commitment can be very successful (Beetham, 1991, p. 94). Yet, this form of tacit consent is not without its problems. It is a process the powerful often are able to use to their own ends, whether through inducements, manipulation, or coercion. Given these concerns, we must ask whether the apparent willingness of children to conform to the demands of their parents confers legitimacy on these power relations, in particular in situations where children have not engaged in joint decision making. As we saw, according to the 'sociological child' thesis, structural and symbolic constraints not only construct childhood and parenting as meaningful social realities, they also construct the legitimacy of parental power, as childhood now is taken to be a period of incompetence, dependence, and vulnerability (James et al., 1998, p. 41ff). If that is the case, if parental power is in part responsible for the widely-held view that children are incapable of making decisions for themselves or incapable of making decisions jointly with their parents, can children's behaviour confer legitimacy on the very power that structures that behaviour?

We have seen that the consent of the governed, whether contractual or tacit, can confer legitimacy on a power relation. Also, children's consent, in both its modes, can confer legitimacy on parents' power. However, we have also highlighted a number of reasons for caution here. On the one hand, children's consent is not sufficient for the legitimacy of parental power, in particular as children may willingly consent to power relations that are, on the basis of different criteria, demonstrably illegitimate. Indeed, we have seen how consent may be 'manufactured' by the prevailing influence of the powerful. On the other hand, we rightly expect parents to help foster and develop their children's capacities more generally, including the decision making capacities exercised in the giving or withholding of consent, and parents may do so without engaging their children in a process, such as joint decision making, that engages children consensually. That is, parental power may be considered legitimate in some situations even when children have not given their consent.

Legitimacy and the family

In the first part of this chapter, we saw that whether or not coercive power is exercised in accordance with legally valid rules is not itself sufficient to answer all our questions about the legitimacy of power. Now we can see that whether or not power is exercised with the consent of the governed also is not sufficient to determine the legitimacy of power relations. We must not restrict legitimacy to matters of legality or consent, therefore. This point merely reminds us of the need to move to a level of normative evaluation from which we can better examine the practices and taken-for-granted assumptions of parent–child relations.

So far in this chapter, I have been critical of 'liberal' ideas about the public and private sphere, insofar as liberals conclude that relations between parents and children are characteristically private and therefore should not be analysed in terms of their legitimacy. However, I have already indicated my commitment to a 'liberal' approach to practical reason and practical judgement when faced with moral dilemmas, one that is, with some qualifications, informed by Rawls's account of reasonableness and Nagel's account of public justification in a context of actual disagreement (see Chapter 3). But this leaves us in a quandary. If the liberal approach to practical reason is intended for our deliberation of issues that arise in what liberals take to be the political domain, as Nagel and Rawls suggest, how can we employ such an approach to the evaluation of parent–child relations, which liberals take to be external to the political domain? In addition, if we recall, we had reasons to be critical of what some liberals had to say about both practical reason and moral dilemmas.

As I argued in Chapter 3, the lexical ordering of principles in Rawls's work is incompatible with what we have discovered so far concerning the irreducible plurality of moral claims. Therefore, we cannot assume that, when we engage in practical reason, we must identify a single moral claim that is fundamental and therefore that has priority over competing claims. We should also remember that the liberal account of practical reason was attractive initially as a way in which to work through real, genuine moral dilemmas, as Nagel himself attempts to do. It is because no one moral claim is fundamental that we are faced with moral dilemmas, and it is through practical reasoning and practical judgement that we can attempt to resolve such dilemmas. This suggests we should adopt the following approach to the predicament we find ourselves in. In what follows, I want to show that the moral dilemmas, for which the liberal account of practical reason is required, arise not only in the political domain, but also in relations between parents and children. I also want to show that the highest level of moral objectivity, which is required when faced with moral dilemmas and which is attainable through the exercise of practical reason, is required here as well.

Moral dilemmas in different domains

As we saw in Chapter 3, we can be faced with moral dilemmas, such that, even when we do what is right all things considered, it is rational to feel 'regret' at 'the item that is not acted upon'. I now want to examine the varied contexts in which moral dilemmas arise.

First, moral conflicts do indeed arise when we are required to justify the coercive imposition of social institutions. For example, Berlin tries to show how there can be moral losses involved in pursuing even our most cherished political objectives. He accepts that we should on occasion curtail negative freedom, in part because one should be committed to other goals, such as social justice, equality, and the reduction of poverty. Nonetheless, a clear conceptual distinction should be maintained between these values. 'Nothing is gained by a confusion of terms', Berlin argues: 'To avoid glaring inequality or widespread misery I am prepared to sacrifice some, or all, of my freedom [...] but it is freedom that I am giving up for the sake of justice or equality or the love of my fellow men (2004 [1958], p. 172). Justice may require that we sacrifice some negative freedom so as to promote social and economic equality, but when we do so, this is to sacrifice one thing (freedom) for something else (equality).

It is one thing to show that we can be faced with moral dilemmas when we do what is right in public life and when we use the coercive power of the State to implement our decisions. It is quite another thing to conclude that, because of the distinctive nature and qualities of the political domain, such moral dilemmas are more likely there than in private life. But this is precisely what Nagel has argued. Our actions in public life 'have to be much more impartial than private ones, since they usually employ a monopoly of certain kinds of power and since there is no reason in their case to leave room for the personal attachments and inclinations that shape individual lives' (Nagel, 1978, p. 84). One implication of Nagel's position here is that, in the public sphere, we may be expected to be ruthless, to get our hands dirty, both because we are expected to work towards attaining the best outcomes for the wider society but also because restrictions on the use of coercion and manipulation that do apply to individuals in the private sphere are significantly weaker in our public roles. And thus, in the public sphere, we will face the most difficult-to-resolve moral dilemmas because of the seriousness of what is at stake.

Let us question this liberal tenet that the most serious moral dilemmas are a feature of the public sphere but are not characteristic of intimate, private relations, including those of the family (see Coady, 1991). The first thing to note is that, as we have seen in the first half of this chapter, parents exercise power over their children in the family, and at times they coerce and manipulate their children. Therefore, if coercion or manipulation are more closely associated with moral dilemmas of the most serious kind, 'dirty hands' dilemmas, then parents can be faced with such dilemmas in their relations with their children. It is not only public officials but also parents who may have to act impartially and who may be justified in violating moral rules towards others, including their children, in order to do so. Indeed, as we saw, when parents act paternalistically they will violate some moral rule towards their children.

Second, parents may also face moral dilemmas even when not exercising coercive power. Moral dilemmas can arise simply because of a clash of values. We are familiar with cases of individuals trying to work through a moral conflict that has arisen because of their unique commitments and obligations as parents. For example, as a parent, I *ought* to encourage my child to pursue standards of moral excellence, and in doing so I may promote a substantive moral doctrine. However, I also *ought* to promote my child's autonomy. And these moral requirements can come into conflict, when to promote my child's autonomy requires also encouraging my child to question the standards of excellence, and underlying substantive normative convictions, I had wished to promote (see Chapter 10).

Third, moral dilemmas may arise when the moral demands of the intimate sphere come into conflict with the moral demands of the public sphere. Perhaps the most famous example, provided by Jean Paul Sartre, is that of the son who must decide between going to fight for the French Resistance and staying to care for his elderly mother (1957 [1946]).[2] To turn this example on its head, many parents have gone to fight in wars and in doing so left their children in the care of others, and they too were faced with moral dilemmas: I have a duty to care for my children, but I also have a duty of patriotism to my fellow citizens, and it is possible for the two to come into conflict. This is a moral dilemma that is of the most serious kind, it is not explained simply or solely by one's public role and its demands, and it does not arise because of the exercise of coercion or manipulation.

What does all of the above tell us? We have seen that moral dilemmas of the most serious kind arise for us in the intimate, private relations of the family, including in parents' dealings with their children. Therefore, we should reject Nagel's argument that serious moral dilemmas are characteristic of the political domain and not the private sphere. A further implication is that the moral regret that should be felt in situations where there has been some item not acted upon, the moral regret of moral dilemmas (Williams, 1965), is characteristic of the private sphere as well as the public. At the same time, in situations such as these, although we are faced with a dilemma, and although we will be left with regret regardless of our decision, nonetheless, a decision and an action are required. So how do we justify our moral judgements and our actions? To address this question let us return again to practical reason and practical judgement.

Moral objectivity and resolving moral dilemmas

In Chapter 3, I argued that we should attempt to resolve dilemmas through a combination of theoretical analysis along with the type of practical reasoning and practical judgement associated with a number of liberal thinkers, in particular Rawls and Nagel. At that point, I acknowledged a number of possible criticisms of such an approach, and I asked the following questions: If we adopt a 'liberal' approach to practical reason, will we be more likely to give priority to the duty to protect individual liberty when it comes into conflict with perfectionist and utilitarian aims, and to give priority to general considerations, such as general rights and general duties, when they come into conflict with personal commitments? And if that is the case, will such a 'liberal' approach be inappropriate for consideration of parent–child relations, where personal commitments are central and values other than individual liberty are relevant?

To begin with, I want to consider what type of reasoning is appropriate to justify the coercive imposition of society's basic institutions. Let us first consider those liberals who believe that, if we are to be reasonable, we should remain *neutral* between competing moral claims. Such liberals call for an epistemological 'restraint' that distinguishes 'between what justifies individual belief and what justifies appealing to that belief in support of the exercise of political power' (Nagel, 1990 [1987], p. 312). For such liberals, when we engage in practical reasoning, we put to one side our substantive moral commitments, and instead we are willing to 'submit one's reasons to the criticism of others' (ibid., pp. 315–16). It follows, for many liberals, practical rationality requires us to remain neutral when faced with different and incompatible value systems and ways of life.

In contrast, others do not accept that practical reason also requires neutrality. For Aristotelians, Thomists, and other communitarians, we must *not* put to one side substantive commitments, for it is these that are the first principles of all practical reasoning. For example, as the member of a Catholic community, I reason from within a moral tradition that not only provides moral principles but also places such principles in an order of priority for me, such that, in any given situation, I will arrive at the correct decision (MacIntyre, 1988; Lutz, 2004). Catholics can claim that their own moral doctrine sets a demanding and exacting moral standard, and also that it requires Catholics be impartial when they make moral decisions of right and wrong and good and bad. For these reasons, it is argued, Catholicism is sufficiently objective for the task of justifying the coercive imposition of legal rules concerning, *inter alia*, family structure and the bearing and rearing of children. Yet, in many cases, Catholics and non-Catholics come to quite different conclusions with regard to what behaviours are permissible and obligatory in these spheres. So we are led to wonder whether liberals are correct to conclude that we should, instead, remain neutral with respect to different and perhaps conflicting moral doctrines.

According to Ronald Dworkin, liberalism 'requires that the government treats all those in its charge *as equals*, that is, as entitled to its equal concern and respect' (1978, p. 125; emphasis in original). This means or requires 'that government must be neutral on what might be called the question of the good life' (ibid., p. 127). For example, if a proposed policy would restrict freedom of worship and religious education for Protestants but not Catholics, then a Catholic should think of it *not* as a policy 'promoting adherence to the true faith' but *rather* as a policy 'preventing them [Protestants] from practicing their religion'. The virtue of such an approach, its stance of neutrality with respect to the truth or falsity of Protestantism, is that it has some chance of 'being accepted by all parties concerned as a true description of what is going on [...] and [...] being accorded the same kind of impersonal value by all parties' (Nagel, 1990 [1987], p. 310). This stance of neutrality *vis-à-vis* the truth of Protestantism is not available to those who reason *as* Catholics when considering the legitimacy of the State's power.

The liberal argument is that the coercive imposition of institutions can be legitimate only on the basis of the highest standard of moral objectivity. However, are they correct to equate the latter with *neutrality* between competing conceptions of the good life? It is arguable that they have, in a highly questionable manner, simply insisted that one moral claim be given priority over others. As we have already seen in Chapter 3, Rawls is criticised for smuggling in his own substantive, and controversial, moral commitments into his account of political reasoning, as the latter presupposes both that moral justification is based on consent, and that a morally worthwhile life is autonomous (Dryzek and Niemeyer, 2006; Thunder, 2006). In addition, his critics argue that, as Rawls does explicitly put to one side the question of their truth or falsity, the 'reasonable' citizen is given the freedom to regard non-liberal beliefs and values as false or invalid or flawed (MacIntyre, 1988, p. 345ff; Barnhart, 2004, p. 265).

I want to take an approach that departs from liberal neutrality but also from Aristotelian or Thomist communitarianism. I think it is possible to reinterpret Nagel's account of practical reason and separate it from his commitment to liberal neutrality. When we look at what Nagel proposes, it could be argued that he offers a method of moral debate suited to addressing moral conflicts. It is not of necessity biased towards any one moral stand-point, not even liberal neutrality. For Nagel, we must be willing to submit our reasons to the criticism of others, to present the basis of our own beliefs so that others have what we have and can arrive at the same conclu-sion, but also to accept that the investigation of our disagreement be open-ended rather than a bare confrontation between impersonal points of view (Nagel, 1990 [1987], pp. 315–16).

I believe this is best understood as a pluralist method suited to address-ing moral conflicts, including the conflicts between liberal and non-liberal values. There will remain the suspicion that it is biased in favour of 'liberal' values and policies. Perhaps we can only respond satisfactorily to this concern by attempting to address moral conflicts with such a method. When we do engage in a series of case studies in the final chapters of this book we shall see that, in certain cases, this procedure of 'public justifi-cation' can justify decisions to give priority to non-liberal values. This is the case, for example, when individual liberty is 'trumped' by considera-tions of personal well-being, or general welfare, or perfectionism. Indeed, as we saw in Chapter 6, Nagel himself showed that his approach would oppose prohibitions against discussion of intelligent design in the class-room (Nagel, 2008, p. 201), even though the teaching of intelligent design can be considered antithetical to liberal values and a liberal way of life.

The other concern is that, even if the liberal account of practical reason is suited to moral issues arising when we coercively impose basic institu-tions, it is ill-suited to parent–child relations within the family. Indeed, Nagel himself has distinguished between justifications for the beliefs that I follow in my private life, on the one hand, and justifications for the exer-cise of coercive power, on the other hand. However, what this distinc-tion serves to hide from view is precisely the sort of situation we need to address in this book. This is the type of situation faced when we ask, 'Do my Catholic beliefs justify my exercise of power over my children in sharing a Catholic way of life with them?' As I said at the start of this chapter, Nagel comes part of the way towards recognising that there is a problem here for his approach, seeing this is a 'problematic intermediate case' (1990 [1987], p. 322).

Nagel's concern is with how individuals, who have private lives and partial commitments, nonetheless can have reasons to accept as legitimate the coercive imposition of society's basic institutions (1991, p. 36). That is why the family is a 'problematic intermediate' case for him. He is happy to leave me free to live my private life in accordance with my Catholic beliefs, if this is what my personal commitment is, but he does not accept that my Catholic beliefs are sufficiently objective to justify coercive power relations. Yet, there is evidence for power relations, sometimes coercive, in my private or intimate family relations. If we acknowledge that such power relations require justification, how are we to proceed? And in evaluating power relations, can parents and children resolve moral dilemmas by appeal to reasons that may be insufficiently objective were they engaged in a public debate, a debate that included non-Catholics, about the coercive imposition of the family as a basic institution? For example, could distinctively Catholic reasons suffice when the parents and children of a Catholic family attempt to work through their dilemmas concerning the parents' exercise of power?

I think the answer is a qualified, perhaps heavily qualified, 'yes'. Insofar as both parents and children can in this way 'submit one's reasons to the criticism of others' then they are satisfying the requirement that each can arrive at a judgement from the same basis. Note, they do so without being neutral, contra Nagel. Indeed, they do so while not leaving behind their partial, particular commitment to Catholicism. However, this affirmative answer is qualified for the reason that there may always be a need to refer such moral questions to a higher level of objectivity, that is, a basis other than Catholic morality.

We may be justified in doing so, first, when we are concerned that the exercise of power by parents over children is inseparable from the children's acceptance of their parents' values. That is, we may at times consider parents' values to serve an ideological function in that they help both conceal and justify power relations. The second reason is that the most significant moral issues may arise in any sphere, including the family. That is, children are exposed to potentially great harms in the family, and potentially great opportunities are available in and through the family. When that is the case, we are justified in requiring the highest standards of objectivity in resolving moral conflicts that arise here, and so we are justified in requiring that Catholicism be left behind when engaging in practical reasoning and practical judgement.

Conclusions

In this chapter, we have been considering a very important criticism of any attempt to evaluate the legitimacy of parents' power. It could be argued that, in this book, we have evaluated parent–child relations in the way that we would evaluate the power relations of adults in the political domain, whereas the concepts we use when evaluating the power relations of the political domain are simply not appropriate to the normative evaluation of the relations between parents and children.

In response, I have argued that we can and should evaluate the legitimacy of parent–child relations. This is the case because coercively-imposed legal rules are a central feature of the family, including rules that guarantee privacy, protect and regulate parents' rights, and protect and empower children. In addition, parents can exercise power with greater or lesser degrees of child consent. Therefore, when we evaluate parent–child power relations we can and should consider whether parents are acting in accordance with legally enforced rules, and we must also consider what counts as public expressions of consent by children. In addition, even if the highest standards of moral objectivity were required only for the coercive imposition of society's basic social institutions, the family is one such institution, and therefore such standards would be required here as well. However, moral objectivity is required by the seriousness of the issues at stake, and the most serious moral issues can arise in the informal relations of the private sphere, between parent and child, and even when coercive power has not been exercised. When that is the case then, once again, the highest moral standards are required.

And we also addressed the deeper issue of just what the highest standards of moral objectivity consist in. As I have taken on board much of what liberal writers have said on this, and as liberal writers have been accused of bias in their approach to political deliberation and political justification, this is an important question for this book. Although I have defended the idea of reasonableness and the related idea of public justification in a context of actual disagreement, as I said, there will be cases when, in adopting such an approach, we will resolve moral conflicts in such a way that the recognisably liberal value will give way to non-liberal values. Thus, unlike Rawls, for instance, we will not be seeking, through reflective equilibrium, to establish an order of priority between our moral claims; and specifically, it is not the case that individual liberty is the fundamental moral claim. That is not an option here, as we have ruled out the possibility that any one value is, as a general rule, fundamental. In addition, members of non-liberal families are entitled to employ their own non-liberal moral considerations when they evaluate power relations within their own family, but with the following proviso, that at times a higher level of moral objectivity may be required, one that enables us to call into question these very non-liberal values.

Notes

1 The First Amendment states as follows: 'Congress shall make no law respecting an establishment of religion, or prohibiting the free exercise thereof; or abridging the freedom of speech, or of the press; or the right of the people peaceably to assemble, and to petition the government for a redress of grievances'.

2 As Paul Johnson (1988, p. 230) has pointedly observed, Sartre himself never

faced such a dilemma during the occupation of France in the early 1940s: 'He did not lift a finger, or write a word, to save the Jews. He concentrated relentlessly on promoting his own career'.

8

Licensing, monitoring, and training parents

We should distinguish the rights parents have 'over' their children from the 'right to parent'. This is the distinction between parents' power over their children, or more precisely parents' legitimate power over their children, on the one hand, and the right to play the role of a parent and therefore the right to raise or rear children, on the other hand. In this chapter I focus on the latter, the 'right to parent', before proceeding in subsequent chapters to examine the legitimacy of various aspects of parents' power over their children. To take matters in this order makes intuitive sense, for if adults in the first instance do not have a 'right to parent' they cannot also have a right to exercise power over children as a parent.

There are two ways in which we can speak of a 'right to parent'. We can examine whether adults have a right to procreate, a right to *bear* children (Benatar, 2010). Although a very important question, I will not focus on it here, except insofar as it bears on the second way in which we speak of a 'right to parent', namely the right to *rear* children. It is widely accepted that, in one sense or another, this right is conditional. That is, if adults do not satisfy certain requirements, for example the requirement of being a competent parent, society may refuse to grant the right in the first place, or the right already granted may be restricted or rescinded altogether. I will look at three proposals concerning the conditions to be placed on the 'right to parent': that we should license parents, that we should monitor parents, and that we should train parents. Of course, it is also possible to join together some or all of these three proposals, but I want to examine the merits of each independently.

Hugh LaFollette (1980; 2010) has argued that prospective parents should be licensed, and those who will not be competent parents should be refused licences. His position is that parenting is similar to other activities that require licences, such as driving a car or practicing medicine: it is an activity that is potentially harmful to others, it does require a certain level of competence, and we have moderately reliable procedures for determining competence. In contrast, David Archard (2004) makes the case for the monitoring of parents. A child welfare agency should have statutory powers to enter the family home and have access to children, Archard argues, on the grounds that this will deter child abuse while having no negative impact on the liberty of those parents who are not mis-treating their children. And finally, the argument for the training of parents has been made by LaFollette, among others (Engster and Gonzales, 2012). It is argued that the provision of voluntary parenting programmes is a non-coercive method to promote competent parenting and in that way better protect children.

What I will try to show here is that, in many of the arguments concerning the conditions attached to the 'right to parent', one moral consideration is considered fundamental. Those who propose parental licences and parental monitoring assume that the paramount consideration is the well-being of the children affected. In these arguments, our duty to prevent harm to the child is, as a general rule, given priority over other moral considerations, in particular, the parents' right to privacy and the parents' right to parent their own child. Given what we have seen already (Chapter 3) we can say that there is, therefore, a process of moral simplification whereby the significance of other, conflicting moral considerations is diminished. I want to trace the ways in which such moral simplification has occurred. However, I also want to examine opportunities both to acknowledge the presence of moral conflict and to try to resolve such conflicts through practical reasoning and practical judgement. In doing this, I will find little merit in parenting licences, but what shows greater promise is the combination of universal parental training with a restricted programme of parental monitoring.

Empirical evidence

I return below to discuss the evidence for the effectiveness of parental training programmes as a means to protect children's interests. However, I will begin by examining the empirical issues that are most pertinent to arguments for the licensing and monitoring of parents. I will focus on the claim that we can predict which adults would be incompetent parents. In particular, I explore this claim as it is developed by LaFollette when calling for parental licences, although it has relevance for the monitoring of parents as well, as we shall see.

LaFollette argues that, if we have a test that predicts whether adults will be competent parents in the future, we can then grant parental licences to competent parents and refuse licences to those who will not be competent.

The same considerations apply to those proposing the monitoring of parents. For when practitioners monitor parents they are not just looking for evidence of child mistreatment in the past, but also whether the adults are likely to be competent parents in the future. Although LaFollette concedes that we cannot agree on the criterion of 'good' parenting, nonetheless he insists 'we undoubtedly can identify bad ones – those who will abuse or neglect their children' (1980, p. 190). And, according to LaFollette, we can 'predict reasonably and accurately whether people would maltreat their own children' (ibid., p. 188). To do so, 'we can use existing tests that claim to isolate relevant predictive characteristics – whether a person is violence-prone, easily frustrated, or unduly self-centered' (ibid., p. 191). He also argues that 'parents who maltreat their children often have identifiable experiences, for example, most of them were themselves maltreated as children' (ibid.).

LaFollette concludes by acknowledging he 'cannot say emphatically that we now have accurate predictive tests', but this should not deter us, he believes, for 'we could undoubtedly develop them' (ibid., p. 192). To that end, he proposes running a longitudinal study where all potential parents would be required first to take a battery of tests. We would then follow up on these parents to discover which ones subsequently maltreated their children. At that point, we could fashion a usable, accurate predictive test by correlating test scores with incidences of child maltreatment. Subsequently, Claudia Mangel has argued that the desired test already exists, namely the Child Abuse Potential Inventory (CAPI), which, she argues, will predict future abusers with a high degree of accuracy (1988, p. 25). Thirty years after the first publication of his article, LaFollette, quoting Mangel, concluded that the CAPI 'appears to be reasonably accurate', although he then qualifies this initial enthusiasm, stating that with 'further study we could likely devise a reliable test' (2010, p. 337).

Both Mangel and LaFollette refer to the accuracy of predictive tests, although LaFollette admits that, 'as a philosopher', he is 'on shaky ground' making claims about the possibility of producing such predictive tests (1980, pp. 190–1). However, the accuracy of tests used as predictors of child abuse is central to the philosophical and ethical questions raised about licensing parents (see Archard, 2004, pp. 188–9). In the decade immediately following LaFollette's essay, reviews of the instruments used to predict child abuse were unanimous in concluding that such tests are *not* accurate (in Sandmire and Wald, 1990). This is partly a reflection of the fact that any such instrument will produce four categories of results: true positives, true negatives, false positives, and false negatives (see Anomaly, 2014). The type of test needed in order to implement LaFollette's proposals will correctly identify those who will abuse (true positives) and those who will not abuse (true negatives). However, any such instrument will also mistakenly identify some people as future abusers who will not become abusers (false positives) and it will mistakenly identify some as non-abusers who will in fact become abusers (false negatives) (Sandmire and Wald, 1990, p. 56, n. 11).

The extent to which an instrument produces false results depends in part on the prevalence of the behaviour in question. If the prevalence of abusers is low, for example 1 per cent of the adult population, as it is for 'serious' cases of abuse requiring medical care, even instruments with very high levels of accuracy will 'produce a group labeled as abusers with 85 per cent of these judgements being wrong' (ibid., p. 60). That is, in a population of 1,000 families, with a 1 per cent abuse rate, and with an instrument that correctly identifies 90 per cent of actual abusers (referred to as 'sensitivity') and 95 per cent of the actual non-abusers (referred to as 'specificity'), the test will produce 50 false positives, 9 true positives, 940 true negatives, and one false negative: in other words, in a population of 10 abusers, 50 people will be incorrectly labelled as abusers, and 1 will be incorrectly labelled as a non-abuser (see Table 8.1).

So, to begin with the issue of false positives, the number will be high, but does this have great moral significance? As a recent discussion of Sandmire and Wald's critique concludes, 'the cost of rescuing nine children out of 10 from abuse – denying 50 innocent individuals or couples the opportunity to parent – is hardly trivial' (De Wispelaere and Weinstock, 2012, p. 201). Similarly, we can ask, is it 'hardly trivial' that one abuser will be mistakenly labelled as a non-abuser and therefore, wrongly, granted a licence to become a parent? Whether or not it is 'hardly trivial' turns on the relative significance of the values in question, an issue we return to below.

Table 8.1 Hypothetical predictive instrument with high sensitivity/specificity and 1 per cent prevalence of child abuse in 1,000 families (adapted from Sandmire and Wald, 1990)

		Actual Abuse Occurred		
		Yes	No	
Test Predicted Abuse Would Occur	Yes	A 9	C 50	A = True Positives B = False Negatives
	No	B 1	D 940	C = False Positives D = True Negatives
		10	990	

As we have seen, the instrument we use to predict child abuse will produce two types of error. However, we can manage the trade-off between the two when we design the way in which data are collected. For example, if we operate with a very high threshold in identifying abusers, we will reduce the incidence of false positives, for the reason that a parent must score very poorly to pass the threshold, but in so doing we will increase the incidence of false negatives. That is, fewer people who are not in fact abusers will be mislabelled as abusers, but more people who are abusers will be mislabelled as non-abusers. Therefore, we can decide between allowing a greater proportion of false positives or a greater proportion of false negatives. But we cannot do away with the possibility of false results in predicting child abuse.

How important is the fact that any test we use to predict who will one day abuse their children will also produce false results? LaFollette believes that 'we should not put too much weight' on the fact that, so far, we do not have any test that would give us 'the predictive power we might want before establishing a robust licensing program' (2010, p. 337). We should not put too much weight on this because, in the future, we could likely devise an accurate test. However, I think it is fair to say that a better understanding of statistics would lead one to be less sanguine about future possibilities for predicting child abuse. For if the prevalence of serious child abuse is approximately 1 per cent, as others argue, then our ability to predict serious child abuse will be very poor because of the large proportion of false results that our predictive test will return, whatever test we employ.

We have looked at some of the empirical evidence concerning the prediction of child abuse, which is relevant for both parental licences and the monitoring of parents. Before moving on, let us look at the empirical evidence for an alternative policy option, the provision of parenting programmes. This is highly relevant to our current discussion, as LaFollette himself, when he 'revisited' his proposals in 2010, defended what he called a 'limited licensing program'. The 'limited' proposal is to set minimal requirements for a licence, to issue licences to those who successfully complete a parenting course, and to 'reward those with licenses – say with special tax breaks – rather than punish those without' (ibid., pp. 338–9).

Others have argued that there are now a number of parenting programmes available that are evidence-based and effective. In particular, it is argued, participation in these programmes leads to improved parenting behaviour, with beneficial consequences for children's well-being:

In sum, there now exists a large body of empirical evidence that demonstrates the effectiveness of behavioral parent training classes in improving parenting knowledge and skills, promoting positive parent behaviors, reducing harmful parenting behaviors, reducing substantiated cases of child abuse and neglect, improving children's developmental outcomes, and ameliorating child conduct problems. (Engster and Gonzales, 2012, p. 231)

As we shall see below, one reason why a parenting programme is preferable to a licensing system is if the former poses less of a threat to the liberty of prospective parents. Nonetheless, in deciding between the two, we must also compare the effectiveness of parenting programmes and licensing systems in changing parenting behaviour for the better and bringing about improvements in children's well-being. And significant questions can be raised about the empirical evidence for the effectiveness of parenting programmes.

For example, one programme Engster and Gonzales draw attention to, Triple P (Positive Parenting Programme), is at the centre of an on-going controversy over the quality of evidence cited in its support. Recent reviews and meta-analyses of studies claiming to show that Triple P is responsible for improved outcomes for children note, *inter alia*, that many of the authors of these reports are affiliated in some way with the developers of Triple P, that participating parents are not in fact representative, and that very few studies have compared Triple P with alternative active treatments (Wilson et al., 2012; Coyne and Kwakkenbos, 2013). Indeed, there are no definitive answers to two highly relevant questions: Would all families benefit from the programme in the same way that participating families have done and would other programmes lead to similar or even better gains than Triple P? What we can say is that many studies show a close association between parenting style and children's well-being. Nonetheless, we should retain a healthy scepticism concerning these findings. In particular, the appeal of a parenting programme diminishes in direct proportion to the growing uncertainty about its effectiveness.

Legislation, policy, and services

Through the passing of legislation, the implementation of policies, and the provision of services, the State exercises a profound influence on parenting, as we saw in Chapter 7. I want to focus here on the State's exercise of power over adults in connection with their right to parent.

LaFollette's proposal is that the State 'should require all parents to be licensed' (1980, p. 182). He addresses a number of possible objections to his proposal. He does not accept that it will entail 'unnecessary governmental intervention into individuals' lives' for the following two reasons. First, 'the intrusion would not often be substantial, and when it is, it would be warranted'. Yet, we have seen that, in some proportion of cases (those that are false positives), the intrusion would not be warranted, so this is an issue we must return to. His second argument is that such encroachment 'would be no more than and probably less than' the encroachment currently experienced by those who apply to adopt children, and if such encroachment is justified concerning potential adoptive parents it should be justified concerning prospective biological parents (ibid., p. 187). This second point relies on the underlying assumption that there are no significant, relevant differences between the situation of adoptive parents and biological parents, which I return to below.

If a licensing system raises concerns about the infringement of adults' rights, an alternative proposal is for the extensive monitoring of parents. Archard, who supports such an approach, is *not* proposing the '[c]ontinual observation of parenting' but rather a system whereby a child welfare agency has 'statutory powers of entry into the family home, and rights of access to children' (2004, p. 173). His rationale is that this will deter child abuse, as parents will be more likely to treat their children well if they know that they may receive a home visit at any time. Also, Archard concludes, it has no direct implications for parents' liberty of action, as the latter is only affected by courses of action taken as a consequence of the observation. Archard also believes that we should *not* refrain from monitoring families for fear of violating a right to privacy. As we shall see below, although he questions whether parents have a right to privacy at all, he also argues that any infringement of such a right is justified if necessary in order to protect children from harm (ibid., p. 191).

We are focusing on the State's exercise of power over adults in connection with their 'right to parent'. One reason to be concerned about parental licences and parental monitoring is that they may lead to an illegitimate increase in the State's coercive power over parents. Many thinkers, in particular feminists, have been concerned with the ways in which the State should, instead, lessen or remove restrictions on adults' choices concerning parenting. Feminists have argued that, only when the assumption that all women must be mothers is challenged, 'will a woman's destiny truly be her own' (Ireland, 1993, p. 1). Therefore, liberal laws on access to contraception and abortion are, it is argued, one way to protect women's freedom in deciding to become parents (Thomson, 1971). However, as mentioned in the previous chapter, the feminist approach has been criticised for the reason that it has been 'woman-centered, rather than child-centered' (Cassidy, 2006, p. 44). Instead, it is argued, women should consider how their competence as parents will impact on the well-being of children they will bear and rear (ibid., p. 46). Lisa Cassidy agrees with LaFollette that we can anticipate whether or not we will be competent parents, and she goes further than LaFollette in arguing that only those who will be better than averagely competent should parent. However, she is concerned to keep the State out of 'our bedrooms' (ibid., p. 54). All she asks is that women make a normative decision about their own lives, and for that reason this will not be the first step towards what she sees as LaFollette's legal paternalism (ibid., p. 55).

Cassidy's proposal is that women should take responsibility for the decision to become parents, and to do so only when they will be better than averagely competent parents. However, this leaves unexamined the types of situations that have exercised LaFollette and others, namely where compulsory licensing of parents or non-voluntary monitoring of parents have been proposed. First, the State and its agencies must design policies suited for dealing with adults who will not be competent parents but nonetheless will, unless they are prevented from doing so, take steps to become parents. Second, many parents of existing children are not competent, and it must be decided if and in what way the State, through its agencies, should intervene so as to influence the rearing of children, including through non-voluntary monitoring of parents.

Conceptual issues

So far we have looked at methodological questions that arise when we try to predict child abuse, as well as the evidence for the effectiveness of parenting programmes. We have also explored various proposals for the State's role in respect of adults becoming parents and retaining the right to parent, including the licensing and monitoring of parents. Following on from that, there are a number of conceptual issues that I want to explore, and so in this section I will address the following questions. What are the normative reasons for not licensing parents? Why do we value privacy, and in particular the privacy of the family, and is privacy undermined when our behaviour is monitored? Finally, if the State merely promotes decent parenting, can we avoid some of the objections to the licensing and monitoring of parents?

Infringing the 'right to parent'

I want to examine whether parenting licences violate the 'right to parent'. However, first let us consider what the justification or basis for such a right is, and also whether there are reasons to think that parenting licences are, in fact, compatible with such a right. One line of argument is that my right to rear my children is an extension of my right to liberty of action as an adult. Importantly, any such right would be limited, as is the case with all rights of liberty. This is the basic point made by Mill when arguing that 'the only purpose for which power can be rightly exercised over any member of a civilised community, against his will, is to prevent harm to others' (1985 [1859], p. 68). For example, it is argued that, as my liberty is limited by the rights of others, as a parent I have no right to bear or rear children where the 'offspring stand a high chance of being harmed' (Benatar, 2010, p. 90). Therefore, a parental licensing system may be compatible with a 'right to parent' that is based on adults' rights of liberty, insofar as the latter is limited by the rights of others.

Others derive the 'right to parent' from adults' interests. For Brighouse and Swift, adults have interests in parenting, as the parent–child relationship 'involves the adult in a unique combination of joys and challenges; experiencing and meeting these makes a distinctive set of demands on him, and produces a distinctive contribution to his well-being' (2014, p. 88). However, according to Brighouse and Swift, the right to parent is conditional 'on the adult's being a good enough parent, on his discharging his fiduciary duties to an adequate standard' (ibid., p. 94). That is, adults can lose their right to raise children if they are not going to do so properly. In other words, although adults have a right to parent, once again such a right is conditional.

Therefore, a licensing system that prevented some adults from procreating, and removed children from incompetent parents, may well be compatible with such a *conditional* right to parent. Indeed, the conditional nature of the 'right to parent' is already widely recognised in the case of adoption. And this is one of LaFollette's key arguments for a licensing system for parents (2010, p. 336). If we think it justifiable that adults who wish to adopt children may only do so after they have shown themselves to be sufficiently competent, why do we not also think that the same condition applies to those who wish to procreate? It is 'fundamentally unfair' to impose such restrictions in cases of adoption and not do so in cases of procreation, it has been argued (Bottrell and Macleod, 2015, p. 190). Thus, LaFollette and others reject the notion that there is a right to reproduce, or at least that such a right is unconditional.

Is it the case that if licences are justified in the case of adoptive parents they are justified in the case of biological parents? Let us start with the position of Brighouse and Swift, which has many similarities with LaFollette's. The former argue that an adult's 'right to parent' is conditional 'on the adult's being a good enough parent, on his discharging his fiduciary duties to an adequate standard' (2014, p. 94). That is, as parents exercise 'discretionary powers' that affect the interests of their children, they must accept a 'duty of care' for their children (see Miller and Weijer, 2006, p. 437). Nonetheless, Brighouse and Swift insist that children should not be redistributed from 'merely adequate' parents to those who have higher levels of competence, as this disruption of the family home would cause more harm than good to children. This is one of the relevant, significant differences between the situations of adoptive parents and biological parents, and the reason why the authors do not support LaFollette's licensing programme. In the main, children are living with their biological parents, and because this is the status quo that in itself is one reason to leave children where they are. In contrast, in cases of adoption, the question we are faced with is whether the alternative state of affairs (adoption) is such as to justify the disruption of the status quo (whatever the latter is).

Does it follow from Brighouse and Swift's criticism of parental licences that adults have a right to parent their *biological* children? Anca Gheaus has argued that biological parents have a right to raise the children they have a biological connection with. Not only is there a fundamental right to parent in general, a right based on parents' own interests, as Brighouse and Swift argue, but also a 'parent-interest based right to keep one's birth baby' (Gheaus, 2012, p. 446). This is the case for two reasons. 'First, pregnancies involve a variety of costs – physical, psychological, social and financial. Most of these costs can only be shouldered by pregnant women and, to some extent, their supportive partner. Second, during pregnancy many – perhaps most – expectant parents form a poignantly embodied, but also emotional, intimate relationship with their fetus' (ibid.). However, Brighouse and Swift do not accept that these considerations justify a right to parent one's biological child. They concede that genetic parents will find it 'enjoyable' to notice 'family resemblances' in their children, and it can be 'an enriching experience' to share 'the task of parenting with someone who has come together with you to create a child'. Nonetheless, they conclude, first, 'we doubt that the adult interest in parenting a genetic child can compete with the child's interest in being well parented', and second, even if there are reasons to treat genetic parenting as the default, this is 'not because the genetic parent has a weighty claim to parent a child where there is reason to think somebody else would do a better job' (2014, pp. 106–7; see also Bottrell and Macleod, 2015).

For this line of argument, it is not biology but competence that grounds the right to parent. Like LaFollette, Brighouse and Swift conclude that 'the moral right to parent is conditional on one's ... possessing, and being willing to exercise, the capacities needed properly to play the role of parent' (2014, p. 94). Nonetheless, Brighouse and Swift conclude that 'the bar a parent has to meet in order to count as "good enough" to continue parenting a child may not be much higher than the standard "abuse and neglect" condition', but this is the case largely so as to protect children's interests rather than adults' interests (ibid., p. 96). That is, removing children from their family home puts them at risk because of the initial trauma of the transition and because the change may not bring about improvements of sufficient magnitude to make up for that trauma. What Brighouse and Swift do not accept is that parents have a right to parent their *biological* children grounded in their own interests as adults and parents. If it is better to leave children in their original family home, even when the parents are merely 'good enough' in terms of their competence and other potential parents would be more competent, this is because 'being the current parent of a child makes one a better parent for her than one would otherwise be' (ibid.).

The virtue of this line of thought is that it removes a barrier to the just treatment of children. Parents who are neglecting or abusing a child do not have a right to continue to raise the child on the grounds that they are the child's biological parents. However, such clarity in regard to what may be done to protect children has been secured at a not insignificant cost in terms of moral simplification. For even if we accept the conclusion that a mother who neglects her biological child loses her right to raise that child, it does not follow that the mother did not in the first instance have a right to raise that child that was itself based on a biological connection. Indeed, it is commonly assumed that biology does matter in this way. LaFollette himself acknowledges that, for many people, 'the desire to have a child is central to their sense of self' and also that a 'sizable segment of the population would vehemently resist a robust licensing program' (2010, p. 338). Although we accept that parents must meet certain standards of parenting, and this is the case because of our impartial concern for children's well-being, nonetheless, in everyday life we acknowledge that parents have interests in raising their biological children, and this is reflected in the way we live, which presupposes that biological parents assume certain duties and are owed certain entitlements in raising their children.

Concerning the last point, we should recall what Nagel has referred to as the problem of resolving the 'impersonal' standpoint of impartiality and universality, on the one hand, with the 'personal' standpoint of individualistic motives and requirements, on the other hand (1991, p. 4). If we only accommodate the personal standpoint, we will have a mere hard-nosed realism, where we are limited to the baseness of actual motives. However, if, in contrast, we only accommodate the impersonal standpoint, we run the risk of utopianism, where our morality demands a form of life that is beyond most people because it requires us always to be motivated by universal and impartial considerations. For example, if we must give absolute priority to an impartial concern for children's well-being, to the extent that we do not acknowledge parents' rights to raise their biological children, then, as Gheaus notes in respect of Brighouse and Swift's arguments, there is no principled reason why we should not distribute children away from merely competent parents to those who would be more competent.

The challenge is to find some way to incorporate the personal standpoint, and also to recognise its impersonal value: 'You cannot sustain an impersonal indifference to the things in your life which matter to you personally: some of the most important have to be regarded as mattering, period, so that others besides yourself have reason to take them into account' (Nagel, 1991, p. 11). The fact that I am the biological parent of this particular child is something I cannot be expected to be indifferent to, but also it is something that others must recognise as having impersonal value. Some such understanding is reflected in the everyday practice where, by default, parents have a right to parent their biological children. To put it in Nagel's terms, there is an impersonal value in the personal interest I have in raising my biological child. Arguably, this is a source of resistance to parenting licences that LaFollette and others have not dealt with satisfactorily.

Why we value privacy

While a licensing system for parents raises concerns about the right to parent one's biological children, an alternative approach is the non-voluntary monitoring of families. However, this too is not without its problems, in particular, as it raises concerns about privacy. As we saw in Chapter 7, privacy is defined as 'our ability to control who has access to us, and who knows about us' (Rachels, 1975, p. 329). However, there are worries that, if we guarantee privacy in the family, in effect we will shelter parents from scrutiny in their dealings with their children, and this will hamper our efforts to protect children from harm caused by less than competent parents. But we also saw that we can think of privacy as something that can be guaranteed on behalf of children, and this needs to be considered as well. If we monitor parents so as to better protect their children, will this be an unjustifiable infringement of parental privacy? Not only that, will it be an unjustifiable infringement of children's privacy?

First, let us look at two different ways in which to conceptualise privacy. We need to specify what matters are private so as to identify what intrusions count as violations of one's privacy (Solove, 2002, p. 1104). For some, limited access, privacy, 'allows us to maintain the variety of relationships with other people that we want to value' (Rachels, 1975, p. 329). Whether it is a relationship among friends, one that is professional, or that of a husband and wife or parent and child, in each case the following holds: 'the sort of relationship that people have to one another involves a conception of how it is appropriate for them to behave with each other, and what is more, a conception of the kind and degree of knowledge concerning one another which it is appropriate for them to have' (ibid., p. 328). It is also argued that privacy entails intimacy. For Charles Fried, intimacy is 'the sharing of information about one's actions, beliefs or emotions, which one does not share with all' (1970, p. 142). Privacy is valuable because we value relationships, and that is to say, we value intimacy. Without privacy, we cannot be friends or lovers, but also we cannot be parents or children. The precise type of parent–child relationship, for instance, will vary with changing social conventions, as does the type of information that is shared in that relationship and the type of intimacy that is deemed appropriate. Nonetheless, the relationship of parents to their children exists to the extent it is based on privacy and therefore to the extent intimacy can be assured.

However, it is important not to give too much significance to what can be possessed and too little to the caring aspect of intimate relationships. For example, if I share information with my psychoanalyst, I expect that information to be kept private. I may well share more information with my psychoanalyst than with my daughter; but it does not follow (at least, not as a general rule) that I am more intimate with my analyst than my daughter (Reiman, 1976, p. 33). According to this line of thought, the sharing of information is necessary but not sufficient for intimacy, while exclusive access to information is not even necessary for intimacy. That is, even if the whole world had access to personal information about me and were indifferent to me, I can still enter into an intimate relationship with someone 'who did not just want to collect data about me, but who cared to know about me in order to share my experience with me and to whom I cared to reveal information about myself so that person could share that experience with me, and vice versa' (ibid., p. 34). But if privacy cannot be equated with secrecy *per se*, then the monitoring of families need not undermine privacy. Nonetheless, monitoring will undermine privacy insofar as it is incompatible with the forming of caring, intimate relationships (Innes, 1992, p. 6).

A second way to think about privacy is to see it as an aspect of personal autonomy. In the last chapter, we noted that we cannot simply equate privacy with liberty, as a violation of privacy may not also infringe liberty, and vice versa. Nonetheless, for some, privacy is valuable because of the principle of respect for persons as choosers. This has been described as 'a personhood conception of privacy' (Solove, 2002, p. 1116), as it is incompatible with respect for persons as choosers to alter their conditions of action and conceal this from them (Benn, 1975, p. 8). However, it may well be that considerations of personhood and autonomy *as well as* the importance of caring relations explain the value of privacy. If we consider individual autonomy to be a basis for the right to privacy, it follows we have the right to a private life, a life we can share with intimates, as there are limits to the extent to which we may be subjected to the scrutiny and interference of others, that is, non-intimates (Schoeman, 1984, p. 207). At the same time, according to Reiman, privacy 'protects my capacity to enter into intimate relations, not because it protects my reserve of generally withheld information, but because it enables me to make the commitment that underlies caring as *my* commitment uniquely conveyed by *my* thoughts and witnessed by *my* actions' (1976, p. 44; emphasis in original; see also Rachels, 1975, p. 331).

Therefore, privacy can be thought of as an aspect of personal autonomy *and* the capacity to enter into caring relations. Is privacy valuable to children, and may the monitoring of families pose a threat to children's privacy? As we saw in Chapter 7, we can consider whether children enjoy privacy *vis-à-vis* their parents, that is, whether parents do or do not infringe their children's privacy. And the monitoring of families may be one way to protect children's privacy in this sense, that is, insofar as it protects children from unjustified intrusions by their parents. However, based on what we have said here, we can also think of children's privacy in terms of their capacity to enter into caring relations with their parents. It is the case that children do not bring about the parent–child relationship by their acts and will, but they do have the capacity to assent to and contribute to this intimate relationship. This is important as it allows us to see that the value of privacy within the family lies partly in children's own interests, and not exclusively in parents' interests. Therefore, if we can take this on board when we consider the merits of monitoring families, we must consider not only how this affects children's interests in being safe from abuse and neglect, but also how it affects children's interests in preserving relationships of privacy and intimacy in the family.

The State's promotion of decent parenting

The proposed licensing of parents has been challenged on the grounds that it may infringe the 'right to parent', in particular the right to parent one's biological child. The proposed monitoring of parents has been challenged on the grounds that it may be incompatible with privacy and intimacy in the family. It should be noted that these objections arise in part because of the non-voluntary nature of the proposals: no such objection need arise if I predict I will be an incompetent parent and, for that reason, I choose not to have a child, as some feminists propose. Therefore, it is worth considering what other ways the State may promote competent parenting without interfering with the liberty, or privacy, of parents and children.

First, let us consider whether the non-voluntary aspects can be removed from the proposed licensing programme. When he 'revisited' his proposals in 2010, LaFollette recommended a non-compulsory, non-coercive approach to parenting licences. As we saw, he now proposes providing incentives for attendance at parenting programmes and to issue licences to those who complete such programmes. In his original proposal, he envisaged the State employing its coercive power to prevent adults from becoming parents if they do not pass the required tests. The limited licensing programme would employ the State's non-coercive power instead. It would reward competent parents and therefore encourage parents either to provide evidence of their competence or to improve their competence levels through attending parenting programmes. In a similar fashion, others have argued that the State should provide 'public benefits', such as 'child cash or tax benefits or a paid parental leave', to those who successfully complete parenting programmes (Engster and Gonzales, 2012, p. 232).

If we go down this route, questions then can be asked about how such a parenting programme is to be designed and implemented, and also its likely benefits. For example, some programmes involve universal provision and voluntary enrolment. If such programmes are effective, this would facilitate the State's exercise of power in controlling the environment in which parents exercise power over their children, but do so without interfering with parents' liberty. However, one problem with such an approach is selection bias: that is, those who elect to attend such programmes are not representative of the wider population (Wilson et al., 2012; Coyne and Kwakkenbos, 2013). Those who elect to attend are more ready to adopt what the programme has to offer and the programme is more likely to have greater success here than it would with parents unwilling to do so. Therefore, a not insignificant level of uncertainty remains as to whether such programmes would work for all. An alternative approach is to have programmes based on selective provision and a system of referral whereby those most in need are encouraged, or required, to attend. Such an approach responds to worries about selection bias, but only because of a willingness to countenance interfering with the liberty of adults, and in doing so it resurrects concerns about violating the 'right to parent' and the right to privacy.

Ethical questions

So far we have explored conceptual questions, relevant empirical evidence, and legal, policy, and service issues concerning parental licences and the monitoring and training of parents. In this section I examine two ethical questions that concern, in the main, what the State and its agencies should do, and less so the decisions to be made by parents and children themselves. I ask, should the State license parents even when it cannot predict child abuse with complete accuracy? And should the State monitor parents even when doing so interferes with family privacy? The forgoing suggests that these two ethical questions force us to face conflicting moral claims. In what follows, I will first tease out what I take to be the most significant issues raised by each question, before, in the concluding section of the chapter, offering a defence of specific practical judgements in each instance. In the conclusion I will in addition return to the option of training programmes for parents.

Should the State license parents even when it cannot predict child abuse with complete accuracy?

In order to prepare ourselves to answer this *ethical* question, we must start with a *statistical* one. Statistical considerations play an important role in any evaluation of LaFollette's proposed licensing programme for parents. What we have seen is that, even a highly accurate instrument, one that identifies qualities and characteristics known to be synonymous with child abuse, will falsely label a large number of adults. Adults who are not potential abusers will be mis-labelled as abusers, and adults who are potential abusers will be mis-labelled as non-abusers. These concerns were raised about his proposals soon after the initial publication of his article in 1980. It is noteworthy that, thirty years later, when LaFollette 'revisited' the topic, he did not consider this challenge at all. In his original article, LaFollette does recognise that 'no test' will pick out all those who are competent and only those who are competent. He also believes that 'if the procedures are sufficiently faulty' we should cease to regulate the activity until 'more reliable tests are available'. And yet his conclusion, which can be judged as either unjustifiably optimistic or simply rash, is that 'tests need not be perfect' (1980, p. 184).

When LaFollette refers to the 'accuracy' of the test, as we saw, he does not consider the *proportion* of those wrongly identified by the test, whether wrongly identified as incompetent or as competent. Rather, as I shall try to show, he is interested in a different matter, namely a weighing of the *costs* to the individual wrongly identified as incompetent against the *benefits* to the innocent individuals protected from harm by the licensing programme:

> What counts as a moderately reliable test for these purposes will vary from circumstance to circumstance. For example, if the activity could cause a relatively small amount of harm, yet regulating that activity would place extensive constraints on people regulated, then any tests should be extremely accurate. On the other hand, if the activity could be exceedingly harmful but the constraints on the regulated person are minor, then the test can be considerably less reliable. (ibid., p. 184, n. 2)

In what is an idiosyncratic use of this terminology, LaFollette here equates false positives with less reliable/accurate results, and concludes that a test may be justifiably less reliable/accurate (that is, we tolerate a greater proportion of false positives) when this is necessary so as to better protect the innocent from harm.

The implication of what LaFollette is saying is that, when the harms we are trying to prevent are very serious, we should alter our testing procedure so as to minimise the number of false negatives returned, although this will in turn lead to a larger number of false positives. So, as child abuse is such a serious harm, we should set very high the bar required to pass our test to predict child abuse, which will make it more difficult for potential abusers to pass (it will reduce the number of false negatives), but also more likely that non-abusers will be wrongly identified as potential abusers (it will increase the number of false positives). This is all very well as far as it goes, as this type of trade-off is a feature of the ethical evaluation of the implementation of any such policy. However, making the trade-off in this way cannot be equated with ensuring the greater accuracy of the test. The accuracy of the test is a matter of the *proportion* of those wrongly identified, whether or not they are wrongly identified as competent or incompetent. LaFollette's proposal does not require that the test be made more accurate; it requires only that the inaccuracies be concentrated in one field, namely where non-abusers are wrongly identifying as potential abusers.

Therefore, LaFollette is proposing that we should be willing to accept as legitimate the State's exercise of coercion in preventing adults from becoming parents, in cases where those adults are potential abusers *and* where those adults are wrongly identified as potential abusers. However, one serious shortcoming with the line of argument is that we cannot justify this proposal without first knowing, with the greatest precision possible, the proportion of those affected who have been wrongly categorised as incompetent. This detailed information is completely absent from LaFollette's argument. In addition, we must also include information on all those falsely categorised as competent parents. Even with LaFollette's preferred approach, such errors will occur. This is, once again, necessary information. If we are asked to accept that interfering with adults' 'right to parent' is justified on the grounds that it protects children from harm, we need to know what proportion of children will *not* be protected from harm by such a licensing scheme.

Moreover, even if we did have detailed information on the proportion of false results returned by our predictive test, there is still a substantial problem with LaFollette's argument. This is the case because we may have difficulty reaching agreement on how to determine the relative significance of two outcomes: the constraints wrongly imposed on adults, on the one hand, and the harms prevented to innocent children, on the other hand. We may have difficulty reaching agreement because of differences in value judgements, differences between those who will give priority to the duty to protect children from harm and those who instead will give priority to the duty to protect adults' liberty (see De Wispelaere and Weinstock, 2012). Such a difficulty is not acknowledged in LaFollette's work, and this is the case, I will try to show, because he is engaged in a process of moral simplification.

As protecting children from abuse is the paramount consideration for LaFollette, then the possibility of falsely labelling some adults as potential abusers is deemed a risk worth taking. But, in his argumentation he has diminished the significance of one moral consideration, namely the value of individuals being free to make decisions about their own lives, in this instance, the value of being free to decide to be a parent. To illustrate this point, let us return to Mill's defence of individual liberty. Mill's argument is that we have a duty to protect others' liberty, except when their actions will harm others. So, we *do* have a duty to protect adults' right to parent when *inter alia* their actions will not harm their children. LaFollette has simply not considered the weight of this item in assuming that, when we try to predict who will harm their children, the fact that we falsely label some adults as incompetent parents need not concern us when our aim is to protect children from harm.

Should the State monitor parents even when doing so interferes with family privacy?

As a licensing programme will prevent some adults from parenting who are, in fact, competent to parent, Archard proposes the monitoring of families as a defensible alternative policy. Extensive monitoring would identify situations where children have been harmed and where the children should be removed from the family home. He acknowledges that such monitoring is 'objectionable if it is thought that parents have a right to privacy' (2004, p. 191). Notwithstanding his own 'argument against such a right, its violation would clearly be less objectionable than the removal of children at birth from their natural parents – especially where, as is inevitable with the licensing programme, this is mistakenly done to fit [competent] parents' (ibid.).

At one point, Archard presents his position as an argument *against* the parental right to privacy, in that privacy is appropriate to relations between adults but not to relations between parents and their children (see Chapter 7). However, Archard also acknowledges that parents 'need some degree of privacy and exclusivity in the discharge of their duties of care' (2010, p. 48); and he acknowledges that monitoring does infringe a right to privacy (2004, p. 191), and it is this that is the more accurate account of his position. What his position amounts to is that, in the first instance, parents do have a right to privacy and therefore we are duty bound to protect that right, although, all things considered, we should be willing to infringe that right in attempting to fulfil our duties to promote the well-being of children.

It matters a great deal that we present the argument in this way. Archard mentions only to dismiss the possibility of 'continual observation of parenting' (ibid., p. 173). However, it should be noted that this is one way in which to monitor parents so as to promote children's well-being, and in this case also the parents' right to privacy is infringed. Although Archard believes such continual monitoring is not 'feasible' in our society, in actual fact it is not inconceivable: we do have the technology needed for continual monitoring of parents, as video technology could be fitted in every room of every home, so that parents would be under continual surveillance when they interact with their children. What would the implications of continuous observation of parents be? Well, first, the exercise of coercive power by and through the State's agencies would increase dramatically. The second likely implication is that parents who abuse their children would be less likely to do so and more likely to be caught if they did so. But the third implication, a point that Archard himself makes, would be a potentially devastating impact on the intimacy of the parent–child relation (never mind its impact on other intimate relations in the home).

When we see what implications continual monitoring would have on the parent–child relation, it becomes clear that privacy and intimacy *are* basic requirements of that relation, and that to violate privacy is a *prima facie* bad. Archard may be right that his proposed method of less intrusive family surveillance is justified, but it does not follow that this indicates either that parents do not have a right to privacy or that whatever violation of privacy does occur is of little significance. The question is whether this violation of privacy is to be preferred to the state of affairs that will result if parents are never monitored. What his argument seems to show is that there are good reasons to believe parents do have a right to privacy, but also that his proposals are justified in part because of their only minimal impact on privacy alongside their not inconsiderable potential benefits to children.

Conclusions

When we evaluate the legitimacy of parental licences and the monitoring and training of parents, we are tasked with deciding how the State may exercise power over parents and children so as to better protect children from harm. As we have seen, the State can exercise power in different ways and such power can take various forms. The State can merely exercise control, for example by providing non-compulsory parenting courses designed to promote competent parenting. In contrast, the State can exercise coercive power, such as when it monitors parents and when it implements a licensing system for parents, and in each case imposes sanctions on those who do not meet required standards. I will now consider whether such proposals are justified and whether the exercise of power by the State over parents and children in these ways is legitimate.

Is LaFollette justified in defending a licensing system for parents? As we saw, to answer this question we must consider that, if we implement a licensing system, we will in a certain proportion of cases wrongly categorise some adults as incompetent parents. Therefore, we must consider whether the infringement of the liberty of adults wrongly categorised as incompetent is, all things considered, justified given the potential benefits to innocent children. In order to make this judgement, we can employ Rawls's and Nagel's approach to practical reason. If you are a wrongly categorised adult, is it reasonable to expect you to accept the licensing system responsible for this categorisation on the grounds that this is a small burden to bear given the hoped-for benefits to children?

We must acknowledge that there is a genuine moral dilemma here. It is a *prima facie* bad for the State to interfere with adults' liberty and prevent them becoming parents when in fact they would be competent parents, but also it is a *prima facie* bad not to protect innocent children from abuse at the hands of incompetent parents. Moral considerations are pulling us in different directions and, as we have seen elsewhere in this book, we have not identified a general rule to resolve the conflict between protecting individual liberty and promoting individual well-being. If it was the case that the one and only way to protect children from abusive parents was through a licensing system, we may well then conclude that the attendant infringement of adult liberty is justified. However, given that the impacts of the licensing system on wrongly categorised parents is a *prima facie* bad, we are required to search for alternatives that do not have these negative consequences and yet will protect children. We should explore other ways of protecting children from harm that do not involve imposing such burdens that are, in the first instance, unjustified.

Archard's proposals are, in contrast, a model of pragmatic common sense in this regard. I argued above that we can present his proposals for the monitoring of parents as an effort to balance the value of privacy, on the one hand, and the value of protecting children from harm, on the other hand. If we do not give sufficient consideration to both values, then we are not being reasonable, in Rawls's sense of that term. In particular, it is not reasonable to expect parents to accept continual monitoring of their activities. This is the case, not because we should not expect parents to care about protecting their children, but because continual monitoring would have such dire consequences for the privacy and intimacy that are necessary features of family life. If parents are to be monitored, then it must be restricted and limited.

The same considerations justify the State's provision of parenting support programmes, and also providing incentives to parents to encourage attendance. And this should be done as an alternative to the compulsory licensing of parents, in the first instance as non-compulsory parenting programmes do less harm to parents and children than a licensing system. Nonetheless, it must be borne in mind, the evidence for the effectiveness of voluntary, universal programmes is less than satisfactory, in particular as those who elect to have themselves trained are not going to be representative of parents generally or of incompetent parents in particular. Therefore, by themselves, they are not sufficient. Thus, an argument can be made that the State should provide voluntary parenting programmes and provide incentives for parents to take part, but also implement a non-voluntary monitoring system that does not do significant harm to privacy. Note that in both instances the State is exercising power over parents and children, and in one instance the power is coercive. It is not the State's exercise of coercive power that lacks legitimacy, but its doing so without offering reasonable solutions to the moral dilemmas we have faced here.

9

Children and the provision of informed consent

While in the previous chapter we examined the 'right to parent', and situations where such a right may be justifiably restricted, in this chapter we turn to one area where parents exercise power over their children and examine when it is legitimate to do so. When researchers try to recruit children as participants in a scientific study or when physicians recommend a course of medical treatment for children, a question then arises as to who may authorise such activity. May parents make these decisions on behalf of their children? May children make them independently of their parents? Or should such decisions be made jointly? To address these questions, in this chapter I explore the topic of informed consent, and more precisely, how it is that informed consent authorises children's research participation and medical treatment.

Earlier in this book, we made a distinction between, on the one hand, children's liberty of action, and, on the other hand, both children's voluntariness and their competence in making a given decision (Chapter 1). The distinction is important for a number of reasons. As we saw, parents cannot act paternalistically towards children incapable of liberty of action. In contrast, parents can act paternalistically towards children capable of liberty of action but incompetent, which is called soft paternalism, while if they act paternalistically towards those who are competent this is called hard paternalism. Although of course parents may act non-paternalistically as well, nonetheless whether or not children are competent can be crucial in determining what type of power relation does or may exist with their parents. As the issue of competence helps determine how much power and what type of power parents may rightly exercise over them, it is therefore important, in addition, in determining to what extent children's behaviour can or should be voluntary. And as both voluntariness and competence are, as we shall see now, central to informed consent decisions, both are pivotal to the authorisation of research participation and medical treatment.

How should we define competence? In this chapter, I will argue that people are competent to make a decision if they are able to reflect on the alternative courses of action and the likely consequences of each, and also, crucially, they are aware of the plurality of moral values and the possibility for conflict between those values, and are reasonable in the face of such conflicting moral claims. We shall also consider voluntariness. In this chapter, I argue that people act voluntarily if they will the action without being under the liberty-infringing influence of another. One issue to examine here is whether and in what ways parents can, through the exercise of their power, help their children become more competent and yet without limiting their children's voluntariness.

As in the previous chapter, I will first try to establish the background to this topic, by examining legal, policy, and service issues and empirical evidence relating to children's informed consent. Then, after exploring a number of central conceptual issues, we will be better placed to address two ethical questions concerning children's informed consent: When are parents entitled to take decisions about medical treatment and research participation out of their children's hands? And, in medical practice and research, must consent be sought from both children and their parents?

Legislation, policy, and services

First, I want to investigate some important legal, policy, and service issues concerning informed consent. I start with the legal status of minors and, in particular, the legal rights of minors to make informed consent decisions. It is helpful to compare the legal status of adults and minors on this issue. Although adults are entitled by law to make decisions about their own research participation and medical treatment, nonetheless in any given case an adult may be found incompetent to make such a decision. Indeed, every day, health care providers, researchers, and relatives are tasked with deciding whether adult patients and adult subjects are competent to make such decisions (Buchanan, 2004). Therefore, there are two legal issues to address: the age at which individuals become entitled by law to provide autonomous consent, and the criteria and mechanisms used in judging whether a given individual is competent to make a specific informed consent decision.

In most jurisdictions, age is used as a proxy for both competence and voluntariness. That is, on reaching a certain age, all things being equal, individuals are entitled to the legal protections of those considered to have the necessary competence and voluntariness to make legally-binding commitments. This is the case for decisions about, *inter alia*, marriage, voting, employment, the holding and transferring of property, as well as decisions to authorise medical treatment and research participation. A recent development in both law and medical practice has been to lower, or bring forward in time, the thresholds for competence and voluntariness. For example, adolescents are entitled to provide informed consent for research participation independently of their parents in Denmark, if certain conditions are met, when they are over the age of fifteen, and in New Zealand when they are over the age of sixteen (Felzmann et al., 2010, p. 62). In this way, a substantial number of adolescents are categorised as being entitled by law to provide autonomous consent. With respect to medical care, the term 'mature minor' is used to refer to the legal construct that 'considers adolescents, as far as possible, as equivalent to adults for the purpose of medical decision making' (Partridge, 2014, p. 300). Once the adolescent has passed the new, lower threshold, they are considered entitled to consent to medical treatment.

A separate but related change is the development and use of criteria and mechanisms to identify individual minors entitled to provide autonomous consent independent of their parents. In the UK, the so-called 'test of Gillick competency' can be applied in deciding whether a child under the age of sixteen is 'deemed mature enough to understand the nature and implications of a clinical treatment or procedure' (Hunter and Pierscionek, 2007, p. 659; see General Medical Council, 2007).[1] The explanation for this innovation is at least two-fold. First, there is growing recognition of children's capacity for liberty of action and competence, and also children's rights to have a say in matters that affect them (United Nations, 1989, Article 12). The second explanatory factor concerns practitioners' duty of care to their patients. The Gillick case (*Gillick* v. *W. Norfolk and Wisbech AHA* [1985]), and the so-called 'Fraser guidelines' for providing treatment to a child, developed in response to this case, applied initially to the provision of contraceptive advice to girls under the age of sixteen, and specifically, in cases where the doctor cannot persuade the patient to inform her parents or allow the doctor to 'inform the parents that she is seeking contraceptive advice' (Cornock, 2007, p. 142). Crucially, in availing of this option, the doctor must be motivated by a duty of care to the patient. A doctor should only provide such advice if otherwise 'her [the patient's] physical or mental health or both are likely to suffer' and 'her best interests require him to give her contraceptive advice, treatment, or both without parental consent' (ibid.).

The test of Gillick competency applies to decisions about medical treatment, and as yet it has not been established in law that it can be employed in research (NPSA, 2007). If Gillick competency were to be employed in research, however, it is recommended that only a third party, with no involvement in the study in question, should decide whether or not a young person is competent. This is the case, it is argued, as researchers have a vested interest in recruiting participants and also because many researchers will not have the necessary training to make such a decision (Hunter and Pierscionek, 2007). The fear that unscrupulous or careless researchers may mis-use the test of Gillick competency may be explained by concerns over the robustness of the test itself. I shall return to this issue below when we consider the empirical evidence for children's competence.

As we have seen, the literature on informed consent focuses on both the age at which individuals become entitled by law to make informed consent decisions, and the criteria and mechanisms used in judging whether a given individual is competent to make a specific informed consent decision. Of course, these considerations can, on occasion, pull in opposing directions. Thus, if individuals have reached a certain age they may be entitled by law to provide autonomous consent. Nonetheless, any such individual may be deemed incompetent in a given instance, when the relevant criteria and mechanisms are applied. Not only that, individuals below the legal threshold may be deemed competent based on the application of the same criteria and mechanisms.

Empirical evidence

Empirical findings are important when we consider the lowering (or raising) of legal thresholds as well as when judgements are made about the competence and voluntariness of any given individual. The rationale for lowering the age threshold for autonomous consent is that many adolescents have the capacities required to make informed consent decisions. Do the findings support such a development?

First, there are many studies claiming to show that adolescents have the capacities required to provide informed consent. It is argued that many adolescents have developed beyond the stage of 'autonoetic consciousness', which involves the ability to understand one's own situation, the consequences of alternative courses of action, and the relevant information in making decisions (Metcalfe and Son, 2012). Instead, many adolescents have attained fully developed agency, 'a notion of self that is partly constructed out of our descriptions and some articulated sense of our lives' (Baker, 2013, p. 317). That is, such adolescents have the capacity to make decisions that will shape their lives and their identities. While Baker has focused in on the moral agency of children here, others have addressed the empirical evidence for children's decision making capacities more generally (Taylor, 2013, p. 286). And empirical studies have returned mixed findings in regard to how the competence of adolescents compares to that of adults (Halpern-Felsher and Cauffman, 2001; Miller et al., 2004). Nonetheless, some have observed *no differences* between tenth graders (fifteen to sixteen years of age) and adults in terms of their 'comprehension of the research procedures, risks and benefits, voluntary nature of participation, and confidentiality protections' (Bruzzese and Fisher, 2003, p. 13; see Weithorn and Campbell, 1982).

Adolescents may differ little from adults when we consider cognitive functioning in isolation, as above. However, it is argued that they differ markedly when we consider both cognitive and affective dimensions together (Piker, 2011, p. 205). Indeed, on that basis, many adolescents do *not* have the necessary decision making capacities to provide informed consent. There is evidence of 'faulty perceptions of risk, inadequate capacities to gauge the long-term outcomes of their decisions, and more limited control of their impulses' (Partridge, 2014, p. 300). These conclusions are based in part on studies of children's brain development. One study found that high risk behaviours among children may be explained by a later maturing of the prefrontal areas of the brain responsible for executive control in combination with the important role played at this age by limbic areas of the brain responsible for the high importance given to rewards and to affective considerations (Galvan et al., 2006). Similarly, risky behaviour among adolescents has been traced back to comparatively under-developed cognitive control and the greater significance of social cognition. That is, adolescents understand and evaluate risky behaviour not only in terms of the possible negative consequences for their own well-being but also in terms of the approval and commendation they may receive as a result from their peers (Rodrigo et al., 2014).

Therefore, we cannot say that the available data establish with certainty that adolescents have sufficient competence for independent decision making in research and medical care. At the very least, there is a strong suggestion that adolescents differ from adults in their decision making competence. In any case, even if adolescents are considered equivalent to adults for the purpose of decision making, as is required by the 'mature minor' construct, it does not follow that each and every adolescent will be judged competent. Rather, when we lower the thresholds, we commit ourselves to treat adolescents and adults alike, but, as we have seen, many adults, in given situations, are judged incompetent to make informed consent decisions. Lowering thresholds cannot provide the final word on whether any one adolescent is considered competent to provide informed consent. Therefore, the next issue to address is how we can make reliable decisions about the competence of individuals.

As we have already seen, in the UK the 'test of Gillick competency' is employed in medical decisions for those under sixteen years of age (Wheeler, 2006, p. 807). However, as alluded to above, this approach has attracted much criticism. It is considered 'subjective', both because the decision as to whether an individual minor is competent is left up to the individual physician and also because 'there are no objective guidelines to assist with decision making' (Hunter and Pierscionek, 2007, p. 659). As Sarah Neill points out, the UK government has not produced guidance on how to assess competence beyond the following statements drawn from the Gillick case: 'a competent child is one who "achieves a sufficient understanding and intelligence to enable him or her to understand fully what is proposed" in the medical treatment concerned; the child must also have "sufficient discretion to enable him or her to make a wise choice in his or her own interests"' (*Gillick* v. *W. Norfolk and Wisbech AHA* [1985] AC 112, in Neill, 2005, p. 48). What is meant here by 'understanding', 'intelligence', 'discretion', and 'wise choice', and how any of these would be identified or measured in a non-arbitrary way, is not clarified. The lack of any satisfactory answer to these questions may force us to look elsewhere for guidance.

One promising alternative is the MacArthur Competence Assessment Tool, which is designed to assess whether, in making a decision that does not conform to our expectations, the decision maker has nonetheless followed a rational process (Berg et al., 1996, p. 358). Developed initially for medical decision making, it is offered as a structured instrument for assessing decision making capacity. The instrument tests whether the patient has the capacity to (1) communicate a choice, (2) understand the relevant information, (3) appreciate the situation and its consequences, and (4) reason about treatment options. For each of these four criteria, the patient is given a task and the physician has a number of questions to ask (see Table 9.1). For example, to assess the patient's capacity to reason about treatment options, the patient is required to engage in a rational process of manipulating the relevant information, while the physician asks such questions as 'How did you decide to accept or reject the recommended treatment?' and 'What makes [chosen option] better than [alternative option]?'

The MacArthur test is the most widely-used instrument, it is argued, because it is a structured interview that 'incorporates information specific to a given patient's decision making situation' (Appelbaum, 2007, p. 1837). However, critics suggest that the MacArthur test is not suitable to the difficulties some patients face. For example, although adolescents and young adults (aged thirteen–twenty-one) suffering from anorexia nervosa scored highly on the MacArthur test in one study, their refusal to accept treatment suggested that they were not fully competent. That is, it is claimed, the test does not work with those for whom, because of the effects of their medical condition on their decision making, death is relatively unimportant (Tan et al., 2003, p. 704).

However, this criticism may not do justice to the difficult issue being grappled with by Appelbaum and others, namely, how to resolve a tension between two competing values. For Appelbaum, the decision about whether an individual is competent 'should ideally reflect a societal judgment about the appropriate balance between respecting the patient's autonomy and protecting the patient from the consequences of a bad decision' (2007, p. 1836). I return to the tension between these two values below. However, for now we can say that individuals willing to make decisions that will bring about their own death may be incompetent. But they may not. This is the case because, for Appelbaum and others, we do not make a judgement of competence solely by reference to the question of how the decision will affect the individual's own well-being. It is possible that risky behaviour can be based on competent decisions.

So far we have looked at the empirical evidence for children's competence to provide informed consent. We have access to the findings from studies evaluating children's competence as well as the criteria and assessment tools employed by professionals to judge the competence of individual minors. One objection to such an approach is that it seems to treat competence as an all-or-nothing quality. That is, it assumes that either given individuals have passed the threshold or they have not; and that either a given population of children (children in a specific age range say) fit the category or they do not. An alternative approach is to acknowledge that adolescents have competence in a formative state, and also it can be nurtured and developed with the help of parents and other adults (Piker, 2011). That is, individual children can be more or less competent in their decision making, and the power of parents can be more or less limiting of children's voluntariness. To examine this possibility, I want to consider the evidence for joint or collaborative decision making between parents and children.

It is argued that adolescents are more likely to seek out the support of their parents rather than a professional when making medical decisions. For example, in a meta-ethnology that synthesised the findings from qualitative studies of adolescent contraceptive use, parents played a more important role than health care providers with regard to adolescents' decision making (Daly, 2014). However, the studies showed that parents' influence could be either negative or positive. Adolescents were negatively affected by parental silence and mixed messages around contraceptive use. In contrast, mothers that were viewed 'as a support provided information about contraception and pregnancy prevention [...] were open, talked about sex proactively, began conversations when their teens were young, and provided their daughters with a reason to delay sexual activity' (Daly, 2014, p. 629).

Table 9.1 Legally relevant criteria for decision making capacity and approaches to assessment of the patient (adapted from Appelbaum, 2007)

Criterion	Patient's task	Physician's assessment approach	Questions for clinical assessment	Comments
Communicate a choice	Clearly indicate preferred treatment option	Ask patient to indicate a treatment choice	Have you decided whether to follow your doctor's [or my] recommendation for treatment? Can you tell me what that decision is? [If no decision] What is making it hard for you to decide?	Frequent reversals of choice because of psychiatric or neurologic conditions may indicate lack of capacity
Understand the relevant information	Grasp the fundamental meaning of information communicated by physician	Encourage patient to paraphrase disclosed information regarding medical condition and treatment	Please tell me in your own words what your doctor [or I] told you about: The problem with your health now The recommended treatment The possible benefits and risks (or discomforts) of the treatment Any alternative treatments and their risks and benefits The risks and benefits of no treatment	Information to be understood includes nature of patient's condition, nature and purpose of proposed treatment, possible benefits and risks of that treatment, and alternative approaches (including no treatment) and their benefits and risks

Appreciate the situation and its consequences	Acknowledge medical condition and likely consequences of treatment options	Ask patient to describe views of medical condition, proposed treatment, and likely outcomes	What do you believe is wrong with your health now? Do you believe that you need some kind of treatment? What is treatment likely to do for you? What makes you believe it will have that effect? What do you believe will happen if you are not treated? Why do you think your doctor has [or I have] recommended this treatment?	Courts have recognised that patients who do not acknowledge their illnesses (often referred to as 'lack of insight') cannot make valid decisions about treatment Delusions or pathologic levels of distortion or denial are the most common causes of impairment
Reason about treatment options	Engage in a rational process of manipulating the relevant information	Ask patient to compare treatment options and consequences and to offer reasons for selection of option	How did you decide to accept or reject the recommended treatment? What makes [chosen option] better than [alternative option]?	This criterion focuses on the process by which a decision is reached, not the outcome of the patient's choice, since patients have the right to make 'unreasonable' choices

It is also argued that making decisions in collaboration with their parents can help nurture the decision making capacities of adolescents (Partridge, 2014, p. 305). The evidence cited in support of collaborative or joint decision making points to possible benefits in respect of children's cognitive functioning. One recent study compared outcomes for, on the one hand, adolescents who collaborated with their parents in decision making and, on the other hand, adolescents whose parents made decisions for them. There were no differences between the two groups of adolescents for working memory and academic performance. Nonetheless, collaborative decision making led to improved affective decision making and also less risky behaviour (in this case, 'binge drinking') along with a related 'development of neurocognitive functioning' (Xiao et al., 2011, p. 285). This finding is important given that, as we saw, the differences in decision making between adolescents and adults, in the main, concern affective decision making and risky behaviour.

Partridge concludes that adolescents are 'apprentice decision-makers' and therefore we should not 'isolate adolescents from the guidance of their parents' (2014, p. 306). This is the case, first, because adolescents need to be protected from their own poor decision making; and also, second, collaborative decision making helps adolescents 'to develop into mature decision-makers with the capacity to make medical choices on their own, all the while recognizing the need for exceptions in particular cases' (ibid.). We should note that, on this formulation, joint decision making derives its justification from the primacy given to one value, protecting children from harm. Given the risks posed for adolescents by their own poor decision making, 'we should be more concerned about false positive determinations of maturity' than false negatives (Partridge, 2013, p. 295). Is it the case that we should require children to engage in joint decision making rather than independent decision making, even when we mistakenly think the children lack the competence to make their own decisions, and that this is justified by the fundamental concern we have to protect children from harm? I return to this question below.

Conceptual issues

Our discussion of legal, policy, and service issues, empirical findings about children's competence, professional judgements of competence, and the impact of parenting on children's competence, indicate where conceptual clarification is greatly needed. I will focus, below, on how to define informed consent, what forms of influence endanger voluntariness, the relationship between joint decision making and voluntariness, whether parents have authority over their children with respect to informed consent decisions, and how to define competence.

Informed consent

Informed consent has a number of necessary elements, as laid out by Beauchamp and Childress (2009, pp. 120–1). First, there are two consent elements, both the 'decision' in favour of a plan and the 'authorisation' of the chosen plan. In addition, those seeking informed consent are responsible for the full 'disclosure' of material information and (in therapeutic procedures) the 'recommendation' of a plan, while those whose consent is being sought must have sufficient 'understanding' of both of these. Finally, those consenting must have sufficient 'competence' to understand and to decide, and sufficient 'voluntariness' in deciding. As Beauchamp and Childress emphasise, these are the required elements of informed consent with respect to children as well as adults (ibid., p. 116). Therefore, if children are to provide informed consent, for research participation and medical treatment, the research and medical staff must fully disclose the relevant information and recommend a plan, the children must understand the information provided and also provide their consent, but also the children themselves must be sufficiently competent and their behaviour sufficiently voluntary.

I will focus here on the concepts of competence and voluntariness. For Beauchamp and Childress, competence refers to 'the ability to perform a task', in this case the task of making a decision, and a person may be considered competent 'relative to the particular decision to be made' without being considered competent relative to other tasks or other decisions (ibid., pp. 112, 116). In addition, they argue, judgments of competence are of an all-or-nothing quality; competence is a threshold concept for them. Although competence is relative to a specific task, nonetheless the function of competence judgments, they argue, is to distinguish two classes: 'persons whose decisions should be solicited or accepted from persons whose decisions need not or should not be solicited or accepted' (ibid., p. 111). Similarly, voluntariness is thought of as a threshold. According to their definition, a 'person acts voluntarily if he or she wills the action without being under the control of another's influence' (ibid., p. 133).

Taken together, the threshold criteria of competence and voluntariness would suggest that, if children do not meet the thresholds, morally speaking they should not make decisions in informed consent procedures and instead those decisions should be made by their parents (or other adults in relevant positions of responsibility). In such cases, parents would be surrogate decision makers on behalf of their incompetent children. In the next sections, I want to critically examine more closely this idea that voluntariness and competence are thresholds and to explore alternative ways of thinking about children's informed consent. On the one hand, is it possible for parents to foster and enhance competence where it was not evident before? On the other hand, is it possible for parents to engage in joint decision making with their already-competent children and yet in doing so not undermine their children's voluntariness?

Voluntariness and forms of influence

If children are to provide informed consent, their behaviour must be sufficiently voluntary. What is meant by voluntary behaviour, and what influences are and are not compatible with voluntariness? Earlier we argued voluntary action is free from the liberty-infringing influence of others as well as the excessive influence of unnoticed or uncontrollable urges and compulsions (see Chapter 1). Thus, voluntariness can be undermined by features of a person's illness, for example, debilitating disease, psychiatric disorders, and drug addiction (Beauchamp and Childress, 2009, p. 133). However, as the concept of competence can be used to capture the concern with internal urges and compulsions, I will focus here, instead, on the types of external influences that have an impact on voluntariness, and in doing so explore power relations and their impact on children's voluntariness. In previous chapters, we examined various forms of 'power over', including authority, paternalism, control, coercion, and interference with liberty. Which of these forms of influence do or do not undermine voluntariness?

First, voluntariness is not undermined by *persuasion*. If I persuade my child to make a particular decision, the decision to consent to participate in research, for instance, I do not in that way undermine my child's voluntariness. Rather, my child will come to believe in something through the 'merit of the reasons' I have advanced (ibid.). For example, I may persuade my daughter that participating in the research project will be beneficial for her, or I may convince her that it will be good for other children like her, and so on, and she may make her decision on the basis of the merits of my argument.

In contrast, *coercion* does undermine voluntariness. My daughter is coerced only if she recognises that she has been threatened with sanctions, and if that threat is credible to her and therefore sufficient to explain her subsequent behaviour. For example, I coerce my daughter to consent to participate in a research study if I threaten to impose some punishment should she refuse, and if this threatened punishment is of such a great magnitude from her perspective as to make her not fully responsible for her subsequent actions.

Manipulation can also undermine voluntariness, although it need not. I can manipulate my daughter, and thus sway her to do as I wish, by managing the information provided to her, by lying, by withholding information, and by misleading exaggeration (ibid., p. 134). In such circumstances, we are justified in saying I have interfered with my daughter's liberty, *if* my manipulation is such as to remove certain options from her. However, as we saw, manipulation need not entail interference with another's liberty (see Chapter 5). If I present options to my daughter in such a way that some (e.g. participation in a study) seem preferable to others, it does not follow that other options (e.g. not participating in a study) have been removed. It is possible that my daughter is still free to choose not to participate in the study, and to do so in a meaningful sense, although if my manipulation has been efficacious she will be less inclined to do so.

Without using coercion or manipulation, I can *interfere with my daughter's liberty* simply by removing some of her options. Beauchamp and Childress do not mention this possibility. However, non-coercive interference with liberty will undermine the voluntariness of the subsequent behaviour. If I do not want my daughter to participate in a study there are many non-coercive means available to me to remove that option from her. For example, I can arrange a family holiday to coincide with the scheduled fieldwork. In this way, the option is simply taken off the table; it is no longer an option my daughter can choose. Such an approach is not coercive insofar as I have not threatened a sanction; and it need not involve manipulation either.

Authority is compatible with voluntariness. Beauchamp and Childress also do not consider authority as a form of influence. However, if parents have a rightful claim to authority, that is, legitimate authority, then children owe a duty of obedience to their parents. In addition, as authority refers to voluntary obedience it *is* compatible with voluntariness. I have authority over my daughter when she willingly complies with or obeys me and does so for the reason that she recognises I am 'in authority'. For example, I may command or order my daughter to participate in a study. If she obeys this command for the reason that she believes I have legitimate authority then, and for that reason, she will act voluntarily.

Finally, as *paternalism* can take any of the forms of power mentioned above, then paternalism will undermine voluntariness when it removes an option, including when it is coercive, but otherwise it will not.

So, how should we define voluntariness? For Beauchamp and Childress, a 'person acts voluntarily if he or she wills the action without being under the control of another's influence' (ibid., p. 133). There is one sense in which their conceptualisation is certainly justified. Even when individuals' voluntariness is absent with respect to many decisions made about their life, nonetheless it is possible for a person to act voluntarily in regard to any one decision. This is important as it allows us to examine whether individuals have made voluntary decisions even though much of their life is involuntary in the sense that decisions are made for them and against their wishes. This is true of individuals 'admitted involuntarily' to an institution (ibid.). It is true of anyone subject to the power of another with regards to the major decisions in their life, and therefore it is true of children living in the family home with their parents.

However, there is one sense in which Beauchamp and Childress's definition of voluntariness is too narrow. It defines children's acts as voluntary if they will the action without being under the control of another's influence. However, as we have seen from our discussion of the forms of 'power over', I can control my daughter without either coercing her or interfering with her liberty, that is, without diminishing the voluntariness of her actions. For example, if I persuade her, if I have legitimate authority over her, and even in some cases where I manipulate her, I control her, I exercise power over her, but I do not undermine the voluntariness of her actions. It follows that we should define voluntariness more broadly. As I said, I am concerned here with forms of influence that may limit voluntariness, leaving to one side internal compulsions and their effect on voluntariness. With that in mind, the broader definition of voluntariness is as follows: *A person acts voluntarily if he or she wills the action without being under the control of another's liberty-infringing influence.*

Joint decision making

I want to return now to the idea of joint decision making between parents and children, and examine what impact joint decision making has on children's liberty. To start with we should note that, for some, joint decision making is valuable because it is compatible with a certain type of autonomy, namely 'relational autonomy'. I want to examine whether that is the case and I want to do so by making a distinction between joint decision making and the notion of freedom from interference.

It is argued by some that we should *not* think of autonomy in terms of the individual's self-sufficiency in decision making. Rather, 'self-realization is only achieved relationally'; and 'individuals' identities, interests, ends, and beliefs [should be seen] as fundamentally dynamic, continually constructed and reconstructed in dialogical processes with other people' (Walter and Ross, 2014, p. 19; see Mackenzie, 2008). Autonomy is relational, therefore, rather than a feature of isolated individuals. Thus, according to this line of thought, if parents do engage their child in a process of joint decision making, this will be respectful of the child's future autonomy, even if in the process the parents overrule the child's expressed wishes, and on occasion do so in order to better promote the interests of other family members (Walter and Ross, 2014, p. 21). The argument is that there has been no violation of the child's 'relational autonomy' here, given that the child's self-realisation and interests are both inextricably intertwined with those of other family members.

However, an alternative way to look at such a situation suggests itself. For it is the case that, in the first instance, the parents have violated the child's liberty, although this may be, all things considered, justified so as to promote the interests of other family members. If that is the case, a more general conclusion follows. On some occasions, joint decision making will violate the voluntariness of one or more of the participants. In contrast to the relational autonomy approach, we need to be able to make such distinctions.

Let us move beyond the relational autonomy approach therefore. However, a further problem remains. Let us imagine my daughter *does* reach a decision voluntarily, through a process of joint decision making based on persuasion. Nonetheless, it may be that her initial involvement in the decision making process was involuntary. This would be the case, for example, if she takes part only because I or someone else threaten her with a sanction; or remove other options. Even if the resulting decision making is genuinely voluntary, in our normative evaluation of the situation it matters that I interfere with my child's liberty so as to put in place the decision making process itself. Note this is *not* a problem if my child agrees to engage in joint decision making out of respect for my authority, as willing compliance is compatible with voluntariness. However, as we shall see, the process of joint decision making itself is inimical to authority. I return to this latter point below.

It is illustrative to reflect on what is distinctive about parent–child joint decision making. Two adults may come together, through voluntary association, for the purpose of making a decision jointly, and this is akin to a type of pure contract situation. In contrast, prior to any engagement in joint decision making, children and parents are already in a relationship, indeed, a power relation. What is more, parenting programmes advise parents to coerce their children, and in doing so create opportunities for positive, beneficial activities, including joint decision making. For example, parents are advised to remove bad options so that children cannot choose them (e.g. the bad option of risky behaviour) and parents are advised to threaten their children with sanctions for engaging in such bad behaviour (e.g. the punishment of 'planed ignoring', or the loss of a reward such as story-time, for younger children) (Sanders, 1999).

Therefore, parents can be faced with a conflict of values when they attempt to promote joint decision making. A child can act voluntarily when making decisions jointly, and the intended outcome can be to promote the child's competence as an independent decision maker. However, to promote joint decision making effectively, a parent may well be required to interfere with the child's liberty. That is, we can be faced with a situation where parents should refrain from interfering with their children's liberty in respect of some of the features of the case and in respect of other features they should interfere with their children's liberty (see Williams, 1965).

Authority

We already touched on the idea of parents' authority in this chapter, and I want to explore this in a little more detail now. If parents have the right to authorise children's participation in research and receipt of health care, independent of their children's assent or consent, does this entail that the children have a duty to obey their parents? Do parents have *de jure* authority in this instance? If they do, at the very least, it involves a surrender of private judgement and deference on the part of the children, as the voice of the child is not heard in making the decision in question. The parents who act in this way, at the very least, claim a right to command. It is a *de facto* authority relation, as the parents' actions imply that they are qualified to act on their children's behalf. The remaining question is whether this is *de jure*. And a lot hangs on this, for if parents' authority is legitimate, then children have a corresponding duty to obey their parents.

In the literature on parent–child power relations, a number arguments are made for the 'authority' of parents. However, little or no mention is made of children's corresponding duty of obedience (Archard, 2010, pp. 51–8; Brighouse and Swift, 2014, pp. 67ff.). It is argued not just that parents have a 'right to parent' but that they have rights 'over, or with respect to, their children' (Brighouse and Swift, 2014, p. 93). Brighouse and Swift distinguish the two rights and provide quite different justifications for each. The 'right to parent', they argue, is based on parents' own interests in a certain kind of caring relationship with their children (see Chapter 8). Here the authors are concerned with defending this right against those outside the family most likely to interfere with its exercise, in particular the State and its agencies. In contrast, the rights parents may claim over their children are 'just those rights that it's in their children's interests for them to have' (ibid., pp. 93–4). This is an interfamilial matter, as it concerns both 'what it is that parents must be free to do to, with, or for their children' (ibid., p. 118), and also 'the limits of legitimate parental authority over children' (ibid., p. 116).

Despite providing an argument for parents' authority, nonetheless, Brighouse and Swift will not insist that children have a duty to obey their parents. They associate talk of children's duties with an authoritarian parenting style: 'An unloving carer may perhaps command compliance through fear, but the important developmental aim of disciplining a child is not at-the-moment compliance but over-time internalization' (ibid., p. 73). Parental commands are associated with un-loving parenting and parenting based on fear. If Brighouse and Swift are uncomfortable with the idea of children having duties of obedience to their parents, the cause of their discomfort may be lessened by considering the plural forms of 'power over'. At a conceptual level, we know that coercion cannot be equated with threats of violence, as sanctions take various forms, but not only that, neither can authority be equated with coercion. In any one situation, children may be duty-bound to obey their parents' exercise of non-coercive control and, at the same time, free from any duty to obey their parents' exercise of coercive power. Indeed, even if the parents' use of coercion is legitimate, it does not follow that their children have a duty to obey in this instance. They may have but they may not. Given this plurality, children's duty of obedience cannot be equated with un-loving parenting and parenting based on fear. So we should be more ready to talk of parents' right to command and children's duty of obedience and in that way better prepared to consider the legitimacy of such power relations.

Before moving on, I need to say something about authority, voluntariness, and joint decision making. I said above that parents may command or order children to participate in joint decision making, and also the children will act voluntarily if the explanation for their obedience is their belief that their parents' command is legitimate. Nonetheless, authority is not compatible with the actual process of joint decision making itself if the latter is to be based on persuasion. This is the case because authority involves the surrender of private judgement, or deference. If children acknowledge their parents' authority, they acknowledge their right to command them and that this right to command is independent of the content of that command (Raz, 1986; Wrong, 1995 [1979]). In contrast, the process of joint decision making can be not only voluntary but also one of 'persuasion through rational argument', and the latter is incompatible with authority (Friedman, 1990 [1973], p. 67). If parents engage in a (persuasive) joint decision making process with their children then, with respect to what is decided upon, the children do *not* have a duty to obey their parents independent of the content of the command. The resulting decision should be binding for both parents and children, but this is because it has resulted from a particular type of process, a process that is inimical to authority.

Competence

Having explored some of the issues arising in conceptualising voluntariness, we turn now to the other crucial aspect of informed consent, namely competence. Let us first address the rival standards of competence, ranging from the very weakest to the strongest. The weak standard does *not* require that a competent individual makes a rational decision. It defines competence 'exclusively as an ability to carry out certain mental tasks: to understand the information relevant to making the decision; to appreciate how this information applies to oneself in one's current situation; and to realize that one is being asked to make a decision about the treatment(s) being suggested' (Culver and Gert, 1990, p. 622). As this weak standard does not include any requirement of rationality, an individual judged competent to make a decision may nonetheless make an irrational decision. In contrast, the strong standard requires not only 'the ability to state a preference' and the ability to 'understand one's situation and its consequences' and to 'understand relevant information', but also the ability to 'give a reason', to 'give a rational reason', to 'give risk/benefit-related reasons', and to 'reach a reasonable decision (as judged, for example, by a reasonable person standard)' (Beauchamp and Childress, 2009, p. 114–15). An example of the strong standard of competence was provided above by the work of Paul Appelbaum and colleagues, in particular the MacArthur test of competence.

It should be noted that proponents of the weak standard accept that the rationality of people's decisions *is* relevant when judging whether they should be permitted to make those decisions. For instance, an adult judged competent by the weak standard can still make irrational decisions, and when a refusal of medical treatment is 'seriously irrational, as when the consequences are death or serious and permanent injury', 'the refusal should be overruled' (Culver and Gert, 1990, p. 623). That is, even those who propose the weak standard of competence include all the elements of the strong standard in judging whether or not to permit individuals to make decisions. Therefore, although there is disagreement over whether irrational decisions are by definition also incompetent decisions, and although there is room for disagreement over what counts as an irrational decision (as we shall see), nonetheless there is a consensus position, namely that we are not required to respect seriously irrational decisions, and this is the case for adults and children. Therefore, we are not required to respect what are, according to the strong standard, incompetent decisions.

What makes a decision incompetent in this 'strong' sense? For what reasons are we justified in judging someone else incompetent to make a decision? It is clear from the literature that more than one moral consideration is in play when we try to answer this question, and also that those values can come into conflict. The consensus position above is informed by both the value of individual well-being and the value of individual autonomy. Individuals are entitled to provide informed consent insofar as they have the capacity to make decisions about how to govern their lives generally (i.e. the value of individual autonomy) and also how to promote their well-being specifically (i.e. the value of individual well-being). However, these values 'can sometimes conflict' (Buchanan and Brock, 1986, p. 30). While the value of well-being requires that we sometimes protect individuals from the consequences of their own decisions, autonomy is of value as people want to make decisions about their own life, and the desire to make such decisions 'is in part independent of whether they believe that they are always in a position to make the best choice' (ibid., p. 29).

When judging the competence of a decision, the possible negative consequences for the decision maker do matter. For example, in the UK, the General Medical Council recommends that doctors should adhere to decisions made by competent children. Nonetheless, it warns that 'a young person who has the capacity to consent to straightforward, relatively risk-free treatment may not necessarily have the capacity to consent to complex treatment involving high risks or serious consequences' (2007, p. 12). While there is a general commitment to children's autonomous decision making, doctors must protect children against harms caused by their own risky decisions. However, although it is agreed that the values of well-being and autonomy may come into conflict, there is no agreement over how to deal with such a clash of values, in particular when we consider decisions that are thought to pose a significant risk to the decision maker.

All that we have said so far about moral conflicts strongly suggests that we are not justified in arguing that, as a general rule, one of these values has priority, and that a decision is competent just insofar as it promotes this value. Unfortunately, this is precisely the type of argument that has been made about competence, and it has resulted in the development of two incompatible, entrenched positions on this topic. Some prioritise individual well-being in the conceptualisation of competence, arguing 'that, at least in general, competent individuals are better judges of their own good than others are', and so conclude that we have greater latitude to interfere in other's decisions in situations where 'the severity of the expected harm and the possibility of its occurrence' are high (Buchanan and Brock, 1986, p. 28, p. 37). Others prioritise individual autonomy in the conceptualisation of competence, arguing that individuals are entitled to make a decision that does not conform to our expectations (Berg et al., 1996), what others believe to be 'unreasonable' decisions, and so conclude that 'only patients with impairment that places them at the very bottom of the performance curve should be considered to be incompetent' (Appelbaum, 2007, p. 1836).

I want to suggest an alternative conceptualisation of competence. I have already put forward and defended a specific account of practical judgement, and we can apply this directly now to the conceptualisation of competence. Indeed, we can define competence as reasonable practical judgement. What we have seen is that, in making informed consent decisions, competent decision makers must understand the relevant information and the situation they are in, and provide rational reasons for the course of action they have chosen. They are also faced with moral values that can come into conflict. Returning to practical judgement, according to our conception, in making practical judgements we consult with others where appropriate, we take on board and evaluate the relevant information, but also we address and attempt to resolve any conflicting moral values (see Chapter 3). In bringing these together, it follows, we should judge individuals competent not insofar as their decision will best promote any specific value, but rather insofar as they are capable of reflecting on the alternative courses of action, the likely consequences of each, and also, crucially, the values at stake in making the decision.[2]

And how does the competent individual reflect on these values? It is *not* the case that, as a matter of definition, decisions made where there is a lot at stake require giving priority to one moral value. We should define competence neither exclusively as the ability to promote one's own well-being nor exclusively as the ability to reason autonomously so as to attain whatever it is one takes to be one's good. Rather, competence refers to what is needed so as to work through moral conflicts. Therefore, competence involves an awareness of the plurality of moral values and the possibility for conflict between those values, as well as reasonableness in deliberating in the face of conflicting moral claims. In the next section, I hope to illustrate how the competent individual can work through moral conflicts in this way.

Ethical questions

What are the central ethical questions that arise when we consider children's informed consent? In this section, I will ask whether researchers and physicians are required to seek informed consent from both children and their parents, and also whether parents are entitled to take these decisions out of their children's hands. I will first tease out the main issues that arise when we are faced with these questions and then, in the concluding section of this chapter, turn to specific practical judgements concerning the legitimacy of parents' power over their children in regard to each question.

When are parents entitled to take decisions out of their children's hands?
Parents often take decisions out of their children's hands, and as a result children are not permitted to act as they otherwise would. When may parents exercise their power in this way? Let us look at one example drawn from the literature on clinical trials.

In our example, Mary, who is sixteen years old and recently diagnosed with cancer, wishes to participate in a Phase I oncology trial (Fives, 2016e). As the purpose of such trials typically is to determine the safe dose range and the possible side-effects of an innovative cancer treatment, they 'expose patient-subjects to significant risks of harm without a reasonable expectation of direct therapeutic benefit' (Jansen, 2005, p. 28). Given the nature and purpose of the trial, Mary knows that it is not in her best medical interests to enrol, but wishes to do so in order to contribute to the scientific and medical efforts to cure cancer. Agreeing to participate in a trial 'out of a concern for the good of future patients' is an altruistic decision (ibid., p. 27). Thus, Mary is not suffering from a 'therapeutic misconception' here, as she does not misconceive her participation in the trial as therapeutic in nature (Beauchamp and Childress, 2009, p. 129).

Mary's wish to enrol seems to be in accord with her autonomous pursuit of her own, altruistic, values. If this is the case, and if Mary's parents give priority to the value of autonomy, they will conclude that, in respecting her autonomy, Mary should be free to make this decision herself. However, in our example, her parents judge Mary to be incompetent, and take the decision out of her hands. Their moral judgment is in line with Buchanan and Brock's position, which, in defining competence, gives priority to the value of individual well-being. In a position worked out for elderly and incompetent adults but also applied to the case of children, they argue that incompetent decision making is just decision making that leads to harmful consequences for the decision maker. Although we should respect the autonomy of those who are competent, this is because competent individuals are less likely to make decisions that will harm their own interests: a patient's choice 'should be respected' when there are grounds for believing that such a choice 'is reasonably in accord with the patient's good and does reasonably protect or promote the patient's well-being' (Buchanan and Brock, 1986, p. 36). In deciding whether or not Mary is competent to make this decision, according to this line of thought, we make a consequentialist calculation of the effects of Mary's decision on her own well-being.

Are Mary's parents right? Is their exercise of power legitimate? As her parents act on the grounds that they believe Mary to be incompetent to decide for herself, then to answer this question we need to examine whether Mary shows competence in her decision making. In the previous section, I made the case for reasonable practical judgement as our standard of competence. If Mary is fully reasonable, she will be aware that different values are promoted in different ways by the decision in question. She will be aware also that the decision presents a conflict of values, as choosing to enrol in the trial promotes the autonomous pursuit of her good but is not intended to promote her own well-being. She must also understand the severity of the risks for her well-being and the odds of those risks. In addition, her adherence to her own altruistic values must not be such as to impair her reasoning, as it must be compatible with a willingness to give full consideration to how this altruistic behaviour will affect her own well-being. If this is true of Mary, she is well placed to make a competent decision, that is, a decision that can be presented as an attempt to resolve a moral dilemma. In contrast, if she is unable or unwilling to gauge the severity of the risks to her well-being, or if she is unaware of or refuses to acknowledge that there is a conflict of values here, this would suggest that Mary does not possess the competence required to make this difficult decision.

Must researchers and physicians obtain consent from both children and their parents?

In our example above, we saw that competence could not be defined simply as decision making that was autonomous or simply as decision making that would best promote the individual's own well-being. Rather, competent decision making involved, *inter alia*, sensitivity to moral conflict and a capacity to work through such conflicts with reasonableness, including the conflicts regarding the duty to promote individual well-being and the duty to respect individual autonomy. However, a number of questions remain. If children are competent in the way we have defined, are they entitled to make decisions themselves about research participation and medical treatment, without their parents' involvement?

One possibility is that children's (competent) informed consent is sufficient to authorise their research participation and medical treatment, and so, in such situations, the consent of their parents is unnecessary. However, we must ask, what is the justification for giving children this 'power to' or capacity, but also what is the justification for limiting parents' power over their children in this way? There is a *prima facie* justification for doing so, on the grounds that, if children have the competence to make a decision, they should be entitled to make that decision on their own. However, as the decision maker is a minor, and as parents retain rights and duties as parents, both the 'right to parent' and their rights 'over' their children, then granting children this decision making right can lead to moral conflicts. There may be a conflict between children's right to provide informed consent when they have the competence to do so, on the one hand, and parents' right to make decisions on behalf of their children or decisions that affect their children, on the other hand.

To better appreciate what is at stake here, let us address the more straightforward issue of what is to be done when children are *incompetent* to make a decision. If children are judged insufficiently competent to authorise research participation or medical treatment, does it follow parents should make those decisions on their behalf? According to Buchanan and Brock, a clear locus of authority is needed for those whose decisions 'will be set aside for whom others will be assigned as surrogate decision makers' (1986, p. 27). Surrogate decision makers, all things being equal, will come from among the individual's family members: 'whomever the individual is most closely associated with' (ibid., p. 82). However, we have also seen that joint decision making between parents and (incompetent) children leads to better outcomes for children, in particular, more competent, less risky decision making. Therefore, in situations where children are not fully competent, joint decision making should also be considered seriously as an alternative to surrogate decision making.

Let us return to a situation where children are *competent* to make the decision, but their parents are opposed to their plans. If surrogate decision making is appropriate in situations of incompetence (leaving to one side the question of whether joint decision making would be more appropriate here), it follows that, in the first instance, it is inappropriate for parents simply to take the decision out of the hands of a competent child. Nonetheless, as we saw, children's competence is not the only morally relevant feature of the case, as parents continue to have the 'right to parent' as well as rights 'over' their children. Therefore, there can be a conflict of values here as well. On the one hand, parents should respect their children's competence, while on the other hand parents retain rights to make decisions on behalf of even their competent children.

What I want to suggest is that perhaps joint decision making can be part of the solution to this conflict. In Chapter 7, we spoke of expressive (tacit) consent, where a negotiation process yields a decision that all adhere to. In this chapter, we have spoken about joint decision making between parents and children. Although parents do exert a controlling influence here, nonetheless, if this influence takes the form of persuasion, children do act voluntarily in reaching the (joint) decision. It is true that joint decision making raises its own concerns. As we saw, so as to initiate the joint decision making process, parents may have interfered with their children's liberty by, for example, simply removing other options. Also, finally, we are considering joint decision making in situations where it is not given further justification as a necessary means for the development of the child's competence, as, in our case, the child *is* competent. Nonetheless, despite its limitations, joint decision making may be the best process that both acknowledges a conflict of values when it arises, and provides a context for finding a reasonable resolution to that conflict. Joint decision making is, at the very least, promising as it is not assumed that parents' views must always be given precedence in cases of disagreement; when based on persuasion, it is compatible with voluntariness and therefore meets a basic requirement of informed consent; and it provides a context in which conflicting views can be addressed and agreements sought.

Conclusions

In addressing the issue of informed consent, in this chapter we have examined the legitimacy of the exercise of parents' power over their children. However, there are also implications from our discussion for the exercise of coercive power by the State. If the State does not permit minors to provide autonomous consent, this legal prohibition is backed up by threatened sanctions. The State may, in contrast, guarantee children's enjoyment of certain rights with respect to informed consent. Once again, this is an issue of the State's exercise of coercive power, as, in certain cases, the implementation of children's rights may have to overcome the strong objections of parents and others. Therefore, the highest standards of moral objectivity are required when we consider whether the State's exercise of power in such instances is legitimate.

Difficult moral questions also are raised here when we consider the legitimacy of parents' power. If a parent refuses to allow their children to make an informed consent decision, then once again a high level of moral objectivity is required to justify this exercise of power. In the first instance, it would be unjustifiable to prevent a *competent* child from making such a decision. We have reached this conclusion not by insisting that one moral claim is fundamental and equating competence with decision making compatible with that value. Rather, we started from the premise that competence involves, *inter alia*, an awareness of the plurality of moral values and the possibility for conflict between those values, as well as reasonableness in deliberating in the face of conflicting moral claims. Returning to our example, what this means is that, if Mary's parents take the decision out of her hands, this is a *prima facie* bad.

If parents and children cannot agree, should we simply let parents decide? To do so would go against much of what we are committed to in respect of surrogate decision making. If surrogate decision making is appropriate in situations of incompetence, it is, in the first instance, inappropriate in situations of competence. We must remember that parents have the right to rear their children and the right to exercise control over their children, but, at the same time, competent individuals, whether children or adults, are entitled to make decisions for themselves. Taking all this on board, joint decision making, when it is based on persuasion, may be the most appropriate process for working through a conflict of values.

What general conclusions have been reached here? First, we have offered a general account of competence, and the benefit of adopting this conceptualisation is that it places moral conflict at the centre of decision making. Second, we have seen that competence is not the only relevant item when we consider the right to provide informed consent, as the parents of competent children still retain rights as parents, including the right to make decisions on behalf of their (competent and incompetent) children.

Third, where children are incompetent to make decisions, we should not assume that, as a matter of course, parents should simply make decisions for their children. One option is to engage in joint decision making, whose objective is to promote children's competence. But independent of this, children have a right to liberty when they are capable of exercising that right, even when incompetent. This is a very interesting and complex issue that we will not have time or space to explore to the full here.

Fourth, we have not considered whether children's competence in decision making, both the substance of their commitments and the process by which they reach these conclusions, may be shaped by the very power relations whose legitimacy rests in part at least on judgements of whether those children are competent. However, in the next chapter, we do take up this issue, when we consider attempts made by parents to share ways of life with their children and attempts by the State to shape the citizens children will become.

Notes

1 Similar provisions are made in Australia for adolescents (Felzmann et al., 2010, p. 62). In addition, although the findings in the UK concerning the Gillick case have no application in Irish law, nonetheless, in the Republic of Ireland, a recent consent policy stated that, in 'exceptional circumstances', children under the age of 16 may be allowed to provide informed consent independent of their parents, citing the Gillick case as a rationale for this policy (National Consent Advisory Group, 2013).

2 Much the same conclusion is reached by those who call for a 'demanding' standard of autonomous choice for the (relatively infrequent) occasions where a great deal is at stake for the decision maker and the wider society, for example, when someone wishes to refuse life-saving treatment or request assistance in dying (Campbell, 2016, p. 65). The demanding standard of autonomy involves 'a higher order reflection on, or authentication of, one's first-order desires and preferences', and so, for risky decisions, we would be required 'to reflect on and evaluate the values on which we propose to base our actions' (ibid., p. 62, p. 65).

10

Sharing lives, shaping values, and voluntary civic education

In this chapter, I examine the efforts made by parents to share a way of life with their children as well as those efforts made in the name of the wider society to shape the values of its future citizens. Three questions in particular are addressed. Ought we respect diversity and in addition protect parents' right to religious freedom and, on that basis, their right to share a (religious) way of life with their children? Ought we shape the values of future citizens, and in doing so promote the autonomy of the adults children will one day be, in particular through participation in civic education programmes? And finally, may we interfere with children's liberty, by removing options concerning attendance at and the content of civic education programmes, in particular when our objective is to promote the autonomy of the adults the children will one day be?

It would seem that, in all three instances, there are moral considerations that have prescriptive force for us. First, we ought to protect the rights of adult citizens, including parents' right to religious freedom. And we ought to respect the plurality of forms of life compatible with society's basic rules of justice. Therefore, we ought to protect parents' right to share a religious way of life with their children should they wish to do so, that is, a right to practice their religion with their children and to rear their children in accordance with their religious beliefs. Nonetheless, second, the political community also ought to be concerned about the education of children within that community. Indeed, the community has a right to shape the values of the adults children will one day be, through various forms of education, including civic education. And yet, third, we ought to protect children's rights of liberty, including the freedom to refuse to take part in civic education programmes, even those programmes whose objectives include the promotion of the participants' autonomy.

Although in each instance there is a moral claim that we should act on, it is possible, as we shall see, for these claims to come into conflict. What should happen when the way of life parents wish to share with their children is in conflict with the values to be promoted through civic education, or when such values can be promoted only by violating children's right to liberty? In this chapter, we shall examine the ways in which philosophers address these moral conflicts. In the main, although they acknowledge that moral conflicts arise, they also assume that we can and even must resolve such conflicts in a certain manner, for the reason that, as a general rule, one moral claim is fundamental. However, as we have observed elsewhere, there is no consensus over which moral claim is fundamental and so there is no consensus on the general rule that resolves such moral conflicts. Therefore, instead, we can hope to resolve such dilemmas only through the exercise of practical judgement and practical reasoning.

Empirical evidence

Numerous studies have been carried out concerning civic education, both the civic component of children's formal education as well as specific civic education programmes. In this section, I am interested most particularly in studies examining civic education within a broader political environment of liberal democratic values and institutions. What happens to children who engage in this type of civic education? Below I look at studies that have examined both the process of civic education itself as well as its outcomes.

To begin with I want to look at the evidence for the role played by formal education in fostering civic values. First, does education help promote civic and political knowledge? One study, based on data collected over a fifty year period in the US, between the 1940s and 1990s, measures young people's factual knowledge of political institutions and processes, leaders and parties, and public policies. The study by Delli Carpini and Keeter shows large differences in political knowledge based on young people's education, as well as other variables, including race, gender, levels of political interest, regular use of newspapers and radio, regular discussion of politics with friends and family, as well as a negative association with watching TV news (1996, pp. 144–5). This would suggest that formal education is one explanation for children's development of political knowledge. Why does this matter?

It matters because there is a positive association between levels of political knowledge, on the one hand, and valuable civic attributes, on the other hand, as reported in studies by Delli Carpini and Keeter (1996) and Popkin and Dimock (1999). In particular, children with higher levels of political knowledge can better promote their own self-interest; are more ideologically consistent; rely more on a judgement of political character (a judgement of conduct in political roles) than personal character in making voting decisions; are less likely to distrust the political process; are more tolerant, perhaps because knowledge of civil liberties and civil rights increases commitment to core democratic values; and, finally, are more likely to take part in politics. If it is the case that political knowledge affects civic competence, character, and conduct in these ways, it is all the more important to understand what factors will lead to improvements in political knowledge. Studies have shown that not only civic education programmes but the wider school environment improves political knowledge (Conover and Searing, 2000). In addition, both the wider school environment and civic education programmes can lead to a wide range of benefits for participating children.

Let us first examine the wider school environment. Studies have shown that students' civic consciousness and civic practice have been improved by 'the sense of the school as a community; the students' level of civic engagement in school and extracurricular activities; the level of political discussion in school'; as well as by informal civic instruction in other subjects such as English literature (Galston, 2001a, p. 227). Turning to civic education itself, it too can lead to a wide range of gains for students. These include gains in children's agency, relatedness, and moral and political understanding, each of which is an aim of 'service learning'. Service learning combines practical civic involvement in the community with classroom-based instruction. Its aim is to improve children's agency (through responding to a particular social problem), relatedness (by joining with others to respond to a social need), and political/moral understanding (by reflecting on and discussing proposed responses to a social problem). This hypothesis is supported by findings from a study of eleventh grade students (sixteen–seventeen years of age) from fifty-two schools in Chicago (n=4057), where service learning had a greater impact on commitment to civic participation than children's own previous commitment to civic participation (Kahne and Sporte, 2008). In addition, among twelfth grade students (seventeen–eighteen years of age), service learning led to improvements in personal responsibility to help others, a belief that government should help those in need, a belief that they could be effective leaders, and an 'increased sense of agency – a sense that they could make a difference in their communities' (Westheimer and Kahne, 2004, p. 251).

If one aim of education, and civic education in particular, is to promote the values of democratic citizens, should the education process itself reflect those values? With respect to education generally, it is believed that a participatory, democratic approach is of benefit to students across a number of domains. Many studies have shown that students with positive attitudes towards a domain of study also tend to perform well in that domain: they perform better in subjects they express a liking for (Fives, 2016a; 2016b). As students 'generally learn best when they have a prior commitment to what they are being required to learn', this provides some support for participatory (democratic) approaches to education, where students are given some role in shaping what happens in the classroom (Gutmann, 1999, p. 91). It is argued that a democratic, participatory approach to civic education itself also is beneficial. A discussion-based approach, focusing on local issues, is recommended instead of rote learning concerning institutional and historical matters (Torney-Purta, 1997; Niemi and Junn, 1998). Results from a study of 90,000 students in twenty-eight countries (Torney-Purta et al., 2001) show that 'open classroom climate for discussion is a significant predictor of civic knowledge, support for democratic values, participation in political discussion, and political engagement (measured by whether young people say they will vote when they are legally able)' (Hess, 2004, p. 258). Nonetheless, there are other variables at play, and the benefits of a participatory approach may be explained in part by students' commitments formed prior to and independently of their schooling experience (Gutmann, 1999, p. 89).

Let us turn from the process of education to its outcomes. Can and should it promote autonomy? While some contend that education should promote autonomy in the shape of critical thinking, this is only one of its aims. Democratic schooling should promote 'critical distance from authority', as this is one of the participatory virtues, but it should also promote the so-called disciplinary virtues: 'the imparting of knowledge and instilling of emotional along with intellectual discipline' (ibid., p. 91). In addition, we have only incomplete and imperfect knowledge about how education does in fact promote autonomy. Indeed, Amy Gutmann acknowledges a dearth of evidence to support the claim that education, and in particular democratic education, can promote critical thinking. There are also doubts about whether a system of education can promote autonomous critical reflection as such. That is, to promote critical reflection, we must promote children's ability to assess the strengths and weaknesses of particular choices, as well as their knowledge of their own temperament, interests, and abilities. However, if children are to make informed, critical decisions, they also need knowledge of what particular communities believe to be worthwhile lives (Winch, 2002, p. 34). Therefore, it is argued, it may not be possible to promote critical thinking without also promoting specific ways of life.

What we have seen so far suggests a connection between civic education and both children's autonomy and children's liberty. Civic education is associated with gains in autonomy (children's sense of agency, critical thinking, and moral and political understanding), as is an approach that increases their freedom of choice (a participatory, student-led approach, an approach that gives students a say in what happens in civic education and education more broadly). At the same time, not only should education promote the disciplinary virtues, questions have been raised about whether civic education is in fact effective in promoting children's autonomy, and also whether it can do so without also promoting specific ways of life as worthwhile. This suggests a tension between the various aims of civic education, namely, shaping the values of future citizens more generally, promoting autonomy specifically, and finally protecting children's liberty. We return to this below.

Legislation, policy, and services

I turn now to the legal, policy, and service issues relevant to civic education. In the literature, attention has focused on the possible tension between respect for diversity and the promotion of autonomy through civic education. A further issue, although admittedly one that has attracted less attention in mainstream political theory, is the tension that may arise between the rights of children, on the one hand, and the rights of children's parents or those acting on behalf of the political community, on the other hand.

Diversity poses a significant challenge for civic education in liberal democratic societies, it has been argued. If civic education is designed to promote the autonomy of the adults children will one day be, or if the promotion of autonomy is one of its likely consequences, do the values of civic education take precedence over respect for social diversity in cases where a specific community's way of life does not promote autonomy? This is the 'dilemma of diversity', referred to by Gutmann. Liberal democrats, she argues,

> recognize significant value in the unimpeded pursuit of religious ways of life. Were these ways of life without value, there would be no moral problem. Were they of absolute value, the moral problem would also disappear. Liberal democracy is not committed to enabling all valuable ways of life to flourish, no matter what. The dilemma of diversity arises because the value of a conscientious way of life apparently comes into conflict with the terms of fair cooperation among citizens. (Gutmann, 1995, p. 566)

Are we duty bound to respect diversity when dealing with a community that does not promote the autonomy of its members? As David Archard argues, 'Citizenship requires autonomy, but some at least of the communities do not value autonomy', and for some religious groups in particular, 'The constitutive values and beliefs are not to be subject to critical scrutiny and endorsed or rejected. They are inherited as the true faith and learnt as such' (2003, p. 92). The potential for such tensions are evident in two important legal cases in the US.

The case of *Mozert* v. *Hawkins County Board of Education* (1987) was taken by parents of children in Tennessee public schools. The children in question were obliged to participate in a reading programme, whose objective was to ensure they developed positive values, became good citizens, and also developed the skills of critical reading. One parent of a sixth grader (age eleven–twelve), who referred to herself as a 'born again Christian', first raised objections to stories including mental telepathy, evolution, and secular humanism (1987, p. 1). It was argued that forcing the students to read school books that 'teach or inculcate values in violation of their religious beliefs and convictions is a clear violation of their rights to the free exercise of religion' (1987, p. 2). It should be noted that at some points in the ruling it is the beliefs and convictions of the eleven–twelve-year-old children that are being referred to, while at others it is the beliefs of the children's parents. Although the district court found in favour of the parents, the decision was overturned by the Supreme Court, on the grounds that it was a legitimate State interest to teach students how to 'think critically about complex and controversial subjects and to develop their own ideas and make judgments about these subjects' (1987, p. 7).

The case of *Wisconsin* v. *Yoder*, 406 U.S. 205 (1972) concerned an objection made by members of the Amish community to their children's compulsory participation in formal education beyond the eighth grade (thirteen–fourteen years of age). Although the state of Wisconsin mandates formal schooling until the age of sixteen, the Supreme Court ruled that Amish children were *not* obliged to attend formal schooling beyond the eighth grade. The objection to formal schooling was based on the following contention: 'the values they [formal schools] teach are in marked variance with Amish values and the Amish way of life; they [the Amish community] view secondary school education as an impermissible exposure of their children to "worldly" influence in conflict with their beliefs' (1972, pp. 210–11). Therefore, the Supreme Court ruling entailed that the obligation to attend school beyond the eighth grade interfered with parents' right to freely exercise their religion (Gutmann, 1980, p. 348). The court ruling not only removed compulsory schooling beyond the eighth grade, but it 'also endorsed the nonstandard elementary education offered in Amish one-room schools', that is, parochial schools run privately by Amish parents (Fischel, 2012, p. 108; see McConnell and Hurst, 2006). The implication is that, as parents have a right to freely exercise their religion, they have a right to share that (religious) way of life with their children and do so through control of their children's civic education.

In the two legal cases presented above, there was a tension between the values of respect for diversity and protection of religious freedom, on the one hand, and the promotion of autonomy through civic education, on the other. In the *Mozert* v. *Hawkins* case, the Supreme Court ruling can be interpreted as giving priority to the promotion of autonomy. However, in contrast, in the *Wisconsin* v. *Yoder* case, the ruling could be said to give precedence to parents' rights of religious freedom and therefore respect for diversity.

As I said above, we should also consider the possibility of a different sort of conflict. I turn next to the possible tension between, on the one hand, respect for children's right to liberty and, on the other hand, respect for the rights of children's parents or those acting on behalf of the political community. This tension is evident in the text of the UN Convention on the Rights of the Child (United Nations, 1989), which we have already mentioned (Chapter 7). While acknowledging the rights and duties of parents in the rearing of children (Article 5), the CRC requires signatory States to guarantee certain basic rights of children. These comprise various rights of liberty, including 'the right [...] to freedom of thought, conscience and religion' (Article 14). It should be noted that these are rights guaranteed to individuals *qua* children. That is, to satisfy the commitments of the CRC, it is not sufficient to promote the autonomy of the adults the children will one day be. Rather, as a separate requirement, we must respect children's liberty by, for instance, ensuring they have the right not just to receive but also to impart information, and therefore to communicate with others in ways that they choose.

The CRC's commitments to children's liberty undoubtedly are impressive. However, it is not clear from the document how we should proceed if, in guaranteeing children's right to liberty, we in turn are unable to guarantee the rights of parents or the rights of the wider society. It is stated in Article 3 that 'In all actions concerning children [...] the best interests of the child shall be a primary consideration'. At the same time, parents have the right 'to provide direction' to their children's exercise of their right to freedom of thought, conscience and religion (Article 14). But the CRC says nothing of what should be done in cases where children wish to have access to certain information, and parents, on the basis of their religious beliefs, in providing 'direction' to the children in the exercise of their right, forbid this. Are we to respect the children's decisions here and in that way respect their right to liberty, or instead the rights of parents to exercise their religious freedom and share a way of life with their children?

Conceptual issues

We are concerned here with parents' efforts to share a way of life with their children and the efforts made by society at large to shape the values of future citizens. When we evaluate the exercise of power over children in such instances, what are the conceptual issues to be addressed? As we have seen, there is room for tension between the requirements to respect diversity, promote autonomy, and protect children's liberty. As a result, greater conceptual clarity is needed in these areas. I will focus on whether tensions arise between the promotion of autonomy and respect for diversity, how citizens should deal with moral conflicts, and finally the moral and political status of children.

Is civic education hostile to legitimate pluralism?

Will a civic education programme that promotes autonomy be incompatible with respect for diversity? The first thing to note is that a civic education programme can aim at autonomy in a number of different ways, and the nature of these differences is vital to the question of whether civic education will be in conflict with respect for diversity.

First, we should distinguish between 'promoting' and 'facilitating' the autonomy of the adults children will one day be. The distinction turns on whether, in nurturing the capacity to reflect seriously on the ends or aims of one's life, we aim in addition to ensure 'children can recognize the value and purpose' of doing so (Macleod, 2003, p. 328, n. 6). While Harry Brighouse refers to the possibility of merely facilitating autonomy (2000, p. 81), in contrast, Colin Macleod argues that, through 'Socratic nurturing', adults (parents and others) can promote the autonomy of the adults children will one day be: 'Socratic nurturing aims at developing within children the capacity for reasoned reflection on the meaning, nature, and value of ends and commitments. Socratic nurturing also aims at fostering enthusiasm or at least receptiveness to the actual exercise of these capacities' (Macleod, 2003, p. 318). A second, relevant distinction is that between 'weak' and 'strong' forms of Socratic nurturing. For it is possible to value Socratic nurturing merely as a means to ensure children embrace ends deemed valuable by adults (weak Socratic nurturing). In contrast, strong Socratic nurturing is based in part on the 'importance of expressing respect for the autonomy potential of children per se' (ibid., p. 319).

Therefore, there need be no tension between respect for illiberal ways of life, on the one hand, and 'weak' Socratic nurturing, on the other. Our question is whether in promoting autonomy in the 'strong' Socratic sense, that is, autonomy as an end in itself, there will be an irresolvable tension with the requirement to respect diversity. Two distinct groups of liberal thinkers have attempted to show that, in fact, there is no tension between promoting autonomy and respecting diversity.

For so-called *comprehensive* liberals, such as Joseph Raz, we should promote autonomous ways of life. Raz accepts that, in some instances, communities will resist efforts to promote autonomy among children, but there is no justification for such resistance. As one can prosper in modern societies only if one is also autonomous (1986, pp. 369–70), there is no justification for parents attempting to prevent their children from becoming fully autonomous. If parents deny the necessary 'education and ... opportunities' to their children, then in such instances 'assimilationist policies may well be the only course, even if implemented by force of law' (ibid., p. 424). So there is no conflict between respect for diversity and the promotion of autonomy, according to the comprehensive liberal, for we are not required to respect ways of life that do not also promote autonomy.

For *political* liberals, civic education should promote the values of civility and public reasonableness, values of the public sphere, rather than a liberal (autonomous) way of life as such (Thunder, 2006, p. 676). However, the concept of reasonableness in Rawls's work includes the requirement to recognise and accept the consequences of the burdens of judgment (see Chapter 3). Thus, reasonable citizens acknowledge that disagreements between comprehensive doctrines have a morally innocent source and, for that reason, they do not seek a rational consensus on any one moral doctrine (see Fives, 2010). Others have concluded that the promotion of 'public' values in this way is likely to promote autonomy more generally, and do so at the expense of an unquestioning or unreflective adherence to non-liberal ways of life. Promoting 'core liberal values – such as the importance of a critical attitude toward contending political claims – seems certain to have the effect of promoting critical thinking in general' (Macedo, 1995, p. 477; see Kymlicka, 2003, pp. 51–2). If we encourage children to be critical about political issues, this will spill over into all areas of life, promoting autonomy as something that is valuable in and of itself. Nonetheless, like Raz, Rawls concludes there will be no irreconcilable tension here. For Rawls, there is no incompatibility between respect for diversity and reasonableness (and the autonomy that it brings about). Reasonable comprehensive doctrines are, by definition, those that are compatible with political liberalism, and we are not required to respect unreasonable ways of life (Rawls, 1999 [1987], p. 421).

Therefore, both comprehensive and political liberals conclude that there is no tension between the promotion of autonomy, on the one hand, and respect for diversity, on the other hand, as we are not required to respect ways of life hostile to basic liberal principles. Although they disagree about whether liberal civic education programmes involve the intentional, explicit promotion of autonomy itself or the promotion of 'public' values that in turn promotes autonomy, they agree that all should accept civic education programmes the effects of which are to promote autonomy as valuable in itself. This seems unsatisfactory for the following reason. As it is assumed that we are not required to respect ways of life that are not also compatible with autonomy, at the outset of any deliberations our moral values are placed in an order of priority: autonomy has priority over diversity. And yet it has nowhere been established that, as a general rule, respect for diversity may never trump autonomy.

An alternative approach is to treat this issue *not* as one that can be proven or demonstrated one way or the other, but rather as an open question requiring empirical analysis and a focus on specific issues and situations. This is what Andrew March has attempted, by examining whether Muslims have reason to accept rather than reject autonomy-promoting civic education (2009, p. 11). For March, we can deal with this issue only through a close examination of specific issues and situations. Therefore, when we ask whether the autonomous self is compatible with illiberal ways of life, we can expect more than one answer. Indeed, we may arrive at affirmative and negative conclusions in different situations and when addressing different issues. This is understandable, if we appreciate that what we are doing is attempting to resolve conflicts that arise between incompatible values, and trying to do so in the practical situations where we have to make decisions. One such practical issue is whether or not parents may remove their children from autonomy-promoting civic education programmes. I return again to this issue below, but for now I want to say more about moral conflict itself.

How should citizens deal with moral conflict?

If we ask what purpose civic education serves, most would agree it is to help children become good citizens. Others have addressed the fact that, as political philosophers do not agree about the qualities required of a good citizen, as a result there is disagreement about the nature and role of a programme of education for good citizenship (Archard, 2003; Kymlicka, 2003; Hess, 2004; Westheimer and Kahne, 2004). Here I want to address a different but related point, namely that political philosophers also do not agree on the correct answer to the following question: how should the good citizen deal with moral conflicts? Therefore, we should expect disagreement over how, in a civic education programme, children should be taught to engage with conflicting values.

One tradition of thought gives great significance to the virtues, that is, the good character traits, of citizens. This is the case with Aristotelianism and Thomism, sometimes also referred to as communitarianism (see MacIntyre, 1985; 1988; Fives, 2005; 2006; 2008a). For example, it is argued that the good citizen develops specific dispositions, the disposition to choose correctly and to choose in light of ethical commitments, such as the civil or political commitments of justice and moderation, among others, in Aristotelian thought, and the theological commitments of faith, hope, and charity in Thomist arguments (MacIntyre, 1999; Foot, 2001; Fives, 2008b; 2013a). A genuine political community is composed of good citizens, citizens who develop and exercise the virtues required to attain what are considered goods in that community. And the community may be equated with the State (for example the Greek city-state in Aristotle's time), or alternatively a sub-grouping within a wider political community (for example, the Catholic community in a contemporary, liberal democratic society). The latter distinction is important for our discussion here.

For, if we equate our political community with our moral community, and if the latter is a religious one, it follows that we should educate our children in the values and virtues of our religious community, and we should give this priority over any efforts by the State to impose its own civic education programme if the latter is based on different and perhaps incompatible principles. And we should teach our children to approach moral conflicts in the same way. That is, when values come into conflict, children should give priority to what is the fundamental moral commitment as set out in our religious moral community. In this way, Alasdair MacIntyre argues that, when our moral tradition is in 'good working order', we are not faced with real moral dilemmas, as such a moral tradition provides us with a hierarchical ordering of goods (1988, pp. 106–7, pp. 165–6, p. 337; 2006, p. 170). For that very reason, children should give priority to the values of their own community when they come into conflict with other values, for example, when the Catholic values of faith, hope, and charity come into conflict with the values of autonomy and individual liberty associated with mainstream, Western society and culture.

Utilitarians, in contrast, do not accept that any action is inherently right or that any character trait is inherently good. Instead, acts are right (protecting liberty, say) and character traits are virtues (again, faith, hope, and charity, say) *only* insofar as acting in this way and developing these dispositions has good consequences. That is, although utilitarians recognise the usefulness of social norms and moral virtues, they believe we should adhere to such norms and develop such character traits only if in doing so we promote utility. In any one instance, utilitarians may agree with Thomists that we should promote Catholic values among students in a civic education programme, but they disagree about *why* this is the case. Similarly, we know from the history of political thought that utilitarians have been among the most vocal and influential champions of individual liberty (Mill, 1985 [1859]). However, once again, the utilitarian commitment to rights of liberty is conditional: we should protect rights of liberty, but only insofar as, in doing so, we best promote utility.

We have also referred to the utilitarian approach to moral conflict (see Chapter 3). As we saw, for utilitarians, there is an intuitive level of moral reasoning, where we appeal to *prima facie* principles, and a critical level of moral reasoning, where, by applying utilitarian considerations, we resolve conflicts arising at the intuitive level (Hare, 1978, p. 179). Let us look at one possible outcome of such a process of conflict resolution. A utilitarian approach may encourage conformity among children, and do so through a process of indoctrination, *if* such conformity is thought beneficial, or more beneficial than, for instance, pedagogical approaches that encourage critical thinking or approaches that are student-led and participatory. As we know, the requirement to protect children's liberty can come into conflict with the requirement to promote the autonomy of the adults the children will one day be as well as the requirement to protect parents' rights to share a way of life with their children. The utilitarian resolves this conflict by considering which will have the better consequences in terms of utility. And similarly, utilitarians will teach children to treat one of these as the fundamental value insofar as (and only insofar as) to do so better promotes utility.

Finally, we can turn to liberal political thought, and how liberals deal with the tension between liberty, autonomy, and respect for diversity. As we saw, Aristotelian Thomists do not consider these to be real or genuine conflicts, and they give the promotion of the virtues priority over protecting liberty and promoting autonomy. Nor do utilitarians, who insist that autonomy and liberty, in particular, are valuable only insofar as they promote utility. Similarly, some liberals will not consider these to be real or genuine conflicts either. As we have seen, for Raz, 'the value of negative freedom derives from its contribution to autonomy' (1986, p. 410); and Rawls concludes that principles of justice have a lexical order of priority, and that we are never justified in interfering with an individual's negative freedom so as to promote other values (1971, p. 302). Although Rawls and Raz reach opposing conclusions about which value has priority, their approach to liberalism is such that one fundamental value must be identified, a value synonymous with a liberal way of life. Therefore, for many liberals, there is no real conflict between these values.

However, for other liberals, again, such moral conflicts will be real or genuine rather than merely apparent. Why is this the case? As Thomas Nagel has argued, we have no justification for insisting that, whenever moral values come into conflict, there is only one way in which they can be reconciled. And this is the case because we are unable to place all moral values in a hierarchical order. As the source of values is plural, to insist on such a hierarchy is 'absurd' (see Chapter 3). For liberals of this kind, children should be taught to treat moral conflicts as genuine conflicts between independent sources of moral value. One example of such an approach is evident in Isaiah Berlin's work, as he is able to perceive the independent value of negative freedom, respect for diversity, and even positive freedom. Although Berlin warns about the dangers of some versions of positive freedom, he leaves us in no doubt of the value of 'being one's own master' (2004 [1958], p. 178). In addition, he believes commitment to negative freedom follows from the requirement to respect diversity. As the plurality of values entails that we will always be burdened with choice, we are as a result duty-bound to protect others against interference in their freely made choices (ibid., p. 214). Nonetheless, he also accepts that we may have to restrict negative freedom so as to promote other values. For Berlin and Nagel, therefore, there are independent sources of value that may come into conflict, and their liberal approach to politics both recognises the reality of such conflicts and is committed to resolving them through practical reasoning.

Are children citizens or potential citizens?

The final area where conceptual clarity is required concerns the moral and political status of children. Are children the equals of adults, or do children occupy a lower stratum, morally and politically? Can children be thought of as citizens, with rights and duties of their own, or as future citizens, spared many of the burdens but also denied many of the benefits of full citizenship? This issue is at the heart of concerns around children's liberty when engaged in civic education. If we interfere with children's liberty, for example by not giving children the freedom to choose whether or not to attend civic education classes, are we doing something that is, morally speaking, of the same order of significance as any interference with an adult's liberty?

As we saw in Chapter 7, in Rawls's account of moral development, children do not reach the level of full moral maturity (the morality of principle), but rather occupy the lower (the morality of authority) or intermediate (the morality of association) levels (Rawls, 1971, p. 516). If adolescents do not attain the level of morality of principle, then they are not full or complete moral agents, and this surely affects the rights they may claim. However, advocates of children's rights have noted that many adults do not live up to this ideal of moral agency while many young people can and do (Harris, 1996). As argued for in the liberation thesis, there is no longer any justification for assuming young people incapable of the autonomy adults are said to exercise. In this book, I have taken a different line again. Against the Rawlsian approach, I have argued (see Chapters 1 and 2) that insofar as children are capable of liberty of action, they also have rights of liberty, as the latter are not the preserve of those who have reached the highest level of moral maturity (for example, those who are competent). However, in contrast to the liberation thesis, I also argued that, in some instances, we may be faced with a moral conflict, in that we should interfere with children's liberty, but when we do so something is lost, as a right has been violated. What are the implications of adopting this stand?

While there is disagreement over whether children are the moral equals of adults, it may be that resolving this conceptual puzzle one way or the other is neither necessary nor sufficient in order to answer our substantive questions concerning children's upbringing. As Jonathan Wolff points out, answers to penultimate questions need not wait upon answers to ultimate ones (2011, p. 6). Regardless of whether children are the moral equals of adults, they may have different interests and as a result it may be appropriate to treat them differently. In particular, children may be unique in terms of their strong interest in receiving or participating in education. While adults continue to be able to learn, and even arguably have a duty to strive to improve themselves through education, the situation of children imposes unique demands on parents. Macleod refers to children's 'special evolving interests that are rooted in a particular conception of moral personality' (2004a, p. 57). He concludes that, as children have a special claim on us to develop their moral powers, as a result they have interests qua children in the information and conditions 'conducive to independent reflection and deliberation' (ibid.). Macleod also recognises the moral conflicts that we can be faced with here, for children also have interests in being protected from harm, and parents have rights with respect to their children.

The coherent integration of these considerations is the challenge that we face and to which we now turn. For, leaving to one side the puzzle of whether children are the moral equals of their parents, there are strong enough grounds to conclude that children have rights, including the right to liberty, and yet also that they have interests in being well-educated, including through civic education. It is in this context that we must consider whether parents' power over their children, in particular when sharing a way of life together, is legitimate.

Ethical questions

Now we can address some of the ethical questions that arise when we consider civic education. I will examine both whether the state may interfere with parents' efforts to share a way of life with their children and also whether civic education programmes should be voluntary and child-centred. As in previous chapters, I will first tease out the main issues before, in the concluding section of this chapter, defending specific practical judgements concerning the legitimacy of parents' power over their children.

May the state interfere with parents' efforts to share a way of life with their children?

In order to prepare the way for the ethical work that needs to be done here, I consider two hypothetical scenarios, based loosely on the legal cases and the empirical studies we have already discussed. Let us imagine parents belonging to a religious minority take one of either of the following two positions in respect of a civic education programme for eleventh grade students (sixteen–seventeen years of age), the aims of which include promoting children's capacities for critical reflection, along with other qualities, including relatedness and moral and political understanding, as is the case with 'service learning' (Westheimer, 2004). Some (RM1) refuse to allow their children to participate in the programme at all, on the grounds that this would be an unjustifiable interference with their efforts to share a way of life with their children. We saw such an approach in the *Mozert* v. *Hawkins* and the *Wisconsin* v. *Yoder* cases. Others (RM2) are happy for their children to take part, although they believe that they should be permitted to withdraw their children from such classes, for a number of weeks each year, in preparation for religious ceremonies.

The RM1 approach was adopted by 'born again Christian' parents in the case of *Mozert* v. *Hawkins*. Gutmann notes that, while the objective of the Hawkins curriculum was to expose children to other ways of life and to teach the values and virtues of citizenship, the parents 'rejected the relevance of the distinction between exposure to knowledge and inculcation of belief' (1995, pp. 566, 571). Although the distinction is valid, nonetheless, it is likely that the parents of participants in such a civic education programme *will* find it more difficult to share their way of life with their children. This is the case as it requires that we, as parents, 'surrender some control over our own children for the sake of reasonable common efforts to insure that all future citizens learn the minimal prerequisites of citizenship' (Macedo, 1995, pp. 485–6).

I have argued that we can be faced with moral conflicts when we consider whether parents are entitled to share a way of life with their children. Gutmann recognises that such conflicts can arise, but she also proposes a general rule for their resolution, as we saw in the Introduction. As a 'comprehensive liberal', she defends the following 'appropriate rule' when faced with the 'problem of ordering the religious freedom of parents and the right of children to an adequate education', namely 'that a child's right to education be given priority over his or her parents' right to religious exercise' (1980, pp. 349–50). Her rationale for this general rule is that, insofar as their education promotes autonomy, in the future such children will be 'capable of choosing among available conceptions of the good and of participating intelligently in democratic politics if they so choose' (ibid., p. 349), and although this will interfere with the children's free exercise of their religion in the present, nonetheless 'a concurrent denial of the child's educational right calls into question the grounds of his or her acceptance of those religious beliefs' (ibid., p. 350). In addition, although parents have non-paternalistic rights over their children, which 'derive from parents' rights to live their own lives freely' (ibid., p. 353), such rights are limited by the 'paternalistic' duty to promote their children's autonomy (ibid., p. 350). In short, the requirement to promote autonomy trumps other moral claims.

The situation, for comprehensive liberals, is one of conflicting moral duties. However, it could be argued that Gutmann and other comprehensive liberals deal with this moral conflict by a process of moral simplification. On this argument, as a general rule, we are not required to respect diversity where this comes into conflict with the promotion of autonomy. In addition, Gutmann also does *not* distinguish 'children's [...] rights to religious freedom' and their 'parents' right to religious exercise', but rather runs the two together (ibid., pp. 349–50). This line of argument is highly questionable for two reasons. The first is that children's rights to religious freedom may come into conflict with their parents' right to religious freedom, as happens when children disagree with their parents' beliefs on religious grounds. I return to children's rights below, in the next section, and so, for now, I will bracket the issue of possible conflicts between the rights to religious freedom of parents and their children. The second reason for concern is that it is at least arguable that the duty to promote the autonomy of the adult the child will one day be does *not*, as a general rule, have priority over other moral considerations, and the case for such a conclusion has been made by utilitarians (Scarre, 1980), Kantians (O'Neill, 1989), Aristotelian Thomists (MacIntyre, 1988; 1999), and others, including Archard's version of the caretaker thesis. That is, this is a matter of on-going debate, as it is the subject matter of a philosophical disagreement that has not been resolved. Gutmann can be challenged on the grounds that her proposed general rule for resolving moral conflicts lacks philosophical licence.

Indeed, there may be cases where parents' right to exercise their religion, and the requirement to respect diversity of beliefs and ways of life, should be allowed to trump the duty to promote the autonomy of the adults children will one day be. As we saw, the second group of parents (RM2) agree to their children's participation in a civic education programme but also request that they be permitted, periodically, to withdraw their children from such classes to engage in religious ceremonies considered central to the identity of those who belong to the community in question. Is this justified? It may well be true that, if parents remove their children from school for, let us say, three weeks so as to prepare for a religious ceremony, they are strengthening the children's commitment to and identification with one way of life and moral outlook. In doing this, the parents may lessen the effectiveness of the civic education programme in bringing about one of its core aims, namely the promotion of autonomy. In some cases it may not, of course, but let us assume for argument's sake that it does.

It does not follow that the children ought not to be removed from school for that reason. In fact, to insist that, in *any* case where they come into conflict, we must *always* prioritise children's (future) autonomy over parents' religious freedom and respect for diversity would be highly intolerant as a moral outlook and would require an excessive use of coercive power for its implementation. If we go down this route, then liberal civic education will be actively hostile to the promotion of illiberal ways of life by parents. This would seem to be the case with Mathew Clayton's argument that parents, in raising their children, are not entitled to be guided by ideals that 'rest on the validity of any particular reasonable comprehensive doctrine', whether religious or secular (2006, p. 94).

Should civic education programmes be child-centred and voluntary?

In addressing this second ethical question, I want to start by returning to the hypothetical scenario, outlined in Chapter 1, which once again concerns a service learning civic education programme. As we saw then, some students (S1) request permission to be excused from the classroom-based component of the course, which they feel to be a waste of their time. And a second group of students (S2) are happy to engage in classroom-based instruction, but they request greater input into the design and delivery of the course.

This second scenario highlights the moral conflicts that may arise concerning children's right to liberty, in particular when we institutionalise a civic education programme, conflicts that we put to one side in the previous section. Gutmann defends parents' paternalistic duty to promote their children's autonomy. She believes paternalism entails interference with another's liberty, a definition of paternalism that we have already questioned. However, what is relevant here is her argument that parents ought to interfere with their children's liberty of action 'by reference to the child's present or future interests', interests she equates with 'the capacity for free choice' (1980, p. 338, n. 2). That is, Gutmann recognises that a civic education programme promoting the autonomy of the adults children will one day be nonetheless also may rightly interfere with children's liberty. This is the case because children, '(at least below a certain age), lack adequate reason to make important decisions for themselves'; and 'many decisions freely made by children are likely to result in serious harm to them and to curtail their future freedom unnecessarily' (ibid., p. 340). For that reason, 'society can legitimately exercise more power over children than it can over adult citizens' (ibid., p. 341). To return to the second hypothetical scenario, we can infer that Gutmann's position would be to not allow children to opt out of the classroom component of service learning (S1). However, once again we can say that this deals with a moral conflict by a process of moral simplification. It gives priority to the requirement to promote the autonomy of the adults the children will one day be, but in so doing puts to one side or downplays other morally significant features of the case here, in particular our duty to protect children's liberty.

I want to now turn to a second issue that arises regarding children's liberty. We must consider not only whether children should have the option of not attending civic education classes. In addition, will participation in civic education classes entail interference with children's liberty in the form of the shaping of children's preferences? For Berlin, as we saw in Chapter 4, the scope of my freedom is broader than the specific paths I am disposed to choose. That is, he distinguishes non-interference from non-frustration, as freedom is not the 'absence of frustration [...] but the absence of obstacles to possible choices and activities' (2004 [1969], p. 32). The distinction is important, as one can overcome 'obstacles to the fulfillment of desire' simply by killing desire (2004 [1988], p. 326) or, alternatively, by adapting one's preferences so as to desire whatever options happen to be available (2004 [1969], p. 32). The power of adults can be said to be problematic, on Berlin's view, to the extent that it leads to children's adoption of preferences that would find favour with those adults, and for that reason, the closing off of 'paths' or options that the children otherwise could have chosen. This may happen when parents want to 'share' a way of life with their children. It may also happen when, in a civic education programme, an effort is made to 'shape' the values of the adults the children will one day be.

In some cases, we may come to the conclusion that we ought to act so as to promote the autonomy of the adults the children will one day be, and that to do so requires interfering with children's liberty. However, it is also possible that in other circumstances we will be justified in concluding that we should give priority to protecting children's liberty. Indeed, it is possible to design civic education programmes so that they are, to the greatest extent possible, compatible with protecting the liberty of their young participants, as in our second scenario (S2). Gutmann herself has pointed out that participant-oriented education is, in many respects, more compatible with democracy, as it 'builds upon the students' interests and elicits their commitment to learning' (1999, p. 90). She also rightly warns that this commitment 'should be overridden when disorder and arrogance are so great as to threaten the very enterprise of education within schools' (ibid.).

It is true that, in the extreme case where children's *liberty* becomes children's *licence*, and so threatens to destroy education itself, we should prevent children from acting as they wish. However, this stand does not greatly help us in our efforts to deal with moral conflicts in less extreme cases. In particular, are we justified in retaining control of civic education courses when children wish to take on some of that responsibility themselves? Are there any situations where children should be given greater say on how civic education courses are run and on their content?

Conclusions

We have been examining whether parents have a right to share a way of life with their children and also whether the State may shape the values of its future citizens in particular through civic education. In doing so, we have raised important questions about the State's exercise of power over parents, as well as parents' exercise of power over their children. It is widely acknowledged that, when a society puts in place a civic education programme, we can be faced with moral conflicts between the requirement to promote the autonomy of the adults children will one day be and the right to religious freedom and the duty to respect diversity. However, when children engage with civic education programmes, we can also be faced with moral conflicts concerning the requirement to protect children's liberty. What is more, in this chapter we have found little evidence to support the claim that there is a general rule for resolving such conflicts.

As we saw, Gutmann claims to have identified a general rule for resolving conflicts arising in respect of civic education: 'that a child's right to education be given priority over his or her parents' right to religious exercise'. Her approach is open to question on a number of fronts. Let us imagine a situation where the parents do not actively oppose their children's participation in the civic education programme, but do insist that the children take time away from school for religious purposes (as outlined already). Let us also assume that there is a moral conflict here, although of course in many such situations there may be none. But let us assume there is a conflict. Even here it does not follow that we should give priority to children's right to education and autonomy over the right to religious freedom and the duty to respect diversity. If you are the parent in question, is it reasonable to expect you to accept that you are not entitled to engage your children in religious practices, in particular when you do not actively oppose the civic education programme? We have here different moral claims, and one option open to us is to try to find a compromise between them, in particular by permitting parents to remove their children from school for the short periods of time specified and for the aims outlined.

Nonetheless, in other situations, where parents' decisions are likely to cause significant harm to their children's education and their developing autonomy, we would be justified in reaching a different conclusion. This is the case not because the value of autonomy, as a general rule, is more fundamental than the values of religious freedom and respect for diversity, but rather because it is not reasonable for parents to advance one goal in such a way as to hamper children attaining other goals of great importance. Returning to the example of *Wisconsin* v. *Yoder*, Amish parents who educate their children at home or in private (parochial) schools must answer this kind of criticism. The aims of Amish private education is 'cultural self-determination through control of education', and this is of particular importance to the Amish as 'adult baptism places an enormous pressure on parents to raise children who *want* to be initiated into an exclusive community' (McConnell and Hurst, 2006, p. 236, p. 244; emphasis in original). This does seem diametrically opposed to the promotion of autonomy, certainly in the strong Socratic nurturing sense. Will such an education cause substantial damage to the autonomy of the adults the children will one day be? As I said, Amish parents (and others in similar situations) have to answer this question as the onus is on them to show that their way of life will not cause significant harm to their children's future autonomy. At the very least the evidence suggests that Amish-controlled education does not properly prepare children for further formal education (i.e. high school) (Fischel, 2012). Nonetheless, there is a limit to what we can say about the power exercised by Amish parents as a group, as there is significant diversity within this community. Indeed, some (admittedly a minority) Amish parents have chosen to educate their children in public schools, precisely because of the perceived benefits of exposure to other cultures, and 'accepting them for what they are' (McConnell and Hurst, 2006, p. 245).

We also asked whether or not civic education should be child-centred and voluntary. The first thing to note is that we can provide children with reasons why they should attend civic education classes. Children and young people have a higher-order interest in education as a necessary element of development, along with education for citizenship more specifically (see Macleod, 2004a; Fives, 2013b). Nonetheless, even if it is the case that children have reasons to attend civic education classes, we have to make difficult decisions between measures that protect children's liberty (e.g. giving children greater say in running a civic education programme) and measures designed to promote the autonomy of future adults (e.g. giving professional educators greater control of the programme). In such situations should we *always* prioritise the measures that promote autonomy? Yes, if we assume that education serves only one purpose, or that, of the various purposes it serves, one is fundamental. But this is not the case. What is more, it may be that a certain approach to civic education will lead to less than optimal outcomes concerning the autonomy of future adults, but this may be justified by benefits enjoyed elsewhere, including the greater liberty children experience in running the programme themselves. We should also consider the likelihood of the various outcomes under consideration. Thus while we can be quite certain that specific measures will better protect children's liberty, we have seen that there is uncertainty over the effectiveness of civic education in the promotion of autonomy. What this suggests is that, if we acknowledge we are faced with a genuine moral dilemma, we will have a very strong motivation to explore alternative civic education approaches, in each case examining the benefits and losses in respect of the various relevant values.

We also have to address those who are not opposed to civic education *per se*, but wish to be excused from participation in the classroom-based component (S1). Can civic education be voluntary in the sense that children have a right to opt out of some of its components? If we answer in the affirmative we are acknowledging the importance of protecting children's liberty. However, we need to explore further the moral implications of this decision. Children do not have the right to liberty only insofar as their freely made decisions also lead to good consequences for themselves. Nonetheless, although we do have a duty to respect children's liberty, including when they wish to be excused from certain aspects of their education, to do so may require that we violate other moral duties and as a result lead to moral conflict.

And to resolve such conflicts requires practical judgement and therefore detailed knowledge of the case in question. For example, what if we find that participation in the community service component leads to improvements in relatedness and moral and political understanding but not critical thinking? If that is the case, there are very strong grounds for requiring all children to attend both the classroom and the community components of the course, if it is in the former that we will see the greatest progress in attaining each of the programme aims. Of course, in other cases we may find the aim of improving critical thinking can be attained adequately well without requiring children to attend those parts of the course they find objectionable. Note, in each case we reach conclusions by considering the different possible courses of action and their likely consequences, and the plurality of moral claims that apply, and choose the course of action that offers the most reasonable resolution to competing moral claims.

Conclusion

When political philosophers present their work at conferences and seminars they are often asked for their views on topics or areas that they did not actually address in their paper. For instance, I recently gave a paper on children's informed consent for research and medical treatment. I was then asked for my views on arranged marriages of teenage girls from religious minorities living in liberal, Western societies. It is understandable, for a number of reasons, that such questions are asked. It is understandable, as people want to *test* the arguments you have put forward in one context by seeing what they look like when applied to another, somewhat similar, context. So, my argument about informed consent, and about moral dilemmas faced when we consider informed consent, may have sounded convincing when applied to the fields of research and medicine, but maybe not so convincing when applied to the topic of arranged marriages. That is, would I also say that what we have here, with respect to arranged marriages, is a plurality of values with no clear priority between them, so that we cannot conclude that arranged marriages are unjustified because, let us say as a general rule, we must give priority to the development of young girls' autonomy?

This type of question is itself problematic *if* it is motived by the following assumption about political philosophy. The assumption is that political philosophers can answer complex moral questions without giving very much consideration to the complexities of the cases where the questions are raised. As we have seen in this book, many political philosophers assume that, when we are faced with conflicting moral claims, the job of a political philosopher is to identify general rules to resolve such conflicts. Such an approach assumes that, when we engage in political philosophy we work out ideals in our head and then apply them directly to specific cases: we apply them 'neat', to use Jonathan Wolff's terminology.

Throughout this book, I have argued against such an approach. It is the case that we can do highly abstract and theoretical work, and such work does or should have generality. For instance, when I argued that paternalism as a concept was not sufficient to account for the power exercised by parents, I intended this as a general theoretical claim. At the same time, we can be doing quite applied work, and this requires that we look closely at cases, and make decisions based on practical judgements in those cases. However, when we make practical judgements in specific cases, we also claim a kind of generality in our reasoning. So what should we say when asked to apply arguments made in respect of one case to another case? The honest answer in most scenarios is 'I cannot answer your question with full confidence just yet. It may be that, after careful examination, I will agree that arranged marriages are unjustified because of their impact on young girls' autonomy. However, even if I arrive at this judgement, it will not be based on the assumption that autonomy, as a general rule, has priority over other values'. This is the intellectually honest answer, I think, and the answer that does the least harm to our discipline.

Theoretical conclusions

As I said, political philosophy does require conceptual and methodological work, and such arguments do or should have generality as theoretical claims. What are this book's general findings of a conceptual and methodological nature? The first conclusion is that paternalism is insufficient to account for the legitimacy of parents' power, as there are non-paternalistic forms of parental power, and they too can be legitimate. This finding has important implications for both the liberation thesis and the caretaker thesis, for both equate parental power with paternalism. The implication is that we must break out of what has been a very limiting debate and move beyond categories of caretaker and liberator.

I also concluded that, when we do need to speak of parents' paternalism, then we should use Gert and Culver's pluralist definition. Their definition is of great importance for the discipline of political philosophy, for it draws attention to moral pluralism and moral dilemmas. We have seen that moral dilemmas can arise when we evaluate parental power. According to Williams, a moral dilemma arises 'where there is a conflict between two moral judgments that a man is disposed to make relevant to deciding what to do'. In addition, I would add that we are faced with moral dilemmas when we cannot identify a general rule for their resolution. This amendment is needed, as many believe that we are faced with moral conflicts, but also that we can and should identify the general rule for their resolution. Therefore, in line with Williams, as well as Nagel and Hampshire, I have argued here that moral pluralism can lead to moral dilemmas, and this marks the limit point where theory ends and practical judgement is needed.

Given what I have said about moral dilemmas, when we engage in the analysis of political phenomena we can be faced with an irreducible plurality of morally significant features and of relevant moral considerations. This is the case with the plurality of forms of power, as well as the various justifications of parental power. It is also the case with respect to the variety of concepts relating to children's agency. What I have tried to do is show that the best philosophical efforts to reduce such plurality, to tidy up and place in order these varied considerations, have failed as theoretical exercises. What this means is that they have failed to establish that, as a general rule, we can order our moral claims in the way they have specified. The failure to do so merely represents the failure of ideal theory, of attempts to apply our theoretical constructs *neat* to reality.

Arguments about children's agency, or their lack of agency, are ever-present in the political philosophy literature. However, it is not the case that parents may exercise power over children only insofar as children lack the qualities of an agent and only insofar as parental power makes up for the deficits that legitimate their subordination. This is the case because we know that both soft and hard paternalism may on occasion be justified, and that neither is justified because the subordinate party lacks the qualities of an agent. Not only that, even when parents do exercise power over children to make up for their deficits in competence, they can be faced with moral dilemmas. Even when, in the first instance, it is right for a parent to act so as to make up for a child's incompetence, it may be that the parent will violate a moral rule in regard to the child, for example, the requirement not to deceive one's child or to protect one's child's liberty, and so on.

With respect to power itself, and going against many radical accounts, I concluded that we cannot equate power with coercion. Rather, there are non-coercive forms of 'power over', never mind 'power to' and 'power with'. This has important implications for how we conceptualise legitimacy. Given the irreducible plurality of power concepts, we cannot equate legitimacy with the normative justification of just one of these forms of power. For example, even those who would give priority to coercion must also consider the issue of authority, as even legitimate coercive power may lack authority. What is more, for each form of power, there is a plurality of relevant moral considerations, and they can pull in different directions leading to moral conflict. So even if we are to address the legitimacy of only one form of power, we could be faced with moral dilemmas. For example, if we only analyse the legitimacy of coercive power, we can be faced with conflicts between the requirement to protect each person's liberty, on the one hand, and the requirement to accept wide-ranging infringements of individual inviolability for the sake of maintaining a society that brings with it all the benefits of civilisation, on the other.

Practical conclusions

I have also reached conclusions about substantive issues and have made practical judgements in specific cases. In one sense, these have generality, as I have made an argument in each instance and therefore I am looking for agreement from others. This is a rational enterprise, although I have made a distinction between theory, on the one hand, and practical judgement, on the other. What I have tried to do is provide a rationale for practical judgements that I have reached in respect of particular cases. Although the cases are in many instances hypothetical, they are informed by findings from empirical studies and also from what we have uncovered about legislation, policy, and services in the area in question. And the rationale I have offered in each case has been in line with the ideas of reasonableness and public justification in a context of actual disagreement, borrowed from Rawls and Nagel respectively, although with some adaptations. One important difference between my approach and that of Rawls and Nagel is that I treat parent–child relations as power relations requiring justification. Another important difference is that I have been sensitive to avoid liberal biases when employing an account of practical rationality developed from within liberal political thought.

I first considered the conditions that should be attached to the 'right to parent', and, in particular, arguments for parental licences, the monitoring of parents, and the provision of parenting support programmes. I came down against parental licences and instead considered the merits of alternative measures to best protect children from neglect and abuse. The argument against parental licences follows in part from a statistical consideration, namely that any test we use to predict who will be a bad parent will mistakenly classify many adults as potential child abusers. It is not reasonable to expect adults to accept the possibility that they will be wrongly categorised as abusive, when alternative proposals can safeguard children's well-being without unjustifiably limiting parental rights in this way. So what policies should be implemented? Parenting support programmes are associated with good outcomes in terms of children's well-being, but as those who elect to take such programmes are unrepresentative, by itself it will not provide sufficient protection for children. And although the continual monitoring of parents poses too great a risk to family privacy and intimacy, a limited programme of parental monitoring is a reasonable proposal and should be implemented alongside parental training.

We then considered one area where parents exercise power over their children, namely informed consent decisions for children's research participation and medical treatment. I argued that individuals are competent to make a decision if they are able to reflect on the alternative courses of action and the likely consequences of each, and also, crucially, they are aware of the plurality of moral values and the possibility for conflict between those values, and reasonable in the face of such conflicting moral claims. In the first instance, it is wrong for parents to prevent children from acting on the basis of their competent decisions. Nonetheless, parents retain a right to rear their children and to exercise control over their children, and so we may be faced with real moral dilemmas when parents do not wish to let their children act on the basis of their competent decisions. Also, joint decision making, when it is based on persuasion rather than other forms of influence, may be the ideal process in such cases, both because it is not assumed that any one party (parents, say) are 'in authority' and because it is a context in which to address conflicting values. So, joint decision making does not remove moral conflicts, but may be the best way to deal with many of them in a competent fashion and without undermining the voluntariness of children's behaviour.

When we consider civic education, we are led to ask whether parents have a right to share a way of life with their children and whether the State may justifiably shape the values of its future citizens. And when we try to answer these questions, we may on occasion have to deal with tensions and conflicts between respecting diversity and protecting adults' rights to religious freedom, promoting the autonomy of the adults children will one day be, and protecting the liberty of children. In resolving such dilemmas, we cannot assume that the value of autonomy is, as a general rule, fundamental. It is indeed the case that parents should not be permitted to sacrifice their children's future autonomy for the sake of their (the parents') religious beliefs, and nor should children's licence be permitted to undermine the project of education itself. But nonetheless, there are cases where we should accept some sacrifices in respect of future autonomy so as to better protect the liberty of children or their parents. For instance, in some cases we should allow children greater freedom to influence the design and delivery of civic education classes and to opt out of certain aspects of those programmes, if in doing so we guarantee gains in children's liberty; and we should allow parents to remove their children from civic education classes, for short periods, and so as to engage in religious ceremonies, so as to respect diversity and protect parents' right to liberty.

On practical rationality

There is a superficial similarity between the approach and argument of this book and what post-modernists do. We both agree that there can be conflicts between moral claims and therefore we both believe the role of theoretical reflection is limited. However, where we differ I think is in our account of practical reason and practical judgement. For the post-modernist, all forms of reasoning, practical or theoretical, are both relative and inescapably implicated in power. The post-modernist assumes not only that we cannot escape the way in which we have been constructed as subjects of specific discourses, but that every judgement is an act of symbolic violence, an arbitrary closing off of possibilities. However, post-modernism is undermined by an internal contradiction. Indeed, it can be argued that post-modernist arguments presuppose ethical principles and forms of reasoning that cannot be equated with arbitrary acts of symbolic violence, in particular as post-modernists make their own normative prescriptions and look for our rational agreement when they do so (Fives, 2009).

In contrast, I have assumed that we can make better or worse arguments, arguments that are more or less rationally defensible. In addition, the arguments made here in defence of practical judgements are moral in content. Therefore, I have not adopted a nihilistic attitude to either morality or rationality, for there is no justification for doing so, as shown by the fact that even post-modernists cannot consistently maintain such a position. The overall approach taken in this book has much more in common with what Wolff calls problem-driven political philosophy. Rather than hoping to change the world so as to better fit my theoretical ideas, arguably the approach taken by such public intellectuals as Sartre and Marx (Johnson, 1988), I have instead assumed that my arguments must be informed by the practical reality of people's lives.

However, people's lives are untidy in the sense that when they are tasked with making judgements there can be an irreducible plurality of moral considerations and morally relevant features. It is because of such irreducible plurality that, as Nagel, Williams, Berlin, and Hampshire have observed, we may be faced with moral dilemmas. It is how we respond to moral dilemmas that is the important issue both for the discipline of political philosophy and for how people fare in their own lives. I have tried to outline what I take to be a rigorous approach for the resolution of moral conflicts, and I believe this is an approach that is suited to the situations where people have to make decisions, including the decisions made by parents, by children, and by professionals working with families.

References

Allen, A. (1998) 'Rethinking power', *Hypatia*, 13(1), 21–40.

Anomaly, J. (2014) 'Public goods and procreation', *Monash Bioethics Review*, 32(2), 172–88.

Appelbaum, P. S. (2007) 'Assessment of patients' competence to consent to treatment', *The New England Journal of Medicine*, 357, 1834–40.

Archard, D. (1990) 'Paternalism defined', *Analysis*, 50(1), 36–42.

Archard, D. (1993) 'Self-justifying paternalism', *The Journal of Value Inquiry*, 27, 341–52.

Archard, D. (2003) 'Citizenship education and multiculturalism', in A. Lockyer, B. Crick and J. Annetto (eds), *Education for Democratic Citizenship: Issues of Theory and Practice* (Aldershot: Ashgate), pp. 89–102.

Archard, D. (2004) *Children: Rights and Childhood*, second edition (London: Routledge).

Archard, D. (2010) *The Family: A Liberal Defence* (Basingstoke: Palgrave).

Arendt, H. (1963) 'What is authority?', in *Between Past and Future* (Cleveland: World Publishing Co.), pp. 91–141.

Arendt, H. (1969) *On Violence* (London: Penguin).

Aristotle, *The Nicomachean Ethics* [NE], trans. D. Ross, revised J. L. Ackrill and J. O. Urmson (Oxford: Oxford University Press, 1980).

Arneson, R. J. (2005) 'Joel Feinberg and the justification of hard paternalism', *Legal Theory*, 11(3), 259–84.

Arnold, D. G. (2001) 'Coercion and moral responsibility', *American Philosophical Quarterly*, 38(1), 53–67.

Aunola, K., Stattin, H. and Nurmi, J. E. (2000) 'Parenting styles and adolescents' achievement strategies', *Journal of Adolescence*, 23(2), 205–22.

Bachrach, P. and Baratz, M. (2002 [1962]), 'Two faces of power', in M. Haugaard (ed.), *Power: A Reader* (Manchester: Manchester University Press), pp. 28–37.

Baker, J. (2013) 'Children's agency, interests, and medical consent', *HEC Forum*, 25(4), 311–24.

Baldwin, D. A. (2015) 'Misinterpreting Dahl on power', *Journal of Political Power*, 8(2), 209–27.

Bandura, A. (2006) 'Towards a psychology of human agency', *Perspectives on Psychological Science*, 1(2), 164–80.

Barnhart, M. G. (2004) 'An overlapping consensus: A critique of two approaches', *Review of Politics*, 66(2), 257–83.

Baumrind, D. (1971) 'Current patterns of parental authority', *Developmental Psychology Monographs*, 4, 1–103.

Baumrind, D. (1991) 'The influence of parenting style on adolescent competence and substance use', *The Journal of Early Adolescence*, 11(1), 56–95.

Baumrind, D. (1996) 'The discipline controversy revisited', *Family Relations*, 45(4), 405–14.

Beauchamp, T. L. and Childress, J. F. (2009) *Principles of Biomedical Ethics*, sixth edition (Oxford: Oxford University Press).

Beetham, D. (1991) *The Legitimation of Power* (Houndmills: Macmillan).

Benatar, D. (2010) 'The limits of reproductive freedom', in D. Archard and D. Benatar (eds), *Procreation and Parenthood: The Ethics of Bearing and Rearing Children* (Oxford: Oxford University Press), pp. 78–102.

Benn, S. I. (1975) 'Privacy, freedom, and respect for persons', in R. Wasserstrom (ed.), *Today's Moral Problems* (New York: Macmillan).

Berg, J. W., Appelbaum, P. S. and Grisso, T. (1996) 'Constructing competence: Formulating standards of legal competence to make medical decisions', *Rutgers Law Review*, 48(2), 345–96.

Berlin, I. (2004 [1958]) 'Two concepts of liberty', in H. Hardy (ed.), *Liberty* (Oxford: Oxford University Press), pp. 166–217.

Berlin, I. (2004 [1969]) 'Introduction', in H. Hardy (ed.), *Liberty* (Oxford: Oxford University Press), pp. 3–54.

Berlin, I. (2004 [1988]) 'Final retrospect', in H. Hardy (ed.), *Liberty* (Oxford: Oxford University Press), pp. 322–30.

Bernier, A., Carlson, S. M. and Whipple, N. (2010) 'From external regulation to self-regulation: Early parenting precursors of young children's executive functioning', *Child Development*, 81(1), 326–39.

Bottrell, A. and Macleod, C. (Carolyn) (2015) 'Can a right to reproduce justify the status quo on parental licensing?', in S. Hannan, S. Brennan and R. Vernon (eds), *Permissible Progeny? The Morality of Procreation and Parenting* (Oxford: Oxford University Press), pp. 184–207.

Brennan, S. (2002) 'Children's choices or children's interests: Which do their rights protect?', in D. Archard and C. M. Macleod (eds), *The Moral and Political Status of Children* (Oxford: Oxford University Press), pp. 53–69.

Brighouse, H. (2000) *Social Choice and Social Justice* (Oxford: Oxford University Press).

Brighouse, H. and Swift, A. (2006) 'Parents' rights and the value of the family', *Ethics*, 117(1), 80–106.

Brighouse, H. and Swift, A. (2014) *Family Values: The Ethics of Parent–Child Relationships* (Princeton: Princeton University Press).

Bruzzese, J.-M. and Fisher, C. B. (2003) 'Assessing and enhancing the research consent capacity of children and youth', *Applied Developmental Science*, 7(1), 13–26.

Buchanan, A. (2004) 'Mental capacity, legal competence and consent to treatment', *Journal of the Royal Society of Medicine*, 97(9), 415–20.

Buchanan, A. and Brock, D. W. (1986) 'Deciding for others', *The Milbank Quarterly*, 64(2), 17–94.

Burtt, S. (2003) 'The proper scope of parental authority: Why we don't owe children an "Open Future"', in S. Macedo and I. M. Young (eds), *Child, Family, and State: Nomos KLIV* (New York: New York University Press), pp. 243–70.

Campbell, L. (2016) 'The limits of autonomy: An exploration of the role of autonomy in the debate about assisted suicide', in M. Donnelly and C. Murray (eds), *Ethical and Legal Debates in Irish Healthcare: Confronting Complexities* (Manchester: Manchester University Press), pp. 55–70.

Cassidy, L. (2006) 'That many of us should not parent', *Hypatia*, 21(4), 40–57.

Christiano, T. (2012) 'Authority', *The Stanford Encyclopedia of Philosophy*. http://plato.stanford.edu/entries/authority/ [accessed October 2015].

Clarke, S. (2002) 'A definition of paternalism', *Critical Review of International Social and Political Philosophy*, 5(1), 81–91.

Clayton, M. (2006) *Justice and Legitimacy in Upgringing* (Oxford: Oxford University Press).

Clegg, S. (1989) *Frameworks of Power* (London: Sage).

Clegg, S. (2010) 'The state, power, and agency: Missing in action in institutional theory?' *Journal of Management Inquiry*, 19(1), 4–13.

Clouser, K. D. (1995) 'Common morality as an alternative to principlism', *Kennedy Institute of Ethics Journal*, 5(3), 219–36.

Clouser, K. D. and Gert, B. (1990) 'A critique of principlism', *Journal of Medicine and Philosophy*, 15(2), 219–36.

Coady, C. A. J. (1991) 'Politics and the problem of dirty hands', in P. Singer (ed.), *A Companion to Ethics* (Oxford: Blackwell), pp. 373–83.

Cohen, G. A. (2003) 'Facts and principles', *Philosophy & Public Affairs*, 31(3), 211–45.

Coleman, J. (2002) 'Answering Susan: Liberalism, civic education, and the status of young persons', in D. Archard and C. M. Macleod (eds), *The Moral and Political Status of Children* (Oxford: Oxford University Press), pp. 160–80.

Conover, P. J. and Searing, D. D. (2000) 'A political socialization perspective', in L. M. McDonnell, P. M. Timpane and R. Benjamin (eds), *Rediscovering the Democratic Purposes of Education* (Lawrence: University Press of Kansas), pp. 91–124.

Cornock, M. (2007) 'Fraser guidelines or Gillick competence?' *Journal of Children's and Young People's Nursing*, 1(3), 142.

Coyne, J. C. and Kwakkenbos, L. (2013) 'Triple P-Positive Parenting programs: The folly of basing social policy on underpowered flawed studies', *BMC Med*, 11(1), 11.

Culver, C. M. and Gert, B. (1990) 'The inadequacy of incompetence', *Milbank Quarterly*, 68(4), 619–43.

Dahl, R. (2002 [1968]) 'Power', in M. Haugaard (ed.), *Power: A Reader* (Manchester: Manchester University Press), pp. 8–25.

Daly, A. M. (2014) 'What influences adolescents' contraceptive decision making? A meta-ethnography', *Journal of Pediatric Nursing*, 29(6), 614–32.

De Haan, J. (2001) 'The definition of moral dilemmas: A logical problem', *Ethical Theory and Moral Practice*, 4(3), 267–84.

Delli Carpini, M. X. and Keeter, S. (1996) *What Americans Know About Politics and Why It Matters* (New Haven, CT: Yale University Press).

De Wispelaere, J. and Weinstock, D. (2012) 'Licensing parents to protect our children?' *Ethics and Social Welfare*, 6(2), 195–205.

Donagan, A. (1993) 'Moral dilemmas, genuine and spurious: A comparative anatomy', *Ethics*, 104(1), 7–21.

Dryzek, J. S. and Niemeyer, S. (2006) 'Reconciling pluralism and consensus as political ideals', *American Journal of Political Science*, 50(3), 634–49.

Dunn, J. (1990) *Interpreting Political Responsibility* (Cambridge: Polity Press).

Dworkin, G. (1972) 'Paternalism', *The Monist*, 56(1), 64–84.

Dworkin, G. (1983) 'Paternalism: Some second thoughts', in R. Sartorius (ed.), *Paternalism* (Minneapolis: University of Minnesota Press), pp. 105–12.

Dworkin, G. (2005) 'Moral paternalism', *Law and Philosophy*, 24(3), 305–19.

Dworkin, R. (1978) 'Liberalism', in S. Hampshire (ed.), *Public and Private Morality* (Cambridge: Cambridge University Press), pp. 113–43.

Dworkin, R. (1990 [1986]) 'Obigations of community', from *Law's Empire*, in J. Raz (ed.), *Authority* (New York: New York University Press), pp. 218–39.

Engster, D. and Gonzales, R. (2012) 'Children and justice: a proposal for national parent training classes', *Public Affairs Quarterly*, 26(3), 221–41.

Feinberg, J. (1971) 'Legal paternalism', *Canadian Journal of Philosophy*, 1(1), 105–24.

Feinberg, J. (1980) 'The child's right to an open future', in W. Aiken and H. LaFollette (eds), *Whose Child?* (Totowa, NJ: Littlefield, Adams and Co), pp. 124–53.

Feinberg, J. (1986) *The Moral Limits Of The Criminal Law, Vol. 3 Harm To Self* (Oxford: Oxford University Press).

Felzmann, H., Sixsmith, J., O'Higgins, S., Ni Chonnactaigh, S. and Nic Gabhainn, S. (2010) *Ethical Review and Children's Research in Ireland* (Dublin: Department of Health and Children).

Fineman, M. L. A. (2003) 'Taking children's interests seriously', in S. Macedo and I. M. Young (eds), *Child, Family, and State: Nomos KLIV* (New York: New York University Press), pp. 234–42.

Fischel, W. A. (2012) 'Do Amish one-room schools make the grade? The dubious data of "Wisconsin v. Yoder"', *University of Chicago Law Review*, 79(1), 107–29.

Fives, A. (2005) 'Virtue, justice, and the human good: Non-relative communitarian ethics and the life of religious commitment', *Contemporary Politics*, 11(2–3), 117–31.

Fives, A. (2006) 'Aristotle's ethics and contemporary political theory', *21st Century Society*, 1(2), 201–20.

Fives, A. (2008a) *Political and Philosophical Debates in Welfare* (Basingstoke: Palgrave).

Fives, A. (2008b) 'Human flourishing: The grounds of moral judgement', *The Journal of Value Inquiry*, 42(2), 167–86.

Fives, A. (2009) 'Reasonable, agonistic, or good? The character of a democrat', *Philosophy and Social Criticism*, 35(8), 961–83.

Fives, A. (2010) 'Reasonableness, pluralism, and liberal moral doctrines', *The Journal of Value Inquiry*, 44(3), 321–39.

Fives, A. (2013a) *Political Reason: Morality and the Public Sphere* (Basingstoke: Palgrave).

Fives, A. (2013b) 'Non-coercive promotion of values in civic education for democracy', *Philosophy and Social Criticism*, 39(6), 577–90.

Fives, A. (2015) 'Parents, children, and good leadership: Is parental authority compatible with children's freedom?', in J. Boaks and M. Levine (eds), *Ethics and Leadership* (London: Bloomsbury), pp. 211–32.

Fives, A. (2016a) 'The association of attitude to reading and reading achievement among 9 year olds in Ireland', *Reading Psychology*, 13(1), 27–54.

Fives, A. (2016b) 'Modeling the interaction of academic self-beliefs, frequency of reading at home, emotional support, and reading achievement: An RCT study of at-risk early readers in 1st grade and 2nd grade', *Reading Psychology*, 13(3), 339–70.

Fives, A. (2016c) 'The role of philosophy in public matters', in A. Fives and K. Breen (eds), *Philosophy and Political Engagement: Reflection in the Public Sphere* (Basingstoke: Palgrave), pp. 7–28.

Fives, A. (2016d) 'Working from both ends: The due role of philosophy in research ethics', in A. Fives and K. Breen (eds), *Philosophy and Political Engagement: Reflection in the Public Sphere* (Basingstoke: Palgrave), pp. 161–84.

Fives, A. (2016e) 'Who gets to decide? Children's competence, parental authority, and informed consent', in J. Drerup, G. Schweiger, G. Graf, and C. Schickhardt (eds), *Justice, Education and the Politics of Childhood: Challenges and Perspectives* (Switzerland: Springer), pp. 35–47.

Fives, A., Canavan, J. and Dolan, P. (2017) 'Evaluation study design: A pluralist approach to evidence', *European Early Childhood Education Research Journal*, 25(1).

Fives, A., Kennan, D. and Canavan, J. (2013) 'Why we still need the term "young carer": Findings from an exploratory study of young carers in Ireland', *Critical Social Work*, 14(1), 49–61.

Fives, A., Russell, D., Kearns, N., Lyons, R., Eaton, P., Canavan, J., Devaney, C. and O'Brien, A. (2015) 'The ethics of randomized controlled trials in social settings: Can social trials be scientifically promising and must there be equipoise?', *International Journal of Research and method in Education*, 38(1), 56–71.

Foot, P. (2001) *Natural Goodness* (Oxford: Oxford University Press).

Foot, P. (2002 [1983]) 'Moral realism and moral dilemma', in *Moral Dilemmas and Other Topics in Moral Philosophy* (Oxford: Clarendon Press), pp. 37–58.

Foot, P. (2002 [1995]) 'Moral dilemmas revisited', in *Moral Dilemmas and Other Topics in Moral Philosophy* (Oxford: Clarendon Press), pp. 175–88.

Foucault, M. (1984) 'What is enlightenment?', in P. Rabinow (ed.), *The Foucault Reader* (New York: Pantheon Books), pp. 32–50.

Freedman, B. (1987) 'Equipoise and the ethics of clinical research', *New England Journal of Medicine*, 317(3), 141–5.

Freedman, B. (1990) 'Placebo-controlled trials and the logic of clinical purpose', *IRB: A Review of Human Subjects Research*, 12(6), 1–6.

Freedman, B., Glass, K. C. and Weijer, C. (1996) 'Placebo orthodoxy in clinical research II: Ethical, legal, and regulatory myths', *Journal of Law, Medicine and Ethics*, 24(3), 252–9.

Freeman, M. (1997) *The Moral Status of Children: Essays on the Rights of the Child* (The Hague: Martinus Nijhoff).

Freeman, M. (2007) 'Why it remains important to take children's rights seriously', *International Journal of Children's Rights*, 15(1), 5–23.

Fried, C. (1970) *An Anatomy of Values: Problems in Personal and Social Choice* (Cambridge, MA: Harvard University Press).

Friedman, R. B. (1990 [1973]) 'On the concept of authority in political philosophy', in J. Raz (ed.), *Authority* (New York: New York University Press), pp. 56–91.

Galston, W. A. (2001a) 'Political knowledge, political engagement, and civic education', *Annual Review of Political Science*, 4(1), 217–34.

Galston, W. A. (2001b) 'Value pluralism and liberal political theory', *American Political Science Review*, 93(4), 769–78.

Galston, W. A. (2003) 'Parents, government, and children: Authority over education in the liberal democratic state', in S. Macedo and I. M. Young (eds), *Child, Family, and State: Nomos KLIV* (New York: New York University Press), pp. 211–33.

Galvan, T. A., Hare, C. E., Parra, J., Penn, H., Voss, S., Glober, G., et al. (2006) 'Earlier development of the accumbens relative to orbitofrontal cortex might underlie risk-taking behavior in adolescents', *Journal of Neuroscience*, 26(25), 6885–92.

Gavison, R. (1980) 'Privacy and the limits of law', *The Yale Law Journal*, 89(3), 421–71.

General Medical Council (2007) *0–18: Guidance for All Doctors* (Manchester: GMC).

Gert, B. and Culver, C. M. (1976) 'Paternalistic behavior', *Philosophy & Public Affairs*, 6(1), 45–57.

Gheaus, A. (2012) 'The right to parent one's biological baby', *The Journal of Political Philosophy*, 20(4), 432–55.

Gillick v. West Norfolk and Wisbech Area Health Authority and another [1985] 2 BMLR 11

Göhler, G. (2009) '"Power to" and "Power over"', in M. Haugaard and S. Clegg (eds), *The Sage Handbook of Power* (London: Sage), pp. 27–39.

Gutmann, A. (1980) 'Children, paternalism, and education: A liberal argument', *Philosophy & Public Affairs*, 9(4), 338–58.

Gutmann, A. (1995) 'Civic education and social diversity', *Ethics*, 105(3), 557–79.

Gutmann, A. (1999) *Democratic Education*, second edition (Princeton: Princeton University Press).

Habermas, J. (1990) *Moral Consciousness and Communicative Action*, trans. C. Lenhardt and S. Weber Nicholson (Cambridge: Polity Press).

Halpern-Felsher, B. L. and Cauffman, E. (2001) 'Costs and benefits of a decision: Decision-making competence in adolescents and adults', *Applied Developmental Psychology*, 22(3), 257–73.

Hampshire, S. (1978) 'Public and private morality', in S. Hampshire (ed.), *Public and Private Morality* (Cambridge: Cambridge University Press), pp. 23–53.

Hardimon, M. (1994) 'Role obligations', *Journal of Philosophy*, 91(7), 333–63.

Hare, R. M. (1978) *Moral Conflicts: The Tanner Lectures on Human Values*. Available at: http://tannerlectures.utah.edu/_documents/a-to-z/h/hare80.pdf [accessed 1 December 2016].

Harris, J. (1996) 'Liberating children', in M. Leahy and D. Cohn-Sherbok (eds), *The Liberation Debate: Rights at Issue* (London: Routledge), pp. 135–46.

Hart, H. L. A. (1973) 'Rawls on liberty and its priority', *The University of Chicago Law Review*, 40(3), 534–55.

Haugaard, M. (2002) *Power: A Reader* (Manchester: Manchester University Press).

Haugaard, M. (2012) 'Rethinking the four dimensions of power: Domination and empowerment', *Journal of Political Power*, 5(1), 33–54.

Haugaard, M. (2015) 'Concerted power over', *Constellations: An International Journal of Critical and Democratic Theory*, 22(1), 147–58.

Hayward, C. and Lukes, S. (2008) 'Nobody to shoot? Power, structure, and agency: A dialogue', *Journal of Power*, 1(1), 5–20.

Hershey, P. T. (1985) 'A definition of paternalism', *Journal of Medicine and Philosophy*, 10(2), 171–82.

Hess, D. E. (2004) 'Controversies about controversial issues in democratic education', *Political Science and Politics*, 37(2), 257–61.

Hill, M. (2006) 'Children's voices on ways of having a voice: Children's and young people's perspectives on methods used in research and consultation', *Childhood*, 13(1), 69–89.

Hobbes, T. (1996 [1651]) *Leviathan, or The Matter, Form, and Power of a Commonwealth Ecclesiastical and Civil*, ed. J. C. A. Gaskin (Oxford: Oxford University Press).

Holt, J. (1975) *Escape from Childhood* (Harmondsworth: Penguin).

Horton, J. (2010) *Political Obligation*, second edition (Basingstoke: Palgrave Macmillan).

Houses of the Oireachtas (2012) Thirty-first Amendment of the Constitution (Children) Bill 2012 as passed by both Houses of the Oireachtas, available at: www.oireachtas.ie/documents/bills28/bills/2012/7812/31stAmendofCon(Children).pdf [accessed 1 December 2016].

Hume, D. (1969 [1739–40]) *A Treatise of Human Nature*, ed. E. C. Mossner (Harmondsworth: Penguin).

Hume, D. (1993 [1748]) 'Of the original contract', in S. Copley and A. Edgar (eds), *David Hume: Selected Essays* (Oxford: Oxford University Press), pp. 274–92.

Hunter, D. and Pierscionek, B. K. (2007) 'Children, Gillick competency and consent for involvement in research', *Journal of Medical Ethics*, 33(11), 659–62.

Innes, J. (1992) *Privacy, Intimacy and Isolation* (Oxford: Oxford University Press).

Ireland, M. (1993) *Reconsidering Women: Separating Motherhood from Female Identity* (New York: Guilford).

James, A., Jenks, C. and Prout, A. (1998) *Theorizing Childhood* (Cambridge: Polity Press).

Jansen, L. A. (2005) 'A closer look at the Bad Deal Trial: Beyond clinical equipoise', *Hastings Center Report*, 35(5), 29–36.

Johnson, P. (1988) *Intellectuals* (London: George Weidenfeld and Nicholson).

Jonsen, A. R. (1995) 'Casuistry: An alternative or complement to principles?' *Kennedy Institute of Ethics Journal*, 5(3), 237–51.

Jonsen, A. R. and Toulmin, S. (1988) *The Abuse of Casuistry: A History of Moral Reasoning* (Berkeley and Los Angeles: University of California Press).

Kahne, J. E. and Sporte, S. E. (2008) 'Developing citizens: The impact of civic learning opportunities on students' commitment to civic participation', *American Educational Research Journal*, 45(3), 738–66.

Kant, I. (1908 [1788]) *Critique of Practical Reason: Kant's gesammelte Schriften*, ed. Paul Natorp (Berlin).

Kant, I. (1956 [1785]) *Groundwork for the Metaphysics of Morals*, trans. H. J. Paton, third edition (London: Hutchinson).

Kligman, M. and Culver, C. M. (1992) 'An analysis of interpersonal manipulation', *Journal of Medicine and Philosophy* 17(2), 173–97.

Komrad, M. (1983) 'A defence of medical paternalism: maximising patients' autonomy', *Journal of Medical Ethics*, 9(1), 38–44.

Kymlicka, K. (2003) 'Two dilemmas of citizenship education in pluralist societies', in A. Lockyer, B. Crick and J. Annetto (eds), *Education for Democratic Citizenship: Issues of Theory and Practice* (Aldershot: Ashgate), pp. 47–63.

LaFollette, H. (1980) 'Licensing parents', *Philosophy & Public Affairs*, 9(2), 182–97.

LaFollette, H. (2010) 'Licensing parents revisited', *Journal of Applied Philosophy*, 27(4), 327–43.

Levin, M. (1997) 'Natural subordination, Aristotle on' *Philosophy*, 72(280), 241–57.

Liew, J., Chen, Q. and Hughes, J. N. (2010) 'Child effortful control, teacher–student relationships, and achievement in academically at-risk children: Additive and interactive effects', *Early Childhood Research Quarterly*, 25(1), 51–64.

Locke, J. (1993 [1679–83]) *Two Treaties of Government*, ed. Mark Goldie (London: Dent).

Lukes, S. (2005 [1974]) *Power: A Radical View*, second edition (London: Macmillan).

Lukes, S. (2015) 'Robert Dahl on power', *Journal of Political Power*, 8(2), 261–71.

Lutz, C. (2004) *Tradition in the Ethics of Alasdair MacIntyre: Relativism, Thomism, and Philosophy* (Lanham, MD: Lexington Books).

Macedo, S. (1995) 'Liberal civic education and religious fundamentalism: The case of God v. John Rawls', *Ethics*, 105(3), 468–96.

MacIntyre, A. (1985) *After Virtue: A Study in Moral Theory*, second edition (London: Gerald Duckworth).

MacIntyre, A. (1988) *Whose Justice? Which Rationality?* (London: Gerald Duckworth).

MacIntyre, A. (1999) *Dependent Rational Animals* (London: Gerald Duckworth).

MacIntyre, A. (2006) *Edith Stein: A Philosophical Prologue* (London: Rowman & Littlefield).

Mackenzie, C. (2008) 'Relational autonomy, normative authority and perfectionism', *Journal of Social Philosophy*, 39(4), 512–33.

Mackie, J. L. (1977) *Ethics: Inventing Right and Wrong* (Harmondsworth: Penguin).

Macleod, C. (Colin) (2003) 'Shaping children's convictions', *Theory and Research in Education*, 1(3), 315–30.

Macleod, C. (Colin) (2004a) 'A liberal theory of freedom of expression for children', *Chicago-Kent Law Review*, 79(1), 55–82.

Macleod, C. (Colin) (2004b) 'The puzzle of parental partiality. Reflections on how not to be a hypocrite: School choice for the morally perplexed parent', *Theory and Research in Education*, 2(3), 309–21.

Mangel, C. P. (1988) 'Licensing parents: How feasible?' *Family Law Quarterly*, 22(1), 17–39.

March, A. F. (2009) *Islam and Liberal Citizenship: The Search for an Overlapping Consensus* (Oxford: Oxford University Press).

Marino, P. (2015) *Moral Reasoning in a Pluralistic World* (Montreal: McGill-Queen's University Press).

Marx, K. (1973 [1844]) *Economic and Philosophic Manuscripts of 1844*, ed. D. J. Struick, trans. M. Milligan (London: Lawrence and Wishart Ltd).

Mason, A. (2004) 'Just constraints', *British Journal of Political Science*, 34(2), 251–68.

Mason, J. and Hood, S. (2011) 'Exploring issues of children as actors in social research', *Children andYouth Services Review*, 53, 490–5.

McCarthy, J., Campbell, L., D'alton-O'Connor, C., Andrews, T. and McLoughlin, K. (2015) *Palliative Care for the Person with Dementia. Guidance Document 7: Ethical Decision Making* (Dublin: Irish Hospice Foundation).

McConnell, D. L. and Hurst, C. E. (2006) 'No "Rip Van Winkles" here: Amish education since *Wisconsin v. Yoder*', *American Anthropological Association*, 37(3), 236–54.

Merritt, E. G., Wanless, S. B., Rimm-Kaufman, S. E. and Cameron, C. (2012) 'The contribution of teachers' emotional support to children's social behaviors and self-regulatory skills in first grade', *School Psychology Review*, 41(2), 141–59.

Metcalfe, J. and Son, L. (2012) 'Anoetic, noetic and autonoetic metacognition', in M. Beran, J. R. Brandl, J. Perner and J. Proust (eds), *The Foundations of Metacognition* (Oxford: Oxford University Press), pp. 289–301.

Mill, J. S. (1985 [1859]) *On Liberty*, ed. G. Himmelfarb (London: Penguin).

Mill, J. S. (1998 [1861]) 'Utilitarianism', in *On Liberty and Other Essays*, ed. John Gray (Oxford: Oxford University Press), pp. 131–201.

Miller, F. G. and Brody, H. (2003) 'Therapeutic misconception in the ethics of clinical trials', *Hastings Center Report*, 33(3), 19–28.

Miller, F. G. and Brody, H. (2007) 'Clinical equipoise and the incoherence of research ethics', *Journal of Medicine and Philosophy*, 32(2), 151–65.

Miller, P. B. and Weijer, C. (2006) 'Fiduciary obligation in clinical research', *Journal of Law, Medicine and Ethics*, 34(2), 424–40.

Miller, P. B. and Weijer, C. (2007) 'Equipoise and the duty of care in clinical research: A philosophical response to our critics', *Journal of Medicine and Philosophy*, 32(2), 117–33.

Miller, V. A., Drotar, D. and Kodish, E. (2004) 'Children's competence for assent and consent: A review of empirical findings', *Ethics and Behavior*, 14(3), 255–95.

Morriss, P. (2002) *Power: A Philosophical Analysis*, second edition (Manchester: Manchester University Press).

Mozert v. Hawkins County Board of Education. 827 F.2d 1058 (6th Cir. 1987). Available at: http://users.soc.umn.edu/~samaha/cases/mozert_v_hawkins_schools.html [accessed 19 December 2016].

Nagel, T. (1978) 'Ruthlessness in public life', in S. Hampshire (ed.), *Public and Private Morality* (Cambridge: Cambridge University Press), pp. 75–91.

Nagel, T. (1979 [1977]) 'The fragmentation of value', in *Mortal Questions* (Cambridge: Cambridge University Press), pp. 128–41.

Nagel, T. (1990 [1987]) 'Moral conflict and political legitimacy', in J. Raz (ed.), *Authority* (New York: New York University Press), pp. 300–24.

Nagel, T. (1991) *Equality and Partiality* (Oxford: Oxford University Press).

Nagel, T. (2008) 'Public education and intelligent design', *Philosophy & Public Affairs*, 36(2), 187–205.

National Consent Advisory Group (2013) *National Consent Policy* (Health Service Executive, Ireland). Available at: www.hse.ie/eng/about/Who/qualityandpatientsafety/National_Consent_Policy/National%20Consent%20PolicyMay14.pdf [accessed 1 December 2016].

Neill, S. J. (2005) 'Research *with* children: A critical review of the guidelines', *Journal of Child Health Care*, 9(1), 46–58.

Niemi, R. G. and Junn, J. (1998) *Civic Education: What Makes Students Learn* (New Haven, CT: Yale University Press).

Nijhof, K. S. and Engels, R. C. M. E. (2007) 'Parenting styles, coping strategies, and the expression of homesickness', *Journal of Adolescence*, 30(5), 709–20.

Noggle, R. (2002) 'Special agents: Children's autonomy and parental authority', in C. MacLeod and D. Archard (eds), *The Moral and Political Status of Children* (Oxford: Oxford University Press), pp. 97–117.

Nozick, R. (1974) *Anarchy, State and Utopia* (Oxford: Basil Blackwell).

NPSA (National Patient Safety Agency) (2007) *Information Sheets and Consent Forms. Guidance for Researchers and Reviewers*, Version 3.2 (London: National Patient Safety Agency and National Research Ethics Service).

Okin, S. M. (1989) 'Reason and feeling in thinking about justice', *Ethics*, 99(2), 229–49.

Okin, S. M. (1998) 'Gender, the public, and the private', in A. Philips (ed.), *Feminism and Politics* (Oxford: Oxford University Press), pp. 116–41.

O'Neill, O. (1989) *Constructions of Reason: Explorations of Kant's Practical Philosophy* (Cambridge: Cambridge University Press).

Orwell, G. (1989 [1938]) *Homage to Catalonia* (London: Penguin).

Palmeri, A. (1980) 'Childhood's end: Towards the liberation of children', in W. Aiken and H. LaFollette (eds), *Whose Child?* (Totowa, NJ: Littlefield, Adams and Co), pp. 105–23.

Pansardi, P. (2012) 'Power to and power over: two distinct concepts of power?', *Journal of Political Power*, 5(1), 73–89.

Partridge, B. (2013) 'The mature minor: some critical psychological reflections on the empirical bases', *HEC Forum*, 38(3), 283–99.

Partridge, B. (2014) 'Adolescent pedriatric decision making: A critical reconsideration in the light of the data', *HEC Forum*, 26(4), 299–308.

Pettit, P. (1996) 'Freedom as antipower', *Ethics*, 106(3), 576–604.

Pettit, P. (2011) 'The instability of freedom as non-interference: The case of Isaiah Berlin', *Ethics*, 121(4), 693–716.

Pettit, P. (2012) *On the People's Terms: A Republican Theory and Model of Democracy* (Cambridge: Cambridge University Press).

Pettit, P. (2016) 'Three mistakes about democracy', in A. Fives and K. Breen (eds), *Philosophy and Political Engagement: Reflection in the Public Sphere* (Basingstoke: Palgrave), pp. 187–200.

Piker, A. (2011) 'Balancing liberation and protection: A moderate approach to adolescent health care decision-making', *Bioethics*, 25(4), 202–8.

Popkin, S. L. and Dimock, M. A. (1999) 'Political knowledge and citizen competence', in S. K. Elkin and K. E. Soltan (eds), *Citizen Competence and Democratic Institutions* (University Park, PA: Penn State University Press), pp. 117–46.

Purdy, L. (1996) 'Children's liberation: A blueprint for disaster', in M. Leahy and D. Cohn-Sherbok (eds), *The Liberation Debate* (London: Routledge), pp. 147–62.

Rachels, J. (1975) 'Why privacy is important', *Philosophy & Public Affairs*, 4(4), 323–33.

Raphael, D. D. (1970) *Problems of Political Philosophy* (London and Basingstoke: Macmillan).

Rawls, J. (1971) *A Theory of Justice* (Oxford: Oxford University Press).

Rawls, J. (1993) *Political Liberalism* (New York: Columbia University Press).

Rawls, J. (1999 [1987]) 'The idea of an overlapping consensus', in S. Freeman (ed.), *John Rawls: Collected Papers* (Cambridge, MA: Harvard University Press), pp. 421–48.

Rawls, J. (1999 [1997]) 'The idea of public reason revisited', in S. Freeman (ed.), *John Rawls: Collected Papers* (London: Harvard University Press), pp. 573–615.

Rawls, J. (2003 [1989]) 'The domain of the political and overlapping consensus', in D. Matravers and J. E. Pike (eds), *Debates in Contemporary Political Philosophy: An Anthology* (London: Routledge, in Association with the Open University), pp. 160–81.

Raz, J. (1985) 'Authority and justification', *Philosophy & Public Affairs*, 14(1), 3–29.

Raz, J. (1986) *The Morality of Freedom* (Oxford: Clarendon Press).

Raz, J. (1990) 'Introduction', in J. Raz (ed.), *Authority* (New York: New York University Press), pp. 1–19.

Reiman, J. H. (1976) 'Privacy, intimacy, and personhood', *Philosophy & Public Affairs*, 6(1), 26–44.

Rodrigo, M. J., Padrón, I., de Vega, M. and Ferstl, E. C. (2014) 'Adolescents' risky decision making activates neural networks related to social cognition and cognitive control processes', *Frontiers in Human Neuroscience*, 8(60), 1–16.

Ross, W. D. (2003 [1930]) 'What makes right acts right?', in R. Shater-Landan (ed.), *Ethical Theory: An Anthology*, second edition (Chichester: Wiley Blackwell), pp. 756–62.

Rothbart, M. K. and Jones, L. B. (1998) 'Temperament, self-regulation, and education', *School Psychology Review*, 27(4), 479–92.

Rousseau, J.-J. (1762) *The Social Contract*, trans. G. D. H. Cole. Available at: www.constitution.org/jjr/socon.htm [accessed 1 December 2016].

Rudasill, K. M., Gallagher, K. C. and White, J. M. (2010) 'Temperamental attention and activity, classroom emotional support, and academic achievement in third grade', *Journal of School Psychology*, 48(2), 113–34.

Sanders, M. R. (1999) 'Triple P: Positive Parenting Program', *Clinical Child and Family Psychology Review*, 2(2), 71–90.

Sandmire, M. J. and Wald, M. S. (1990) 'Licensing parents: A reply to Clauida Mangel's proposal', *Family Law Quarterly*, 24(1), 53–76.

Sartre, J.-P. (1957 [1946]) 'Existentialism is a Humanism', trans. P. Mairet, in W. Kaufmann (ed.), *Existentialism from Dostoevsky to Sartre* (New York: Meridian), pp. 287–311.

Scanlon, T. M. (1998) *What We Owe to Each Other* (Cambridge, MA: Belknap Press).

Scanlon, T. M. (2003) 'Rawls on justification', in S. Freeman (ed.), *The Cambridge Companion to Rawls* (Cambridge: Cambridge University Press), pp. 139–67.

Scarre, G. (1980) 'Children and paternalism', *Philosophy*, 55(211), 117–24.

Schoeman, F. (1984) 'Privacy: Philosophical dimensions', *American Philosophical Quarterly*, 21(3), 199–213.

Shaffer, D. R. (2000) *Social and Personal Development* (Belmon: Wadsworth).

Shiffrin, S. V. (2000) 'Paternalism, unconscionability doctrine, and accommodation', *Philosophy & Public Affairs*, 29(3), 205–50.

Simmons, A. J. (1987) 'The anarchist position: A reply to Klosko and Senor', *Philosophy & Public Affairs*, 16(3), 269–79.

Solove, D. J. (2002) 'Conceptualizing privacy', *California Law Review*, 90(4), 1087–155.

Sparrow, R. (2010) 'Implants and ethnocide: Learning from the cochlear implant controversy', *Disability and Society*, 25(4), 455–66.

Steinkamp, N. and Gordijn, B. (2003) 'Ethical case deliberation on the ward. A comparison of four methods', *Medicine, Health Care and Philosophy*, 6(3), 235–46.

Sunstein, C. R. and Thaler, R. H. (2003) 'Libertarian paternalism is not an oxymoron', *The University of Chicago Law Review*, 70(4), 1159–202.

Tan, J. O. A., Hope, T. and Stewart, A. (2003) 'Competence to refuse treatment in anorexia nervosa', *International Journal of Law and Psychiatry*, 26(6), 697–707.

Taylor, C. (1989) *Sources of the Self* (Cambridge: Cambridge University Press).

Taylor, J. S. (2013) 'Introduction: Children and consent to treatment', *HEC Forum*, 25(4), 285–87.

Thomson, J. J. (1971) 'A defence of abortion', *Philosophy & Public Affairs*, 1(1), 47–66.

Thunder, D. (2006) 'A Rawlsian argument against the duty of civility', *American Journal of Political Science*, 50(3), 676–90.

Torney-Purta, J. V. (1997) 'Review essay: Links and missing links between education, political knowledge, and citizenship', *American Journal of Education*, 105(4), 446–57.

Torney-Purta, J., Lehmann, R., Oswald, H. and Schulz, W. (2001) *Citizenship and Education in Twenty-eight Countries: Civic Knowledge and Engagement at Age Fourteen* (Amsterdam: IEA).

United Nations (1989) Convention on the Rights of the Child (Geneva: United Nations office of the High Commissioner for Human Rights).

Veale, A. (2005) 'Creative methodologies in participatory research with children', in S. Greene and D. Hogan (eds), *Researching Children's Experience: Approaches and Methods* (London: Sage), pp. 253–72.

Veatch, R. M. (1995) 'Resolving conflicts among principles: Ranking, balancing, and specifying', *Kennedy Institute of Ethics Journal*, 5(3), 199–218.

Veatch, R. M. (2007) 'The irrelevance of equipoise', *Journal of Medicine and Philosophy*, 32(2), 167–83.

Vygotsky, L. S. (1978) *Mind in Society: The Development of Higher Psychological Processes* (Boston: Harvard University Press).

Walter, J. K. and Ross, L. F. (2014) 'Relational autonomy: Moving beyond the limits of isolated individualism', *Pediatrics*, 133(supplement 1), 16–23.

Weber, M. (1946 [1919]) 'Politics as a vocation', in H. H. Gerth and C. Wright Mills (trans. and eds), *From Max Weber: Essays in Sociology* (New York: Oxford University Press), pp. 77–128.

Weithorn, L. and Campbell, S. (1982) 'The competency of children and adolescents to make informed treatment decisions', *Child Development*, 53(6), 1589–98.

Westheimer, J. and Kahne, J. (2004) 'What kind of citizen? The politics of educating for democracy', *American Education Research Journal*, 41(2): 237–69.

Wheeler, R. (2006) 'Gillick or Fraser? A plea for consistency over competence in children', *British Medical Journal*, 332(7545), 807.

Williams, B. (1965) 'Ethical consistency', *Proceedings of the Aristotelian Society*, 39(suppl.), 103–24.

Williams, B. (1978) 'Politics and moral character', in Stuart Hampshire (ed.), *Public and Private Morality* (Cambridge: Cambridge University Press), pp. 23–53.

Williams, B. (1981 [1979]) 'Conflict of values', in *Moral Luck* (Cambridge: Cambridge University Press), pp. 71–82.

Williams, B. (1985) *Ethics and the Limits of Philosophy* (London: Fontana Press).

Williams, B. (2005) *In the Beginning was the Deed: Realism and Moralism in Political Argument* (Princeton and Oxford: Princeton University Press).

Wilson, P., Rush, R., Hussey, S., Puckering, C., Sim, F., Allely, C. S., Doku, P., McConnachie, A. and Gillberg, C. (2012) 'How evidence-based is an "evidence-based parenting program"? A PRISMA systematic review and meta-analysis of Triple P', *BMC Medicine*, 10(130), 1–16.

Winch, C. (2002) 'Strong autonomy and education', *Educational Theory*, 52(1), 27–41.

Wisconsin v. *Yoder*, 406 U.S. 205 (1972). Available at: https://supreme.justia.com/cases/federal/us/406/205/case.html [accessed 1 December 2016].

Wolff, J. (2011) *Ethics and Public Policy: A Philosophical Inquiry* (London: Routledge).

Wolff, R. P. (1990 [1970]) 'The conflict between authority and autonomy', in J. Raz (ed.), *Authority* (New York: New York University Press), pp. 20–31.

Woodhouse, B. B. (2003) 'Children's rights in gay and lesbian families: A child-centered perspective', in S. Macedo and I. M. Young (eds), *Child, Family, and State: Nomos KLIV* (New York: New York University Press), pp. 273–305.

Wrong, D. (1995 [1979]) *Power: Its Forms, Bases, and Uses* (London: Transaction Publishers).

Xiao, L., Bechara, A., Palmer, P. H., Trinidad, D. R., Wei, Y., Jia, Y., et al. (2011) 'Parent–child engagement in decision making and the development of adolescent affective decision capacity and binge-drinking', *Personality and Individual Differences*, 51(3), 285–92.

Index

agency 3–4, 7, 11, 23–4, 81–97, 99–100, 119, 122, 146, 224–5, 245
  and autonomy 5, 17–18, 24–7, 29–30, 35, 37–40, 45–8, 61, 69–70, 75, 81–92, 94–7, 100–1, 119, 131–2, 134–40, 142, 150, 162, 169, 188–9, 203, 210–11, 214–15, 217–18, 221–2, 225–6, 228–34, 236–44, 247
  children's deficits in 13, 16, 23, 33–5, 37, 39, 42–4, 81, 86, 96, 133, 235, 245
  and competence 8, 14–15, 24–30, 35–6, 41–4, 47, 67, 82, 85–6, 135, 146, 159, 165–7, 197–208, 211, 213–21, 224, 245
  and execution of decisions 23–7, 35–6, 42–4
  and liberty of action 3, 12, 14–17, 23–32, 35–6, 38, 42–8, 52, 81–2, 86, 152, 182–3, 197, 199, 234, 238
  and rights of liberty 22, 33–6, 38–9, 41–4, 46, 159, 222, 228, 232, 234
  and virtue 24–7, 29, 82, 86, 88, 119, 225–6, 231–3, 236
  and voluntary action 24–7, 30, 93, 208
  see also Bandura, A.; Berlin, I.; caretaker thesis; freedom; liberation thesis; paternalism; rationality
Allen, A. x, xi, 114, 121, 249

anarchism 107, 124, 132–3, 136–9
Anomaly, J. 178, 249
Appelbaum, P. S. 26, 202–4, 214–15, 249–50
Archard, D. xiii, 12, 20, 31, 33–8, 46, 81, 153, 155–6, 159, 162–3, 177–8, 182, 193–5, 212, 226, 231, 237, 249–51, 258
Arendt, H. ii, 115, 123, 249
Aristotle 60, 72, 232, 249
Arneson, R. J. 29, 249
Arnold, D.G. 104, 249
Aunola, K. 83, 249
autonomy see agency

Bachrach, P. ix, xi, 19, 117, 249
Baker, J. 200, 249
Baldwin, D.A. 32, 249
Bandura, A. 23, 28, 42, 82, 250
Baratz, M. ix, xi, 19, 117, 249
Barnhart, M.G. 171, 250
Baumrind, D. 83–4, 86, 101–2, 163, 250
Beauchamp, T.L. 26, 30, 156, 159, 207–10, 214, 217, 250
Beetham, D. 108, 150, 160–1, 165–6, 250
Benatar, D. 176, 184, 250
Benn, S. I. 188, 250
Berg, J.W. 202, 215, 250
Berlin, I. xiv, 17, 27, 31, 85, 87, 92–7, 105, 119, 126–7, 129, 152, 168, 234, 239, 248, 250
Bernier, A. 85, 250
Bottrell, A. 184–5, 250

Breen, K. xiii, xv, 253, 259
Brennan, S. 86, 250
Brighouse, H. xiii, 11–12, 33–4, 37–8,
    50, 61, 81, 152, 155–6, 184–6,
    212, 229, 250
Brock, D. W. 135, 159, 214–15, 217–18,
    251
Brody, H. 75, 258
Bruzzese, J.-M. 201, 250
Buchanan, A. 135, 159, 198, 214–15,
    217–18, 251
Burtt, S. 33–4, 81, 133, 155, 158, 251

Campbell, L. xv, 221, 251, 257
Campbell, S. 201, 261
caretaker thesis 4–5, 9, 33–9, 42, 44–9,
    51–2, 55, 70, 85, 87, 132–3,
    145, 162, 237, 244
Cassidy, L. 150, 182–3, 251
Cauffman, E. 200, 255
Childress, J.F. 26, 30, 156, 159, 207–10,
    214, 217, 250
Christiano, T. 109, 251
civic education 222–42
    and critical thinking 134, 225, 230,
        233, 242
    outcomes of civic education 223–6
    and parents' right to share a way of life
        with their children 235–42
    service learning 17, 224, 236–9
    status of children 85–7, 234–5
    see also agency
    and values 228–34, 236–42
    see also Mozert v. Hawkins; Wisconsin v.
        Yoder
Clarke, S. 17, 251
Clayton, M. 238, 251
Clegg, S. x–xii, 117, 119, 251, 254
Clouser, K.D. 71, 251
Coady, C.A.J. 168, 251
Cohen G.A. 145, 251
Coleman, J. 162, 251
competence see agency
Conover, P.J. 224, 251
Convention on the Rights of the Child
        (United Nations) see rights
Cornock, M. 156, 199, 251
Coyne, J.C. 181, 190, 251
Culver, C.M. 11, 15–17, 20, 22–3,
    26, 28–9, 32, 48, 56, 81, 104,
    107–8, 214, 244, 251, 254,
    256

Dahl, R. ii, ix–xi, 12, 19, 32, 117, 251
Daly, A. M. 203, 252
De Haan, J. 57, 252
Delli Carpini, M. X. 223, 252
De Wispelaere, J. 179, 192, 252
Dimock, M.A. 223, 259
Donagan, A. 57, 60, 69, 252
Dryzek, J.S. 93, 171, 252
Dworkin, G. 11–12, 20, 22, 252
Dworkin, R. 134, 164, 171, 252
Dunn, J. 145, 252

Engels, R.C.M.E. 83, 258
Engster, D. 177, 181, 190, 252
ethics 64–80, 87, 99, 162
    see also legitimacy; pluralism;
        rationality

Feinberg, J. 29–30, 37–8, 128, 158,
    252
Felzmann, H. 199, 221, 252
Fineman, M.L.A. 158, 252
Fischel, W.A. 227, 241, 252
Fisher, C.B. 201, 250
Fives, A. 7, 17, 73, 75, 77, 82, 101, 125,
    145, 216, 224, 230–2, 241, 248,
    252–3
Foot, P. 27, 43–4, 56–62, 67, 142, 232,
    253
Foucault, M. ii, x–xi, 98, 100–1, 254
Freedman, B. 75, 254
freedom
    negative and positive freedom 27, 82,
        85–97, 99, 122, 126, 152, 168,
        233–4
    see also agency; Raz, J.; Berlin, I.
Freeman, M. 33, 86, 254, 259, 260
Fried, C. 110, 137, 187, 213, 254
Friedman, R.B. 110, 137, 213, 254

Galston, W. A. 95, 153, 155, 224, 254
Galvan, T. A. 201, 254
Gavison, R. 152, 254
General Medical Council (UK) 199, 215,
    254
Gert, B. 11, 15–17, 20, 22–3, 26, 28–9,
    32, 48, 56, 71, 81, 214, 244,
    251, 254
Gheaus, A. 185–6, 254
Gillick
    Gillick competency, test of 199–202,
        221

Gillick v West Norfolk and Wisbech Area Health Authority and another [1985] 2 BMLR 11 202, 254
Göhler, G. 100, 254
Gonzales, R. 177, 181, 190, 252
Gordijn, B. 74, 260
Gutmann, A. 5, 12, 21, 225–7, 236–40, 254

Habermas, J. 101, 255
Halpern-Felsher, B. L. 200, 255
Hampshire, S. 2, 63, 244, 248, 252, 255, 258, 261
Hardimon, M. 164, 255
Hare, R.M. 69, 233, 255
Harris, J. 33, 45–7, 61, 158, 234, 255
Hart, H.L.A. 56, 255
Haugaard, M. ii, x–xiii, xv, 17, 20, 32, 82, 102, 117, 119, 130, 249, 251, 254–5
Hershey, P.T. 11–12, 17, 21, 255
Hess, D.E. 225, 231, 255
Hill, M. 162, 255
Hobbes, T. 95, 129–33, 255
Holt, J. 33, 44–5, 154, 255
Hood, S. 162, 257
Horton, J. 139, 164, 255
Hume, D. 164, 255
Hunter, D. 199–200, 202, 256
Hurst, C.E. 227, 241, 257

informed consent (children)
  assent 21, 107–8, 112, 156, 162–3, 189, 212
  joint decision making 67, 73, 135, 165–6, 197, 203, 206, 208, 210–13, 219–21, 247
  mature minor 41, 199, 201
  and parental consent 105, 199
  surrogate decision makers 219–20, 227
  voluntariness 8, 26, 135, 197–200, 203, 206–11, 213, 219, 247
  see also competence; Gillick
Innes, J. 188, 256
Ireland, M. 182, 256

James, A. 100–2, 166, 256
Jansen, L.A. 217, 256
Jenks, C. 100–2, 166, 256
Johnson, P. 174, 248, 256
Jones, L.B. 85, 260

Jonsen, A.R. 74, 256
Junn, J. 225, 258

Kahne, J.E. 224, 231, 256, 261
Kant, I. 40, 94, 256
  Kantian 2, 13, 39, 42, 62, 77, 131, 137, 237
Keeter, S. 223, 252
Kligman, M. 104, 107–8, 256
Komrad, M. 17, 256
Kwakkenbos, L. 181, 190, 251
Kymlicka, K. 230–1, 256

LaFollette, H. 153, 155, 176–8, 180–7, 189, 191–3, 195, 256
legitimacy *see* power
Levin, M. 122, 256
Levine, M. xiii
liberalism 9, 124–9, 133–41, 149, 171, 230, 233
  see also Berlin, I.; freedom; Nagel, T.; paternalism; Rawls, J.
liberation thesis 4–5, 9, 33–4, 44–9, 51–2, 55, 70, 132, 145, 155, 234–5, 244
  see also Harris, J.; Holt, J.
Liew, J. 85, 256
Locke, J. 130, 132, 256
Lukes, S. ii, ix–x, xii, 20, 98, 115–20, 255–6
Lutz, C. 170, 256

Macedo, S. 230, 236, 251–2, 254, 256, 262
MacIntyre, A. 26–7, 60, 75, 77, 142, 170–1, 231–2, 237, 256
Mackenzie, C. 210, 257
Mackie, J.L. 164, 257
Macleod, C. xiii, 152, 184–5, 229, 235, 241, 250–1, 257–8
Mangel, C. P. 178, 257
March, A.F. 231, 257
Marino, P. 78, 257
Marx, K. 93, 248, 257
Mason, A. 145, 257
Mason, J. 162, 257
McCarthy, J. 74, 257
McConnell, D.L. 227, 241, 257
Merritt, E. G. 84–5, 257
Metcalfe, J. 200, 257
Mill, J.S. 3–4, 9, 13–14, 18, 75, 90, 92, 126, 183, 193, 232, 257

Miller, F.G. 75, 258
Miller, P.B. 75, 258
Miller, V. A. 200, 258
moral dilemmas *see* pluralism
Morriss, P. x, xii, xiv, 16, 103, 113–15, 121, 258
Mozert v Hawkins County Board of Education 827. F.2d 1058 (6th Cir. 1987) 227–8, 236, 258

Nagel, T. xiv, 2, 6, 56, 63–4, 68, 72, 76, 78–9, 95, 134–6, 148–9, 167–73, 186–7, 195, 233–4, 244, 246, 248, 258
National Consent Advisory Group 221, 258
National Patient Safety Agency (NPSA) 199, 258
Neill, S.J. 202, 237, 258
Niemeyer, S. 93, 171, 252
Niemi, R.G. 225, 258
Nijhof, K.S. 83, 258
Noggle, R. 86–7, 258
Nozick, R. 129, 131–3, 258

Okin, S.M. 150, 258–9
O'Neill, O. 39–42, 55, 61, 81, 237, 259
Orwell, G. 107, 259

Palmeri, A. 11, 48–9, 259
Pansardi, P. x, 114, 259
parental licenses *see* power
parental power *see* power
parenting
    adoptive and biological 157, 182–9
    child abuse (predicting) 177–80, 183, 189–93, 246
    monitoring of 8, 50, 146, 152–3, 156, 176–83, 187–90, 193–6, 246
    and privacy 38, 44, 151–4, 156–7, 160, 174, 177, 182–3, 187–90, 193–6, 246
    support and training for 8, 50, 146, 176–7, 180, 190–2, 194, 196, 200, 246
    see also rights
Partridge, B. 165, 199, 201, 206, 259
paternalism *see* power
Pettit, P. 125–8, 158, 161–3, 259
Pierscionek, B.K. 199–200, 202, 256
Piker, A. 201, 203, 259

Popkin, S.L. 223, 259
power
    as authority ix, 98–9, 109–13, 118, 122–3, 125, 136–40, 142–3, 149, 155, 162, 165, 206, 208–13, 218, 225, 234, 245, 247
        see also anarchism
    as coercion 3, 13–14, 17, 20, 27, 32, 53, 88–90, 94, 98, 100, 102–9, 112–13, 115–19, 124–5, 129–30, 133–4, 136, 140, 142, 147–8, 165–6, 168–9, 192, 208–9, 213, 245
    as control 3, 12, 16–19, 26, 29, 32, 47–8, 51, 83–4, 92, 95, 98, 100, 102, 105–7, 111–17, 120–2, 125, 133–6, 140–2, 190, 194, 207–10, 213, 219–20, 227, 236, 247
    as interference with liberty 1, 3–4, 9, 11–13, 15–20, 27, 30–1, 37–9, 42–3, 45, 47, 50–2, 85, 88–92, 94, 96–8, 100, 102–3, 105–9, 112–13, 116–17, 121, 125–9, 131, 133, 135–6, 140, 142, 152–3, 188, 190, 195, 208–12, 215, 219, 222, 227, 234–9
    legitimacy of xiii, 1, 3, 8–9, 11–12, 21–2, 34, 37, 53, 65, 75–6, 81, 87, 89–90, 109, 112, 118, 121, 123–43, 147–75, 194, 196, 213, 216, 220–1, 235, 244–5
        and consent 160–6
        and legality 151–60
        and normative evaluation 166–73
        and public private division 166–73
        see also anarchism; liberalism; republicanism; social contract theory
    parental power
        and civic education xiii–iv, 8, 17–19, 50, 105–6, 127–8, 139, 146, 222–42, 247
        and informed consent 8, 16, 22, 30, 51, 67, 75, 135, 145–6, 158, 163, 167, 197–221, 247
        and parental licensing 8, 50, 146, 155–6, 176–96
        see also caretaker thesis; liberation thesis; right to parent

paternalistic 1, 3–4, 7, 9, 11–52,
    55–6, 61, 69–70, 79, 81, 87, 89,
    96–100, 102, 106, 109–13, 119,
    122, 125, 133, 140–2, 147, 169,
    183, 197, 208–9, 237–8, 244–5
and interference with liberty 1,
    3, 4, 9, 11–13, 15–20, 27, 30,
    31, 37–9, 42–3, 45, 47, 50–2,
    88–92, 97, 100, 102, 140,
    216–22, 236–42
and moral dilemmas 11–12, 20–1,
    31, 38, 42, 47, 52, 244–5
'soft' and 'hard' 27–31, 36, 46–8,
    197, 245
'power over' x, xiii, 16–17, 33, 98,
    103, 107, 109, 111–18, 120–5,
    136, 140–1, 208, 210, 213, 245
'power to' x, 53, 99, 103, 112–16,
    118, 120–2, 126, 216, 218, 245
'power with' x, 53, 99, 103, 112–16,
    118, 120–2, 245
pluralism
conceptual
    agency concepts 81–97
    power concepts 98–123
and moral dilemmas
    and logical contradiction 56–68
and moral regret 6, 55–62, 66–71, 79,
    168–70
and moral simplification 2–3, 31,
    55–6, 61, 63, 68, 79, 177, 186,
    193, 237, 239
prima facie ought and all things
    considered ought 12, 18, 20, 38,
    43, 57–62, 67, 69, 71, 79, 91,
    104, 126–7, 168, 193–5, 211,
    218, 220, 233
and their resolution 5–7, 22, 54–6,
    59, 61, 64–5, 67–9, 72–3, 75,
    77, 79, 95, 98, 128, 158, 219,
    233, 236, 242, 244, 248
see also Foot, P.; paternalism; Williams,
    B.
privacy see parenting
Prout, A. 100–2, 166, 256
Purdy, L. 33, 259

Rachels, J. 152, 187, 189, 259
Raphael, D.D. 151, 259
rationality
and children's agency 25–7, 29–30,
    35–6, 40, 82, 86, 119, 214

practical reason and judgement 170,
    246, 248
problem-driven political philosophy 8,
    145, 248
theory and its limits 6–8, 64–79, 93,
    145
    see also Nagel, T.; pluralism; Rawls, J.;
    Williams, B.
Rawls, J. 6, 34, 56–7, 72, 75–9, 130,
    147–50, 162–4, 167, 170–1,
    174, 195, 230, 233–4, 246,
    259
Raz, J. 61, 86–92, 94, 96–7, 109, 134–9,
    213, 229–30, 233, 252, 254,
    258, 260, 262
Reiman, J.H. 153, 188, 260
republicanism 2, 121, 124–9, 132, 158,
    162
right to parent see rights
rights
    Convention on the Rights of the Child
        (UN) 154, 157–9, 228
    legal 151–60
    and liberty 15, 23–4, 27–8, 30–1,
        35–47, 52, 55, 61–3, 70, 78, 87,
        159, 183, 221, 223, 228, 238,
        242, 247
    parents' rights (right to parent and
        rights over their children) 8, 132,
        139, 146, 154–5, 157, 160, 163,
        176–7, 181–7, 189–90, 192–3,
        197, 212, 218–19, 237, 246
    Thirty-first Amendment of the
        Constitution (Children) Bill
        2012 (Republic of Ireland) 157,
        255
    see also privacy
Rodrigo, M. J. 201, 260
Ross, L.F. 210, 261
Ross, W.D. 58, 260
Rothbart, M.K. 85, 260
Rousseau, J.-J. 93, 260
Rudasill, K.M. 85, 260

Sanders, M.R. 100, 211, 260
Sandmire, M.J. 178, 260
Sartre, J.-P. 169, 248, 260
Scanlon, T.M. 78, 130, 260
Scarre, G. 4, 13–15, 23–4, 38–9, 42, 55,
    61–2, 69–70, 81, 237, 260
    see also caretaker thesis; paternalism
Schoeman, F. 188, 260

Searing, D.D. 224, 251
Shaffer, D.R. 83, 260
Shiffrin, S.V. 17, 260
Simmons, A.J. 143, 260
social contract theory 2, 124, 129–33,
    148, 161, 163–4
sociology of childhood 98–9, 103, 116
Solove, D.J. 187–8, 260
Son, L. 200, 257
Sparrow, R. 49, 260
Sporte, S.E. 224, 256
Steinkamp, N. 74, 260
Sunstein, C. R. 106, 261
Swift, A. xiii, 11–12, 33–4, 37–8, 50,
    61, 81, 152, 155–6, 184–6, 212,
    250

Tan, J.O.A. 261
Taylor, C. 142, 261
Taylor, J. S. 200, 261
Thaler, R. H. 106, 261
Thirty-first Amendment of the
    Constitution (Children) Bill 2012
    (Republic of Ireland) see rights
Thomson, J.J. 182, 261
Thunder, D. 77, 171, 230, 261
Torney-Purta, J.V. 225, 261
Toulmin, S. 74, 256

Veale, A. 162, 261
Veatch, R.M. 70, 75, 261
Vygotsky, L. S. 83, 261

Wald, M.S. 178–9, 261
Walter, J.K. 210, 261
Weber, M. ix, xii, 130, 160, 261
Weijer, C. 75, 184, 254, 258
Weinstock, D. 179, 192, 252
Weithorn, L. 201, 261
Westheimer, J. 224, 231, 236, 261
Wheeler, R. 201, 261
Williams, B. xiv, 2, 6, 55, 57, 59, 62,
    64–8, 72, 80, 87, 94, 99, 101,
    145, 169, 212, 244, 248,
    261–2
    see also ethics; pluralism; rationality
Wilson, P. 181, 190, 262
Winch, C. 225, 262
Wisconsin v. Yoder, 406 U.S. 205 (1972)
    227–8, 236, 241, 262
Wolff, J. 7, 145, 235, 243, 248, 262
Wolff, R.P. 26, 137, 142–3, 262
Woodhouse, B.B. 153–4, 262
Wrong, D. 16, 103–4, 108–9, 111, 114,
    130, 137, 213, 262

Xiao, L. 165, 206, 262